The Sentencing of Children
Profesional Work and Perspectives

Max Travers

NEW ACADEMIA
PUBLISHING

Washington, DC

Printed in the United States of America

Library of Congress Control Number: 2012944761
ISBN 978-0-9855698-7-7 paperback (alk. paper)

New Academia Publishing
PO Box 27420, Washington, DC 20038-7420
info@newacademia.com - www.newacademia.com

The Sentencing of Children

Contents

Acknowledgements

This book seeks to raise awareness of how children's courts respond to youth crime through examining the professional work around sentencing in the three Australian states of Tasmania, Victoria and New South Wales. There are many people who have supported this project by giving access to research data or suggesting questions to investigate. I am particularly grateful to Chief Magistrate Arnold Shott of the Magistrates Court of Tasmania, and his successor Michael Hill, for supporting the project during 2005 and subsequently, and the individual magistrates and administrators who helped in Hobart, Launceston, Burnie and Devonport. Judge Paul Grant, the President of the Children's Court of Victoria made it possible to observe hearings in Victorian courts during 2008. Ros Porter of Victoria Legal Aid helped in allowing me to "shadow" defence lawyers.

I would like to thank Magistrate Paul Mulroney of the Children's Court at Campbell Town and Judge Mark Marien the current President of the Children's Court of NSW, who replaced Senior Magistrate Scott Mitchell in 2009, for giving permission to observe hearings in New South Wales. Many practitioners working for Youth Justice (Juvenile Justice in NSW), the police, Legal Aid and other agencies also helped. None of the above are, of course, responsible for the contents of this book or the general argument, which is directed to a wider audience, including students taking courses in criminal justice, law, social science, social work and youth studies.

No project involving travel around different states is possible without some form of funding. I am grateful to the University of Tasmania for giving support from the Institutional Research Grant Scheme (IRGS) funded by the Australian Research Council in 2005, and for the opportunity to earn some additional income from advanced honours teaching. Part of a study leave in the first half of 2010, during which I presented papers relating to this project in Japan, England and the United States, was supported by consultancy income obtained from being lead investigator on an Australian Housing and Urban Research Institute (AHURI) grant on regulation and affordable housing.

This study builds on the ethnographic approach to studying legal practice in my doctoral thesis (Travers 1997a), which was partly concerned with juvenile justice, and a later (1999) study about immigration appeals tribunals that looked at different occupational perspectives. I would like to thank my supervisors in the Department of Sociology, University of Manchester, Wes Sharrock and Rod Watson for encouraging me to study everyday work practices, and the many ethnomethodologists and conversation analysts who have conducted research on legal institutions driven by a commitment to examining the detail of routine, practical work. Closer to home, I would like to thank Rob White, who comes from the critical tradition in criminology (for example, White 2008), for suggesting this topic when I moved to the University of Tasmania in 2003. We collaborated in teaching an online course on international youth justice for judicial officers in four countries which resulted in some thoughtful exchanges about the challenges facing children's courts in addressing difficult social problems. We have also contributed, with Michael McKinnon, to a national project, coordinated by Allan Borowski and Rosemary Sheehan, based on interviewing practitioners and policy makers about their views on the criminal and protective work of children's courts (Sheehan and Borowski 2012).

My own project is intended to be complementary, in the sense that it describes the practical issues that arise in sentencing, rather than advancing an argument about policy. That said, the conclusion does consider the implications of sociological research for policy-makers and practitioners, and even advances some recommendations. The book also makes a theoretically-driven argument, drawing on the interpretive tradition in sociology, for how we should conduct research about the criminal justice process. I am not sure how this argument will be received, given the dominance of positivist and quantitative approaches in this field, both in Australia and internationally, and the fact that some criticisms are also directed at critical criminologists. The book seeks to show that there are alternative ways of researching and conceptualising children's courts, based on developing a sensitivity towards ordinary working practices, and that this has implications for criminal justice policy.

I would like to thank New Academia Publishing, and three academic reviewers for their help in developing the manuscript at a time when everyone is under pressure to publish, and there is less time for this unrewarded but vital professional work. Finally, I am grateful to *Current Issues in Criminal Justice* for permission to print material in chapter 4 from a paper published in 2010, "Welfare, punishment or something else?   Sentencing minor offences committed by young people in Tasmania and Victoria" (Vol.22, pp.96-116). I am also grateful to *Youth Justice* for permission to print material in chapter 6 from a paper published in 2007, "Sentencing in the children's court: An ethnographic perspective" (Vol.7, No.1, pp.21-35).

I.

Introduction

Teenager facing jail over graffiti

An 18-year old woman with no criminal record has been jailed for three months for writing one word of graffiti on the wall of an inner-Sydney cafe…Jane Black of Daceyville, admitted using a black Texta marker to write "2shie." The word was 30cm high and 60cm long. In the Downing Centre Local Court yesterday, magistrate Peter Smith jailed her for three months, but another magistrate later granted her bail pending an appeal. She pleaded guilty to intentionally or recklessly damaging a brick wall…The cafe is seeking $200 compensation.

This short report, published in an Australian newspaper without any editorial comment or subsequent reaction from readers,[1] illustrates the difficult issues raised for the courts in many countries by youth crime. Most readers of this book are likely to be welfare-oriented professionals, or students planning to work in social welfare services. Those with liberal or progressive views may feel that the magistrate who heard this case behaved harshly. Some readers may believe that it is morally wrong, and certainly ineffective or counter-productive to send any young person to a detention center, even for offences involving property theft or violence, and that more resources should be directed towards prevention or supervision.

There are also, however, many members of the community who favor tougher penalties for nuisance offences such as graffiti (for which one can be sentenced to imprisonment under New South Wales law). They might be disappointed that this defendant had a right of appeal, or see the sentence and the reporting of this case as having a valuable deterrent effect. There are also some who may privately feel that incarcerating a young person does not go far enough: that only a return to corporal punishment, and ending the "soft" treatment of young people in the family, school and prisons will reduce youth crime.

Although little is made of this issue in the large literature on juvenile offending, this case also highlights the rather artificial nature of the age of adult criminal responsibility. In Australian law in this state, this defendant was a child before the age of 18 (a "girl" rather than a "woman"). The ordinary terms through which we differentiate different levels of cognitive development such as child, youth, teenager, adolescent and young adult, are not strictly speaking relevant to the legal framework governing sentencing.[2] Under the legislation, you are either a child or an adult offender. Children can expect more lenient treatment in what the police sometimes describe as "kiddie's court." This involves getting many chances, with an emphasis on rehabilitation instead of punishment.

Only the most progressive commentators would propose that the justice system should continue a lenient, rehabilitative approach after age 18.[3] There continue, however, to be debates over how we should respond to youth crime, and the effectiveness of children's courts among practitioners and the policy community. If we take at face value the objective of legislation to balance welfare and punishment, why do so many young people in Australia, and elsewhere, spend a significant part of their teenage years in detention centres?[4] Is there anything that we can do differently? This book seeks to encourage and make possible debate about these issues through describing how sentencing decisions are made by magistrates and other professionals in children's courts.

Why This Study?

Many books about juvenile justice are written by those who already have a professional perspective or commitment to a policy agenda, and would like their research to be seen as useful by government agencies (see, for example, Smith 2003, Barry and McNeill 2009, Aarons et al 2009). There has also been a substantial contribution from sociologists with a politically motivated interest in the criminal justice process: who are interested in how it reproduces class and other divisions, and contributes to the subordination of young people (for example, Brown 2005, Blagg 2008 and Carrington and Pereira 2009). Then there are people like myself, working in different social science traditions, who have become interested in these institutions, and how they respond to youth crime, by chance and through curiosity. Although such researchers might well be seen as naive or ill-informed by insiders, they come with the advantage of having few preconceptions, and inevitably will see things differently.

My first encounter with juvenile justice took place in the United Kingdom while I was doing fieldwork for my doctorate in the late 1980s. This was an ethnographic study (Travers 1997a), in which I spent time as a participant observer in a small firm of lawyers. Like any legal aid firm, Gregsons represented a variety of clients.[5] In its criminal work, the firm represented what might be described as career criminals. These included men in their thirties and forties, charged with armed robberies. The youngest I met was in his early twenties. He was the son of a well-known offender serving a long sentence also for armed robbery. This seemed to suggest a family business: that he had learned this trade from relatives, and if things went wrong could draw on a support network.[6] He seemed intelligent, well adjusted and not worried by the prospect of joining his father. I have since learnt that some psychologists would describe this young person as having an "antisocial personality disorder." This suggests that there was something wrong with him, although perhaps it only means that he deliberately engaged in harmful actions without social approval.

This firm of lawyers also represented young offenders, that is those under the age of 18 who had committed criminal offences. These started offending in their early teens, and continued into their early twenties. The offences were generally of a minor nature: taking a vehicle without consent or TWOCing was the most common offence, along with criminal damage, theft, burglaries, and assaults on the police. Some of the legal work in representing these offenders is described in my study. For example, there is a transcript of a lawyer interviewing two 14 year old youths in the cells under the magistrates court. They joined some older youths in taking a car, and setting it alight in a local estate. They had been pursued by the police, and one suffered injuries when a large police officer pinned him to the ground.

This hearing took place in the ordinary adult list in the magistrates court: there was no dedicated children's court, apparently no form of diversion operating (in the late 1990s, New Labour would introduce Youth Offending Teams),[7] and no contact with youth workers. My analysis of professional work used three categories that attempted to convey how lawyers understood different types of clients: "regulars" (meaning repeat clients), "serious offenders" (meaning those charged with serious offences) and "vulnerable clients" (meaning those with behavioral or social problems). This seems interesting, in retrospect, because the lawyers were not treating the young people they saw regularly any differently to adults: they were simply clients seeking legal advice and representation.

After completing the study, I did not think much about juvenile offending. Instead, I pursued a study about the system of tribunals in Britain that hears appeals on immigration and refugee status (Travers 1999). This did, however, involve a shift from looking at legal representation to the work of the adjudicators who make decisions, and how different practitioners work together to produce an outcome. There are many differences between children's courts and immigration appeals tribunals.[8] My study about immigration appeals in Britain explained the legal and evidential considerations involved in hearing appeals relating to the primary purpose rule (ended through legislation during the study) and asylum-seekers. This study looks at the considerations involved in sentencing young people in Australia after a guilty plea. These hearings do not involve reviewing evidence, and reaching a decision on guilt or innocence. Instead, magistrates have to determine the appropriate sentence for an offence within a particular legal framework, and after considering all the circumstances.

Even though immigration appeals tribunals and children's courts follow distinct procedures, and are concerned with different areas of law, they have common organizational problems. In Australia, the most taxing issue facing court administrators is how to reduce the time spent by young people who are remanded in custody. This has grown in all states, and resulted in some defendants spending a few months in custody even though they receive a non-custodial sentence. In the case of Britain's immigration courts during the 1990s, there was a backlog of years not months, resulting in considerable anxiety, even if no actual hardship, for most appellants. For a variety of reasons, this became a political issue, and the New Labour government invested money in new hearing centers to speed up the determination process. Nothing like this has happened in the case of young people spending months as remand detainees in Australia.

When I moved to the University of Tasmania in 2003, there was concern among practitioners and policy makers about the issue of bail. This study was, however, driven by curiosity rather than to solve the problem of youth crime or advance a political message. Offences committed by young people have fallen steadily internationally in the last thirty years (Muncie and Goldson 2006). However, they still commit numerous offences individually and in groups, including shop stealing, thefts, burglaries, and taking cars. They regularly come to police attention in shopping malls, for fighting, or for causing a disturbance at parties. In public areas, they cover any part of the built environment not under surveillance with graffiti.[9] Since young people have been committing these offences since at least the late-19th century (Pearson 1983), it would seem unlikely that any measures pursued today will make a substantial impact on the problem.[10]

What motivates this book is not a search for solutions, but an interest in how professionals working in children's courts respond to youth offending. Here it seems important to face head on the criticisms, presented in moral or ethical terms, that will no doubt be advanced from some quarters, that focusing on professionals means siding with dominant social groups, or even that there is something boring or old hat in looking at institutions when the real action lies outside the criminal justice system (Ferrell et al 2008, p.183). Here, I cannot make much of a defense, other than that there are considerable practical difficulties involved in studying multiple perspectives within institutions. As Howard Becker (1961) noted in his influential paper, "Whose side are you on?," the researcher often has to choose between opposing interests and viewpoints. Although this is often understood as placing a moral duty on the researcher to support the subordinate group, Becker also makes the more subtle observation that it is both scientifically necessary but also impossible for the sociologist to address every perspective.

This being said, few researchers have been successful in addressing the viewpoint of young offenders, certainly without imposing their own adult, and often politically motivated, conceptions of crime.[11] The best studies have been conducted by youth workers who spent long periods getting to know young people, and conducting naturalistic observation of their criminal activities (for example, Parker 1974). When conducting my doctoral research, I remember receiving a blank look after asking a 14 year old, rather foolishly, why he got involved with people who took cars. There is a moral implication in the question, but even worse it showed a lack of familiarity with his social world. Taking cars was probably the main leisure and social activity for young people on the local estates.

A Project in Three Stages

Whereas natural scientists have almost complete control of their materials, social science depends on obtaining support and participation from organizations that have their own view of the subject matter. When pursuing an ethnographic project, you have to obtain access to different agencies and institutions, and in doing so develop a research question. This can take a considerable amount of time, and it may not even be clear during the initial stages that the study will be possible. In this case, the challenge was not simply to obtain access to legal hearings, but to the occupational groups that work in children's courts.

This research study started in Tasmania, the smallest state in Australia. It is an island 240 kilometres to the south of the state of Victoria. Tasmania was politically important as the centre of the penal system during the colonial period (Clark 1963), and joined the other states in 1901 in establishing Australia as a Federation. The state has a population of about 500,000,[12] and has similar demographic and socio-economic features to country regions in larger states, even though it has its own parliament and legal system. The largest city, Hobart, in the south of the island has a population of 200,000 and the second city Launceston in the north a population of 100,000. There are magistrates courts in these population centers and in the smaller northern cities of Devonport and Burnie. There is a common law, adversarial system in Tasmania, and the other states, that is similar to the legal system in the United Kingdom, the USA or Canada. One difference in relation to the United Kingdom is that magistrates in Australia are legally qualified and sit alone (the equivalent would be stipendiary magistrates). In Britain, lay people are appointed as magistrates, and make decisions as a panel advised by a legally qualified court clerk.

In Tasmania, there was no separate children's court with dedicated magistrates in 2005, but criminal cases relating to young people were heard separately in closed hearings by a Youth Justice Division.[13] The main statute that sets out objectives and principles for the sentencing of children is the Youth Justice Act 1997 (Tasmania). Following the advice of someone who knew Tasmanian institutions well, I approached the Department of Justice and the Department of Human Services, and met a senior civil servant in each department. With their backing, I approached the Magistrates Court and Youth Justice, seeking permission to pursue an observational study. In the Magistrates Court, I met a group of magistrates, and gave a short talk about the importance of opening up the criminal justice process to discussion and scrutiny in a democracy. In Youth Justice, I met three senior managers, one of whom had studied sociology and was already sympathetic to the objective of writing about the work of this agency for a broader audience. In the event, I did not pursue the initial objective of spending time inside a Youth Justice office, and accompanying these practitioners to court. This is because it is difficult examining more than one occupational perspective at the same time. On each court visit, I tried to speak to the magistrate after the hearing. I also interviewed Youth Justice workers, Legal Aid lawyers and prosecutors about their work.

Once you embark on a study, it develops its own momentum. In Tasmania, it meant trying to observe a reasonable number of sentencing hearings, even if this also involved spending many hours watching adjournments, not guilty pleas, and the other administrative matters that concern those working in courts. Youth justice matters were listed for particular magistrates on "For Mention" days once a month. Later in the year, I also obtained permission to observe hearings in the smaller courts in the north of the island. Because this took place over the summer break, I was able to do this more systematically. I arranged three visits each to the courts at Launceston, and at the smaller courts in Burnie and Devonport in which all court business comes before a single magistrate.[14]

Victoria is a much larger state than Tasmania, with a population of around five and an half million. Around four million live in or around the city of Melbourne. There is a central children's court with dedicated magistrates, although most hearings are heard by generalist magistrates in metropolitan and country courts. Victoria has the lowest rate of imprisonment among Australian states for both adult offenders (Freiberg and Ross 1999) and juvenile offenders (Richards and Lyneham 2010, Australian Institute of Health and Welfare 2011). There is, however, no agreement among academic commenators on whether this reflects a lower crime rate or a difference in sentencing practices; and, if the latter, on what historical, institutional and cultural factors explain this distinctive judicial culture.[15] This study will contribute to these discussions in chapter 9, through demonstrating from a qualitative analysis of a few sentencing hearings, that there is greater leniency in Victoria. The main statute on young offenders is the Children and Young Persons Act 1989 (Victoria).

Whereas the children's courts in Tasmania and New South Wales are closed to the public, anyone can attend hearings in Victoria subject to reporting restrictions. However, I followed a similar procedure in obtaining permission to speak to practitioners. This involved meeting the President of the Children's Court and obtaining the support of Legal Aid. In Victoria, my focus was on the work of Legal Aid lawyers. I began by "shadowing" Legal Aid lawyers as they took instructions from clients before hearings and represented them in court. This is a valuable method for understanding routine work in a court. It allows the researcher to observe episodes of work, but also to ask questions if space becomes available during the day. The only drawback was that, in Victoria, Legal Aid lawyers are most involved in new matters, or in representing defendants on minor charges. In addition, I met magistrates after some hearings, and interviewed or had informal conversations with practitioners from different agencies. I observed hearings at the central children's court and at three metropolitan courts. I also visited a country court, and observed one hearing of the Youth Koori Court, an initiative that seeks to make criminal proceedings more meaningful for Aboriginal defendants.[16]

New South Wales is the most populous state in Australia, with a population of around seven million. Four and an half million people live in the Sydney metropolitan area. There are similarities to Victoria in that there is a central children's court with dedicated magistrates, based in Parramatta and Glebe, but generalist magistrates hear cases relating to young people in metropolitan and country courts. The main piece of legislation on criminal conduct by children is the Young Offenders Act 1997 (New South Wales). I began by writing to the Senior Magistrate of the children's court in Sydney. This led to a meeting with a magistrate there, who subsequently moved to become the local magistrate in the children's court at Campbelltown. I attended the court Christmas party which proved a good opportunity to meet a range of practitioners, and hear them talk informally about the challenges for the past year in their professional work. At the same time, I approached Legal Aid and the Department of Juvenile Justice.

These contacts eventually led to some valuable interviews with practitioners working in these agencies. I spent a few days during the following year observing sentencing hearings, and also some trials in Campbelltown. I also visited the central children's court at Parramatta, and spent a week attending hearings and meeting practitioners in the country court at Armidale.[17] I also observed some reporting sessions in Glebe of the Youth Drugs Court, an initiative involving diversion of defendants to an intensive program of rehabilitation.

For each of the three stages of the project, the process of gaining access through writing letters and obtaining permission from different institutions, and also obtaining approval from an ethics committee, took about a year. This suggests that some patience, and a scientific purpose, is required to pursue this type of study. In addition, the amount of time spent does not guarantee that you have advanced beyond a basic understanding of professional work. Aaron Cicourel is best known for a (1968) study in which he was funded to spend three years as a full-time observer in two police stations. He reports that, even with this level of access, he only started to understand the work, and gain the trust of the officers, towards the end of his fieldwork.

Ethical Considerations

The material in this book has been approved by the children's courts in three states. This seemed a good procedure to follow in a study about potentially sensitive issues. It was also necessary, before conducting each stage of the study to obtain permission from an ethics committee.[18] There have been debates taking place in Australia and elsewhere about whether the system of ethics review that regulates research in universities has become too restrictive. Social scientists have argued that the system of ethics review exaggerates both the likelihood and magnitude of potential risks (Israel 2004, Schrag 2010, Van den Hoonard 2012), since the guidelines were originally designed to protect hospital patients participating in clinical trials.

Two examples from this project illustrate how this system can affect researchers. Children's hearings in Tasmania and New South Wales were closed to the public, partly to protect young people from coming into contact with victims (a case where the complainant or victim was excluded is described in chapter 6). In these states, the courts were happy to give permission to observe hearings provided that the identities of parties were anonymised. However, when I sought approval from an ethics committee to pursue this project in Tasmania, it was initially suggested that I should obtain written consent from every defendant and practitioner, and also from the parent or guardian where available of each defendant. After making representations, the ethics committee agreed that consent could be obtained if parties at hearings knew that a researcher was present, and could object.

During the second stage of my project in Victoria, I encountered the same problem. A new committee in Tasmania insisted on this requirement even when reporting hearings in an open court. Fortunately, I could also apply under the regulations to an ethics committee in Victoria, and this took a different view. However, in each case I was told that, when observing interviews between professionals and clients, it would be necessary to obtain written consent from the young person, and from a parent or guardian (by telephone if necessary). This demonstrates the obstacles facing someone who wants to study young people in a research project, even without seeking to interview them.

In Tasmania, there was an additional problem of how to approach using audio-recordings, which I obtained for a few hearings. Anyone who gave consent for me to attend would not necessarily know that I might also be listening to the audio-recording. For this reason, I decided only to use this more detailed record, as against the notes taken during or after hearings, after the court had written to defendants, and practitioners involved, giving them an opportunity to object. This procedure was approved by the ethics committee under its procedures for amending applications. It provided a safe-guard for someone who might be concerned about a potentially sensitive event being reported in an academic study.

There will be some readers who will not see these constraints as obstacles, but as sensible precautions. The reality is that asking magistrates to obtain written consent from everyone at an hearing makes it impossible to pursue this type of research. Asking organizations to obtain consent forms from clients observed, and to collect forms from their parents, both imposes an administrative burden and makes it impossible to conduct truly naturalistic research. Some researchers find working within these restrictions so difficult that they abandon projects about children or young people: an example of how regulation can have unintended consequences, since no one disputes that observational or interview-based studies can make a valuable contribution in developing or evaluating government policies. Many sociologists and criminologists would also argue that it is wrong, on ethical grounds, that one should require permission from a parent to interview a 16 or 17 year old youth. In many countries, young people can vote, and even in Australia one can obtain medical treatment as a 16 year old without parental consent.[19]

Some Objectives

The main objective of this study is to describe the nature of professional work around sentencing, drawing on observations of hearings and interviews with professionals. Chapter 2 locates this in the context of debates about juvenile justice policy in five English speaking countries. There is also, however, a theoretical objective: to promote a greater appreciation of the interpretive tradition within criminology (see also Travers 2005). Qualitative research has received some degree of criticism in recent years within criminology for not being sufficiently rigorous and scientific, and most of the limited funding available for research is directed towards quantitative projects.[20] A recent Australian text presents qualitative research as producing interesting insights on mixed methods projects that cannot usually be included in journal articles (Bartels and Richards 2011), suggesting that it is hardly central to the criminological enterprise. Chapter 3 offers a justification for conducting ethnographic fieldwork, based on the in-depth study of different institutional perspectives, in an age of evaluation research informed by different theoretical assumptions. It also discusses methodological issues such as the relationship between ethnography and discourse analysis, the extent to which interpretive ethnography can address power relations, and the ethical issues that arise in doing justice to the views of children. The chapter also advances a middle position between the "intellectual excesses" that often characterize the debate between qualitative and quantitative approaches. It suggests that, even if it is not possible to be completely objective, careful description of everyday practices can achieve a kind of objectivity in writing about children's courts.

Chapter 4 introduces the different professional groups working in children's courts. These include magistrates, juvenile case workers, defense lawyers and prosecutors. Other studies have examined the work of professionals doing similar work, although without always fully appreciating the practical circumstances of their work. How do magistrates make sentencing decisions? How do case workers write pre-sentence reports? How do these groups work together collaboratively? How do they understand the nature of success or failure in their work? Drawing primarily on interviews, the chapter will attempt to go beyond the idealized accounts one finds in professional manuals and critical studies by sociologists, and consider the nature of professional work.

The central part of the study looks at the practical considerations involved in sentencing different types of offenders. This concept was originally developed by Alfred Schutz (1962) as a means of getting some purchase on the meaningful character of the world, as this is experienced in everyday life. We see the people around us as typical of particular categories, which allows us to predict how they will behave. Schutz also notes that, in most situations, this is done automatically: we immediately see people as types without needing to reflect or make an interpretive judgment. In the case of children's courts, sentencing is centrally concerned with determining the appropriate response to criminal offences by children.

In addition, the legal framework directs magistrates to identify different types of offenders. Chapter 5 looks at how the children's court responds to minor offenders. Chapter 6 looks at the considerations involved in sentencing repeat or serious offenders. Chapter 7 looks at those young people who are particularly vulnerable, or already subject to child protection orders. Chapter 8 looks at bail hearings and contested trials. Each chapter contains transcripts obtained through observing actual hearings. Together they make it possible to see the work of practitioners, and also the nature of offences by young people, in some detail.

These chapters mostly describe the work of children's courts in these three Australian states in general terms, without identifying the source of data extracts.[21] This is possible because to a large extent the legislation in the three states, and the procedures in hearings, are quite similar. In fact, my impression from teaching an international online course on juvenile justice, is that the law and procedures in other countries do not differ substantially from those in Australia. Nevertheless, there are significant differences in outcomes between children's courts. Chapter 9 argues that there are real differences in sentencing practices, particularly between Victoria and the other states. There are also significant variations between regions within states, and between individual magistrates.

The concluding chapter considers the implications of the data presented in the study, and the ethnographic approach adopted, for understanding children's courts. It also makes some recommendations for juvenile justice policy in Australia and internationally. These are based on the assumption that, even though they have been falling for 20 years, rates of detention are too high, and that more could be achieved, perhaps by adopting the approach developed in Victoria. You do not, however, need to agree with this viewpoint: the objective of this study is to present a balanced account of what actually happens, and how practitioners understand their work, that makes it possible to debate policy alternatives.

2.

Welfare versus Punishment: A Continuing Debate

Most of this book describes sentencing in Australian children's courts, with the aim of making visible the realities experienced by decision makers on the ground as they are faced with actual young people. Before doing so, however, it is important to understand the debates about policy that take place about youth justice internationally. There is a large literature, particularly in the United Kingdom and the USA, written by welfare professionals and academics arguing for a less punitive and more welfare oriented juvenile justice system. This chapter will argue that this debate between those who see young people in need of special protection and help, and those who believe that they should be punished like adults, has always been central.

Although some commentators have argued that it is outdated, and we need a new framework (for example, Smith 2005), the first part of this chapter argues that it offers an useful means of thinking about the history of juvenile justice, and what happens in five English speaking countries.[1] Whether you agree with the recommendations at the end of this study will depend on where you stand in this debate. The second half of the chapter will approach the debate from a more critical standpoint. It will contrast three models for thinking about the development of policy in particular countries and internationally, and ask why there seems to be no resolution or end in sight for this continuing debate.

Policy Debates in Juvenile Justice

During the 19th and early 20th centuries, many government offi-cials and social reformers in Britain and the USA argued, against established institutions and practices, that children and young people should be treated differently from adults. They succeeded in establishing the welfare-oriented children's court which sought to protect young people from bad parenting and social deprivation (Platt 1969). Although children could be detained for long periods, this court was concerned with welfare rather than punishment. Children were not convicted of criminal offences but helped by social workers.

During the 1960s in America, and later in other countries, there was a movement to reform the children's court. In a series of landmark cases, parents challenged decisions to send young people to children's homes for long periods even though they had only committed minor offences (Bernard 1992, Lemert 1970). Similar reforms followed in other countries over the next two decades. This often involved establishing separate legislation for child protection and juvenile crime. In each side of the refashioned children's court, there was more oversight by magistrates and a greater emphasis on due process, including the right to legal representation. In the criminal legislation, children were treated as being responsible for their actions like adults.

This latest reform movement is sometimes presented as resulting in a move back to punishing children, which can be demonstrated by the fact that increased numbers are sent to detention centers, as against being "helped" in children's homes. From this perspective, legislation that uses the term "punishment" sends the wrong signals, and encourages magistrates to impose punitive orders. This was not, however, the objective of the reformers. Instead, they argued, in a way that has some similarities with the UN Convention on the Rights of the Child, that legislative changes were required in order to treat children with more dignity and respect. The great achievement of the first children's courts was to rescue children from adult prisons, but in doing so they were denied legal rights and protections. The reformers in the 1960s gave children these rights, but also believed that children should be punished, even if they received more lenient penalties than adults.[2] The American courts even determined that children could take legal action, on their own behalf, to protect themselves from unintentional abuses in the name of welfare.

Since then, the most influential reform movement in juvenile justice has been restorative justice. This originated in practice and as a theoretical perspective in criminology in New Zealand and Australia, but has resulted in many initiatives worldwide. A key principle is that offenders should be brought into contact with victims, and the wider community, and either apologize for their actions or compensate the victim. However, it has perhaps been most effective in establishing conferencing, in which there is an opportunity to talk about the offence through a mediator, as a more meaningful way of communicating with offenders than traditional court hearings.

Although restorative justice is claimed to be wholly new, as happens in many initiatives in this competitive professional field, in reality it draws on elements of welfare and justice systems. It has been successful, politically as much as professionally worldwide, because it appeals to, or at least is seen as having some positives, by each side of this debate. Conferences appeal to those with a welfare orientation because they seem to treat young people more holistically, and are run by the social services rather than the police or lawyers. But they also appeal to the police, and traditionally minded magistrates in courts, because they impose greater demands on defendants than receiving a police caution, and often result in higher penalties than could be imposed by courts.[3]

There is a continuing debate internationally over whether juvenile justice should place greater emphasis on welfare or punishment (Muncie 2009, Taylor et al 2010, Roberson 2011). Many professionals and academics would like the system to become more welfare-oriented, by recombining the two sides of the children's court (for example, Pitts 2001, Smith 2003). There are, however, pressure groups and politicians who would like to see the system become more punishment-oriented, both by giving fewer chances, and attempting to deter offenders. One can see an extreme example in the radio "shock jocks" who advocate bringing back corporal punishment. From this perspective, detention centers are too concerned with welfare and rehabilitation, or parents are blamed for not "disciplining" children. Faced with political pressures from those lobbying for welfare and punishment, government agencies often strike a pragmatic balance that preserves existing practices and institutions (Travers 1997b).

A Contemporary Reform Movement

Most studies published in the growing academic field of juvenile justice are dissatisfied with how we currently respond to youth offending, both in their own countries and internationally. In particular, they argue that juvenile justice systems are excessively punitive: too many young people are incarcerated, and insufficient resources are directed towards rehabilitation, or preventative measures such as early intervention (for example, Pitts 2001, Goldson 2008, Muncie 2009). Social work academics have made some persuasive contributions, often based on empirical research, arguing for more resources and a greater emphasis on rehabilitation (for example, Barry and McNeill 2009). There have also been calls to incorporate the principles in the 1989 UN Convention on the Rights of the Child into legislation or administrative systems.[4]

Here are a few examples of criticisms from recent studies published in Britain and the USA:

> This book was born out of a profound sense of frustration at the state of the youth justice system in England and Wales. This frustration is epitomized by the depressing trend of the current era towards an ever greater reliance on the most punitive means of control available, which permeates the entire spectrum of youth justice practice... (Smith 2003, p.1).

> The UK's record in the matter of the United Nations Convention on the Rights of the Child is deplorable. Having ratified the treaty in 1991, Britain has been chastised twice, in 1999 and 2002, for a continual abrogation of its obligations, on everything from misuse of child custody to violence against children...(Brown 2005, p. 32).

> There will always be a need for detention and long-term lockup to ensure community safety, but we've come to rely on them [in the USA] as our best response rather than treating them as only one part of an overall approach to juvenile delinquency. We rely on them so heavily, in fact, that we have invested more resources in bricks and mortar than we have in the treatment programs these youths

actually need to successfully turn their lives around (Aarons et al 2009, p.180).

Although the number of young people in custody is much lower in many countries than during the 1960s, many commentators are concerned that detention rates have risen in recent years. There are some sobering figures reported by John Muncie (2009). According to one report about the USA, "juvenile incarceration increased by 42 percent during the 1990s reaching an estimated 105,600 in 2006" (Muncie 2009, p.356). In Britain, the under-18 prison population rose from 1,328 in June 1992 to 3,175 in October 2002, although it has subsequently fallen (Muncie 2009, p.339). There are also reports of a growing international punitiveness as countries have adopted policies originally introduced in the USA. A striking example is the Netherlands in which "between 1995 and 2001, the number of youth custodial places increased from 900 to 2100"(Muncie 2009, p.368).

It is perhaps going too far to describe those concerned about these changes as a global reform movement. Nevertheless, there is a growing academic and policy literature that asks governments to live up to their international obligations, and only send young offenders to detention as a last resort. Reformers have also tried to combat the arguments made by some academics during the 1970s that rehabilitative programs are usually unsuccessful: that "nothing works" (Martinson 1974). There is a large literature today, produced by social workers, and criminologists, that claims to demonstrate, often with some passion and evangelical zeal, that many programs do work (Ward and Maruna 2007). This suggests that governments world wide should be investing more resources, and energy, in these programs as against pursuing the soft option of incarcerating persistent young offenders.

The Debate in Five English Speaking Countries

The welfare-punishment debate takes different forms across the world, these days often influenced by UNICEF which has commissioned reports about countries in which concerns have been raised about the experiences of young offenders (see, for example, UNICEF 2008). Without giving too much detail, this section provides a summary of current issues and developments in five English speaking countries. Partly because I have relevant materials and information to hand, I have chosen to focus on England, Scotland, the USA, Canada and Australia.[5]

This summary is not intended as a comprehensive review, and the limited details given illustrate the difficulties of describing juvenile justice systems since these vary within countries, even before looking at the experiences of minority groups. The summaries will, however, demonstrate the continuing relevance of the welfare-justice debate. They show that, despite some differences in terminology, juvenile justice systems in these countries have similar institutions, professional occupations and legislative frameworks. There are "youth courts" or "children's courts" that are separate to the adult system, even if critics argue that the boundaries are being eroded. There are also similarities in how policies have developed. In each country, there has been a shift from the welfare to justice model in the last forty years, even if this has only taken place in Scotland quite recently. There are concerns about growing punitiveness in each country (Muncie and Goldson 2006).

England

During the first half of the 20th century, the juvenile justice system in England combined punitive and welfare elements. There was, however, considerable support during the 1960s for creating a welfare-oriented system in which social workers made key decisions. The 1969 Children and Young Persons Act, enacted by a Labour government is seen as the high mark of this movement, although the changes were not implemented, or watered down when the Conservative party was elected in 1970. There was a growing emphasis on punishment, and an increase in youth detentions. Surprisingly, however, the numbers in custody fell dramatically during the 1980s, even though there was a right wing government, with a populist law and order agenda, led by Margaret Thatcher. This is explained in most texts as arising from the sensible policy adopted by the police of giving repeat cautions rather than sending young offenders to court. The public accepted this approach since fewer offences were committed (partly due to demographic changes), but also through benign neglect by the media.

There was a shift in policy during the early 1990s, partly in response to the fears generated after the disturbing Bulger case in which two ten year old boys were convicted of murdering a toddler (Davis and Bourhill 1997). It is, however, the New Labour government elected in 1997 that is blamed by many commentators for sending more young people to detention. This was, perhaps, unfortunate since the ambitious aim behind the New Labour program, established in legislation such as the 1998 Crime and Disorder Act, was to combine elements of the previous welfare and punishment models. Instead of benign neglect, repeat offenders were referred to Youth Offending Teams. Many were required to attend restorative conferences in which they could meet and apologize to victims (Crawford and Newburn 2003). Many received help from the social services at this early stage of their offending career. Unfortunately, despite this ambitious diversionary program, increasing numbers were sent to court after committing further offences, and an increasing proportion of these received custodial sentences.

Policy debates about juvenile justice in England will be influenced, at least for the next few years, by the riots that took place in several cities during August 2010. Nevertheless, it is possible to distinguish rioting from ordinary youth crime. We know that at least some rioters had not been in trouble with the police before.[6] There have, so far, been no substantial changes to the juvenile justice system following the election of the Conservative/ Liberal Coalition government in May 2010. This government does, however, recognize the cost to the taxpayer of incarceration. It is committed to reducing the deficit created through effectively nationalizing major banks in response to the the 2008 Global Financial Crisis (Streek 2011). The mechanism suggested in a Green Paper (Ministry of Justice 2010) to achieve a reduction in detentions is for local authorities rather than central government to bear the costs. It is possible that more young people will be detained given the tough response of some magistrates to the riots.

Scotland

Juvenile justice "north of the border" offers an interesting contrast to England, in that the recommendations in the 1964 Kilbrandon report were followed through, resulting in a welfare oriented system (McNara 2006). Scotland was, for many years, almost unique among jurisdictions internationally as not viewing children capable of criminal misconduct. Instead, the Scottish Children's Hearing System saw young offenders as requiring protection rather than punishment. Decisions were made by a lay panel, comprising a children's reporter (or advocate), a child and legal guardian and a social worker. One should not exaggerate the differences between jurisdictions oriented to welfare or justice principles since serious and persistent offenders were still sentenced to detention (even if this was described differently). Nevertheless, the ethos of the system was distinctive in emphasizing rehabilitation over punishment.

In recent years, there has been a shift towards the justice model, caused in part by greater media attention to youth crime, even though according to most measures it has been falling with the proportion of young people in the population. There have also been concerns about delays in arranging hearings. To address this problem, a new institution has been established called the "Youth Court." The objective in a pilot during 2003 was "to deal with persistent 16 and 17 year old offenders." These young people "would be fast tracked to an adult Sheriff Court (sitting as a Youth Court) within ten days of being charged" (Piacentini and Walters 2006, p.44). Critics have argued that this marks a retreat from welfare principles, and that there is far less emphasis on talking to offenders, or considering welfare issues, in the new court. However, offenders under the age of 16 are not viewed as capable of committing a criminal offence.

The USA

There is a much higher rate of juvenile detention in the USA than in other countries, although there are wide variations among the 52 states or jurisdictions (Roberson 2011). This may suggest that comparison is difficult. There are certainly exceptional features such as the racial divide in America, and the fact that in some states young people have been imprisoned for life or even executed until quite recently (Amnesty International 2005). The administration of justice is more politicised than in many countries because judges and often prosecutors are elected, and have to respond to populist concerns about pressures to get tough on youth crime.

Nevertheless, the institutional and legal frameworks in juvenile justice are similar, in many respects, to those in other English speaking countries. America was the first country to move to the justice model from the late 1960s, out of concerns that young people were being incarcerated for long periods in the name of welfare. There are numerous diversionary schemes and restorative justice initiatives in the USA, although these vary between particular courts and states. There are children's courts that balance welfare and punishment considerations within the justice model. In recent years, there has been much criticism by professionals with a welfare orientation about the increasing practice of transferring persistent offenders to adult courts (for example, Corriero 2006, Aarons et al 2009). However, Aaron Kupchik (2006) demonstrated in an empirical study, to be considered in more detail in the next chapter, that in practice outcomes are similar. This is a good example of how institutional change is often more important symbolically, in this case through satisfying those calling for greater punitiveness, than in changing outcomes or sentencing practices.

Canada

Juvenile justice has also become an arena for debate in Canada, although in this country the Federal government has tried to steer a middle way through national legislation that has been gradually adopted in the ten provinces and two territories (Department of Justice 2009). Canada had a welfare-oriented system, but this was criticized for resulting in unfair outcomes during the 1970s. The 1982 Young Offender's Act introduced the justice model in which young offenders were seen as responsible for their actions, and capable of being punished. This resulted in a rise in juvenile detentions to the extent that for a time incarceration rates in Canada were higher than other countries. At the same time, the legislation was criticized for resulting in leniency towards serious and persistent offenders.

The Federal government attempted to fine-tune the Act, and eventually replaced it with the 2003 Young Offenders Act. As in every piece of juvenile justice legislation, it begins with an attempt to balance the principles of welfare and punishment:

> The purpose of the youth criminal justice system is to prevent crime by addressing the circumstances underlying a young person's offending behaviour, rehabilitate young persons who commit offences and reintegrate them back into society, and ensure that a young person is subject to meaningful consequences for his or her offences, in order to promote the long-term protection of the public.

Those committed to a welfare model would prefer legislation to acknowledge that young people cannot commit criminal offences. Nevertheless, this legislation has proved successful because of the new emphasis placed on diversion to restorative conferences, which has resulted in a dramatic decline in youth custody.

Australia

In Australia, there was always a legislative separation between the protective and criminal side of children's courts in the seven states and two territories, since these institutions were established in the late 19th century (Seymour 1988). However, by the 1980s there were growing concerns that children could be locked up at the discretion of social workers without having committed serious offences, and without having legal representation (for example, Carney 1984). During the 1980s and 1990s, legislative changes took place establishing the justice model in each state (Borowski and O'Connor 1997).

At the same time, almost every state established procedures for diverting offenders to restorative conferences. The exception was Victoria which, intriguingly, has a considerably lower detention rate, at least for non-Indigenous offenders (Richards and Lyneham 2010). One consequence of the reforms was that a new agency was required to manage rehabilitation and punishment. In some respects, juvenile case workers have a similar role to social workers in the old system.[7] They provide support to families, and address social issues relating to offending. However, they have distinct objectives that come from a system that balances welfare and punishment. They are responsible for both rehabilitating offenders, but also for administering orders intended as punishment.

Since this move to the justice model, there have been some calls for change by academics and professionals who would like more emphasis on welfare in the legislation (Sheehan and Borowski 2012). One argument raised is that a significant proportion of young people who commit crimes have "protective" issues, even if they are not subject to child protection orders. There are concerns about the detention rate which has risen in the last few years, even though it has steadily declined since the 1970s.[8] There are particular concerns about the very high rates of imprisonment among Indigenous young people. There are also complaints, as in every jurisdiction, that the courts and welfare services are under-resourced, and in some states and many regions cannot offer effective rehabilitative programs. All these concerns, as in the other jurisdictions considered, can be understood as part of a continuing debate between welfare and punishment values in juvenile justice systems.

Understanding Policy Development

Tracing the history of policy development in any one country, let alone comparatively, is difficult because there is so much happening in each decade. There is either new legislation generated through the political process or institutional pressures creating momentum for administrative change. It is easy when given a lot of detail, particularly about legislative change, to miss the underlying processes or dynamics. One way to address this in sociology is to employ models, or what Max Weber (1997, p.88) called "ideal types," that approximate to what may be happening, without claiming to represent this accurately. Three models that are used by different academics, and some practitioners, are those of neoliberalism, continuous improvement and the cycle of juvenile justice.

Neoliberalism and Criminal Justice

The most developed criticisms of juvenile justice policy have been made by progressive academics in Britain and the United States. The basic idea is that economic and social inequality has increased globally since the 1980s, caused by a change in government economic and social policies known as neoliberalism, and with it a punitive response to crime (Harvey 2007, Wacquant 2009). This is often explained by "the death of the social" thesis:

> [This] suggests a number of interrelated – sometimes contradictory – youth and criminal justice processes that have occurred to varying degrees across most western societies. These include the privatizing of the state sector and the commodifying of crime control; the widening of material inequalities between and within states thus creating new insecurities and fuelling demands for centralized authoritarian law and order strategies; the devolving of responsibility for crime control to individuals, families and communities (as captured in the notion of 'responsibilisation'); and the espousing of scientific realism and pragmatic, 'what works' responses to crime and disorder in the hope that an image of an 'orderly environment' can be secured which in turn will help to attract further 'nomadic capital' (Muncie 2009, p.355).

The strength of this kind of sociological analysis is that it connects apparently disparate developments in law and governance, and ultimately explains these as arising from underlying economic forces resulting in growing inequality. It is also possible to explain any counter-examples, such as countries in which detention rates have fallen, in terms of resistance or "contradictory" processes. There are, however, several aspects of the development of juvenile justice policy that cannot easily be explained within this theoretical framework.

One is that, even though statistics can be misleading, it would appear that internationally detention rates have been falling since the 1970s. There is not necessarily a clear correlation between neoliberalism, defined as a set of policies employed by British and American governments from the 1980s, and rising punitiveness. Another is the exceptionally high detention rate in America which cannot easily be explained by the concept of neoliberalism. A third problem for the theory is that "responsibilisation" may just be a slogan. There is no sign that the welfare state in Britain or elsewhere has been privatized or down-sized substantially. Under New Labour, and before the Global Financial Crisis, there was a steady rise in public expenditure. Despite these explanatory weaknesses, this critical theory does draw attention to global material inequalities that may ultimately inform responses to youth crime.

Continuous Improvement

It is perhaps inevitable that most texts about juvenile justice policy only give one side of the argument. There are also managers in government agencies who see organizational processes in terms of continuous improvement, one of the key ideas in management theory (Deming 1986). Critical theorists often portray managers in negative terms, suggesting that management initiatives, and in particular risk assessment, are responsible for a rise in youth detentions. Managers, themselves, believe that progress is being made towards a more effective juvenile justice system. A good example from Britain is a 2010 speech by the head of the Youth Justice Board which, at the time, was facing abolition. He presented the experience of the last few years, seen as an unmitigated disaster by critics, in upbeat language:

> Building on these foundations we are now seeing really impressive improvements in the three main outcome indicators for youth justice. First time entrants, having initially risen, are now showing dramatic month on month reductions up and down the country…Secondly, we are also seeing very marked reductions in the frequency of proven reoffending…the reductions here are important, and we should celebrate the achievement that lies behind these figures. Lastly, the number of children in custody is also reducing. Now we could debate all day what is the proper target to aim for here. It is our view in the YJB that there will always be a place for custody for the most damaged, and most damaging children, in our community. But at the same time there is also clear evidence that there are children in custody for whom a community sentence would be just as

effective, or more effective, than custody, and whose needs (and therefore the underlying causes of their offending) can be better met outside of custody (Drew 2010).

Although little empirical research has been conducted, one would also expect that many ordinary practitioners believe that detention is necessary as a last resort. This book contains some evidence that case workers and magistrates, as well as police officers, believe that young people are responsible for their actions and should be treated firmly. These practitioners would not support a return to a welfare-oriented system: they are comfortable with balancing welfare and punishment considerations within the justice model.

The Cycle of Juvenile Justice

A third way of looking at juvenile justice has been advanced as an academic model by Thomas Bernard (2002). Whereas critical theorists see growing penalization, and managers continuous improvement, Bernard believes that there is a regular cycle in policy making. This arises because there is a debate between welfare and punishment models, but also because whatever measures are taken there will always be youth crime. Over time pressure will build up for a change, if only to make practitioners feel better and for governments to demonstrate they are doing something. A new language will arise, and new professional groups will benefit with the new legislation, but the pendulum will swing back over a thirty year cycle.

Although this may seem unduly cynical, it works quite well in explaining shifts in policy within America, while remaining vague on the specific mechanisms that trigger change. It also, however, serves a liberal viewpoint in the same way as critical theorizing. If the last change in the USA to the justice model took place in the late 1960s, and this has happened in other English speaking countries in subsequent decades, perhaps we are now ready for a shift back to the welfare model, in the sense of investing greater effort and resources in rehabilitative and preventative programs. There is widespread dissatisfaction among professionals about the high rate of detentions. The reductions to public spending caused by the

Global Financial Crisis, particularly in Britain, make it difficult to imagine alternatives, although there are now compelling economic reasons to close detention centres.

The Relevance to Practice

Some British criminologists have argued in recent years that the welfare-punishment debate is outdated (for example, Smith 2005). This is either because in the view of the critic both models are equally punitive,[9] or that everyone accepts and takes for granted this framework so it no longer tells us anything interesting. From this perspective, criminologists should focus on new developments, such as managerial concerns with efficiency and effectiveness (Pratt 1989). Even so, the welfare-punishment debate continues to be relevant to most areas of juvenile justice practice. It also remains a central theme in theoretically motivated studies in sociology and jurisprudence (for example, King and Piper 1995), because ordinary people think in these terms.[10] At an organizational level, agencies often seek to balance the two principles when making operational decisions (and, in doing so, they have wide discretion within the legislative framework). Should courts be friendly places in which young people and the magistrate sit around a table, or look grim and forbidding? What sort of regime is appropriate for a youth detention centre? How much emphasis should be placed on care and control in case work? Moreover, individual practitioners balance these considerations in their own practices. There are different ways of approaching the task of working with young offenders, depending on whether one sees their behavior as criminal or resulting from unfortunate social circumstances.

Discussion in the policy literature about the value of the welfare punishment debate sometimes raises sociological questions about the nature of professional work. Muncie (2009, p.303) has suggested, for example, that "welfare and justice are often employed as justificatory devices without either being *in any way* achieved" (my emphasis). To evaluate this statement, you would need good descriptions of what happens inside institutions such as police forces, children's courts and youth detention centers. There is not much empirical research of this kind, and in recent years it tends to be conducted as part of evaluations, commissioned by agencies, that inevitably present a positive view of achievements. In the next chapter, I will be making a case for the value of observational research on juvenile justice that goes further than evaluations in investigating what happens in practice.

3.

Why Observe Sentencing Hearings?

The justification and rationale for conducting observational research as a social scientist when studying institutions such as the police, prisons or courts is that, when observation is used alongside interviewing, it becomes possible to understand what actually happens in the criminal justice process (Emerson 2001, Hammersley and Atkinson 2007). Although there is an overlap between these two research methods, the distinctive feature of ethnography is that it involves spending a long period of time engaging in naturalistic observation. Interviewing can produce insightful findings about some area of social life, but it may miss what is important, because the researcher has not seen the activities that take place in that setting, or heard people talking amongst themselves.[2] This is why criminologists should observe courtroom hearings, in addition to other stages of the criminal justice process. It also allows them to make a practical contribution, either by suggesting improvements in practices or procedures, identifying problems or shortcomings, or simply giving practitioners the opportunity to reflect on their professional work.

Nevertheless, despite the many ethnographies and interview studies that have been published about the criminal justice system, less research of this kind is conducted than in previous decades. Even in the USA and Britain where qualitative research is well-established in university programs, you can no longer assume that ethnography is taught as a research method on criminology majors, or that everyone sees this as vital or necessary for understanding the criminal justice process.[2] Recently there have been criticisms by quantitative researchers or government agencies about excessive subjectivity and looseness (for example, Wiles 2002), and attempts to concentrate scarce funding in quantitative or mixed methods evaluation research that is presented as most useful to policy makers.[3]

To make matters worse, within the fields of ethnography and interviewing, there has been a change in theoretical focus. During the 1960s, grounded theory developed and became a respectable methodology through presenting qualitative research as scientific and objective (Strauss and Corbin 1998). The basic technique is to identify analytic themes through coding interview transcripts and fieldnotes. By contrast, since the 1980s there has been a reaction not only against grounded theory, but also against other forms of ethnographic research that claim to produce objective knowledge (for example, Clifford and Marcus 1986, Denzin 1992, Gubrium and Holstein 2003). It has become common for qualitative researchers, especially in the USA, to question objectivity or even celebrate the fact that there is no such thing as truth. Traditional forms of ethnographic reportage and representation have been criticised on philosophical and political grounds. New styles of "ethnography" have been developed such as performing plays (McCall and Becker 1990) or writing about your own experiences and emotions that do not require conventional fieldwork.[4]

Because of this institutional and intellectual climate, it seems appropriate to explain why ethnographic research is worthwhile, and can produce objective findings. The first section of the chapter will approach this task by considering how evaluation has been used in juvenile justice. It will describe the methods used, drawing on British and Australian evaluations of restorative justice. It will also consider some criticisms made by professional evaluators, and by those who view evaluation as politically conservative, or as having unintended damaging consequences.

The second part of the chapter will consider how ethnography as a research method can be employed in researching juvenile justice, focusing on the interpretive traditions of symbolic interactionism and ethnomethodology.[5] It will re-visit the labeling tradition and suggest that, despite leading in some versions to relativism or a celebration of deviance against conventional society, it also generated valuable research about the criminal justice process based on appreciating professional perspectives and observing actual work. This has resulted in two ethnographies by American researchers about children's courts (Emerson 1969, Kupchik 2006) that make visible the institutional practices concealed by statistics and in policy debates.

The chapter will then consider some general methodological issues: the relationship between ethnography and discourse analysis; the extent to which interpretive ethnography should address power relations; and the difficulties of doing justice to the views and experiences of children. The chapter concludes by considering the extent to which qualitative research can be objective. The aim is to explain the assumptions informing this study, while acknowledging that there are many different ways of conducting empirical research about children's courts.

The Rise of Evaluation Research

A central preoccupation for agencies delivering government services at the present time is to demonstrate value for money, and to improve efficiency and effectiveness (Newburn 2007, Ashworth and Redmayne 2006). This results both from a response to difficult economic times, but also from an international movement that has been successful in professionalizing or "modernizing" government. This movement originated in the USA, but became influential across the world when the New Labour government in Britain, elected in 1997, took up and vigorously promoted the main ideas (Davies et al 2000). A key idea is that the effectiveness of any program or policy should be tested using scientific methods ("evidence-based policy").

Methods and assumptions

Although evaluations often use a combination of methods, and some are explicitly concerned with process rather than outcome, the primary methods and assumptions come from the quantitative tradition in social science.[6] One way to make sense of the movement is that it is not only driven by policy-makers, but by academics with an evangelical commitment to a particular understanding of scientific method. They have used their numbers and influence, particularly in the USA, in lobbying for this to become the only acceptable way of conducting policy research. The "gold standard" from this perspective is the randomized trial in which outcomes are measured and compared using statistical techniques for young offenders who have been assigned to different programs. Through following these procedures, it is claimed that we can obtain objective knowledge of "what works," and insight into specific factors that explain successful programs. Proponents of evaluation believe that application of this knowledge will lead to more effective and cost-efficient policies.

There is a large and sophisticated technical literature on the evaluation of rehabilitative programs for young offenders in Britain (Davies et al 2000) and the USA (Sherman et al 1999). To give some examples from Australia, there was considerable interest when restorative justice was being developed as a policy initiative, in demonstrating its effectiveness using scientific methods. Strang et al (1999) conducted a rigorous evaluation in comparing the offending histories of those who attended conferences and court hearings in the Australian Capital Territory (ACT).[7] Using similar methods, researchers working with Janet Chan (2005) measured the recidivism rate of those attending conferences in New South Wales and compared this to outcomes following court appearances. This study demonstrated not only that diversion reduced or delayed offending but also that Indigenous defendants benefited from diversion, even though they remained over-represented among those appearing in court and being sentenced to detention.

On some occasions, evaluators employ qualitative methods more systematically or in greater depth than providing contextual information for a quantitative study. Process evaluations are concerned with identifying whether a program is being implemented properly. This makes it possible to compare outcomes for properly constituted programs. Even without this scientific goal, agencies have funded studies about the practical problems that arise in implementing legislation. A good example is the well-resourced evaluation of the implementation of referral orders in England and Wales reported in Crawford and Newburn (2003). A large team of researchers interviewed practitioners about the practical issues involved in establishing this new program, young offenders subject to the orders and their parents, and those victims who attended conferences. The objective was evaluative rather than simply descriptive. The researchers found that there were many variations in the way Youth Offender Panels were constituted, depending on the resources and approach of local agencies. They found that practitioners, and young offenders and their parents, were generally positive about the experience of attending a conference. They discovered, however, that few victims attended, either because it was practically difficult to arrange conferences, or they did not want to meet offenders. One recommendation from the evaluation was that "we need to know more about what victims, in what circumstances, are more likely to benefit from active participation in restorative programs, and how best to facilitate this"(Crawford and Newburn 2003, p.241).

What's wrong with evaluation?

The objective of producing useful knowledge that leads to "continuous improvement" in the delivery of government services may seem like commonsense to many readers of this book. Evaluation has, however, been much criticized, and not simply by critics of government policy, for not delivering on its claims. Nick Tilley, one of the most experienced evaluators in the United Kingdom, has complained that most studies fall short of technical competence, and result in bad policy:

> Unless useful lessons for future action are learned from evaluation, there is little point in investing heavily in it. Useful lessons will only be learned if the evaluation is technically adequate, honestly published, and properly read. Much crime prevention evaluation that has been undertaken in the past falls short of even basic technical adequacy...At best this has involved wasting resources that could have been put to other uses. Worse, shortcomings in the evaluation have been overlooked, misleading conclusions drawn and effective practice abandoned, or ineffective practice spread. Worst of all, well-intentioned but harmful interventions have been encouraged (Tilley 2009, p.160).

Pawson and Tilley (1997) also make some critical observations, as evaluators, on the simplistic assumptions about causality that inform the "gold standard" of the randomized experiment. In their view, it is impossible to generalize from particular studies (in the terminology of quantitative research, they have no "external validity"). An example is that a rehabilitative program might work, but only because of the offenders selected, or the skill of a charismatic instructor. What is required is greater sensitivity to the processes that produce outcomes. This may sound as if they are advocating in-depth ethnography as a means of improving on the limited and potentially misleading knowledge that can be obtained from quantitative evaluations.

There has also been much criticism of evaluation on political grounds in Britain. According to one independent audit, spending on youth justice had increased by 45 percent under the New Labour government, but without significantly reducing reoffending rates (Solomon and Garside 2008). This suggests rather more than an implementation problem, but that the policies being pursued to reduce offending, through for example referral orders, do not work even though the evaluations are mostly positive. Muncie (2009, p. 298) argues that "evaluation comes to rest solely on indicators of internal system performance" rather than looking at the big picture.[8] This is also a methodological criticism since evaluations do not normally examine "the unpredictability and variability of local contexts and the complexity of the social and political in general" (Muncie 2009, p.325). Instead, they seek to produce clear-cut finding for agencies.

Given that quantitative methods, and the natural science model, are seen by many criminologists as the "gold standard", it seems worth pushing this point slightly further. From a different scientific perspective, the problem with evaluations is not their political bias, since this can hardly be avoided in social science research, but the fact they usually reveal little about what happens on programs or how practitioners understand their work. Unfortunately, the organizations funding studies do not usually want to hear about problems that cannot be solved. In the case of children's courts, most practitioners will readily admit, for example, that sending a young person to a detention centre rarely works, and in many cases leads to more offending through mixing with hardened offenders. This does not mean that there are alternative programs which are more successful, or that we should tolerate anti-social behavior. The thoughtful practitioner also knows that it would require major resources to address the root causes of offending in poverty and disadvantage, and even then there is no agreement on "what works" or the extent to which social services should intervene.

This kind of pessimistic or realistic finding is of little use to government agencies tasked with reducing crime, or even to the critic advancing some optimistic reform agenda. On the other hand, studies that describe in some detail what actually happens inside institutions such as children's courts make it possible to reflect on our achievements and shortcomings in addressing this social problem. Morally or politically, as Howard Becker (1972, pp.194-5) has observed, it seems important in a democratic society to demonstrate again and again that the welfare state and criminal justice system can never meet our expectations. Any study that describes ordinary practices and procedures in some depth, and goes beyond statistical information about outcomes, is valuable both for practitioners and the wider community in reminding us about these institutional realities.

Making Visible Institutional Practices

According to a primer used in teaching undergraduate courses in cultural anthropology during the 1970s, ethnographers

> conduct…research in the field, not in a laboratory or office. They go to natural settings to observe everyday activities and record casual conversations among the people there. They interact with people, watch what they do, listen to them talk, participate in their activities, and, in that context, describe their cultural knowledge (Spradley and McCurdy 1972, p.23).

A central objective is to shift perspective through spending time with a particular group:

> Ethnography is not merely an objective description of people and their behavior from the observer's viewpoint. It is a systematic attempt to discover the knowledge a group of people have learned and are using to organize their behavior. This is a radical change in the way many scientists see their work. Instead of asking, 'What do I see these people doing' we must ask 'What do these people see themselves doing'. And we cannot answer this question with our own concepts, for that would implicitly introduce our view of their actions (Spradley and McCurdy 1972, p.9).

One striking feature of the history of criminology in recent times has been the extent to which there has been a narrowing in the range of methods employed in empirical research. Ethnographies based on spending time inside institutions, or in communities, are still undertaken (for example, Yates 2004, Sanders 2005), and some achieve considerable impact and become set as standard texts on undergraduate courses.[9] However, there are fewer than in previous decades. As a consequence, there is an absence of living, breathing human beings either in the textbooks used by students or the mainly quantitative studies published in mainstream journals.

These concerns were advanced by a number of interpretive traditions during the 1960s towards quantitative studies conducted by mainstream criminologists.[10] There was also a considerable amount of ethnographic research that investigated different institutions and social worlds, including the criminal justice system. Without repeating all the methodological arguments, it seems appropriate to review some theoretical assumptions of these traditions, and consider how they conceptualized and researched juvenile justice.

Labeling theory re-visited

Labeling theory was developed during the early 1960s by sociologists working in the sociological tradition that, through the writings of Herbert Blumer (1968), has come to be known as symbolic interactionism. This was a time of political unrest in the USA, in which a younger generation wanted change in many areas of social life.[11] Graduate students in sociology were also reacting against a system of funding research, and an intellectual climate, that seemed to result in uniformly positive portrayals of established institutions and professions. Because of this labeling theory, and many of the ethnographies about social institutions published at the time, had a debunking, critical character.

A good example is Erving Goffman's *Asylums* (1961). This is a study in the labeling tradition in that it looks at the process by and through which people were admitted to mental hospitals, and how they responded to treatment. It is also a savage critique of the inhumanity of these institutions, and the scientific pretensions of organized medicine given that a diagnosis depends on contingent social factors as much as applying medical knowledge. In a similar way, studies of criminal justice, and particularly the theoretical statements by labeling theorists and sociologists of deviance, are intended to present the criminal justice system in a bad light. Becker (1972) draws attention, for example, to the contingencies involved in passing criminal laws against marijuana, and in enforcing those laws. The certainties of respectable citizens that there must be social, psychological or medical causes of deviance are shown to have no scientific basis if police officers target particular populations. Researchers in this tradition were also interested in appreciating the social worlds of those being labeled as criminal or deviant in their own terms. One view advanced by David Matza (1964) is that criminal behavior was quite normal amongst young people, and they simply grew out of this. He recommended that agencies such as the police and courts should avoid, wherever possible, stigmatizing offenders, since this may result in creating hardened delinquents.[12]

Labeling theory was criticized during the 1960s for being relativistic, and appearing to suggest that crime did not really exist as a social problem, but was simply a social construction.[13] However, this was only one side to the tradition. Labeling theorists also conducted a large number of empirical studies about the criminal justice process. Instead of accepting what organizations and agencies said about themselves, or accepting official statistics at face value (Kitsuse and Cicourel 1963), researchers conducted observational research inside the police, courts, prisons and other agencies.[14] Many of these studies do not have a critical or debunking intent. Instead, drawing on a broader tradition in Chicago School ethnography, as developed by Robert Park during the 1920s, and later Everett Hughes during the 1950s,[15] they present an appreciative portrait of different occupational groups, including those of police officers, lawyers and judges, in addition to the social worlds of those being labeled through their institutional work.

There were theoretical debates within labeling theory, as well as different empirical programs. Not every symbolic interactionist, including Blumer (1972), was happy with the radical version of constructionism informing some theoretical statements. The interpretive tradition known as ethnomethodology, which emerged during the 1960s in sociology alongside labeling theory, was also often explicitly opposed to the relativism implied in the term "constructionism." The emphasis was instead on respecting how people understand and experience the world in what Alfred Schutz (1962) called the natural attitude: as a constraining reality that we must accept and cannot easily be changed.[16] From this perspective, Melvin Pollner (1974) critiqued the apparent assumption in Becker's *Outsiders* that there could be a secret deviant, someone behaving against social rules or expectations who had not come to the attention of law enforcement agencies. Instead, Pollner argued that deviance could logically only exist within the terms of the model if it resulted in a criminal conviction by a correctly constituted court of law. He was also arguing against those who saw sociology as having a political role in deciding questions relating to deviance. It made more sense to examine how members of society made these decisions, without taking sides.

There were also researchers who advanced a methodological critique of labeling theory. Becker (1961) himself argued that it was important for the interactionist to adopt a balanced approach in studying different perspectives within organisations, even though it was difficult to avoid taking sides. There is a whole literature, written around the same time as labeling theory, about the techniques one could employ in order to achieve balance and objectivity in researching different institutional perspectives (for example, Bruyn 1986, Glaser and Strauss 1967). Earlier models include classic Chicago School ethnographies such as *The Taxi*

Dance Hall (Cressey 1932) in which a variety of perspectives were addressed sympathetically in understanding a social institution.

Ethnomethodologists went further than interactionist studies in addressing the detailed considerations employed by practitioners in their routine work. Aaron Cicourel's (1968) *The Social Organisation of Juvenile Justice* did not simply report occupational viewpoints, but also described in some detail the work of police officers making decisions to arrest and charge young offenders, made possible because he was based in their office for a considerable period of time. In one chapter, Cicourel looked at a series of documents produced about a young offender, pseudonymously called "Smithfield," over a three year period (Cicourel 1969, pp.203-41). After receiving probation orders for burglaries, and being placed in a foster home, he was ultimately sent to the "Youth Authority," the equivalent of today's detention centre.

The reports presented in this chapter come from different police officers and teachers, and there are also what we would describe as "Pre-Sentence Reports," that describe his family background and relationship with peers, and contain recommendations for sentencing. Over time, the factor that seemed decisive was his "antagonistic attitude," and failure to respond to the chances given. Cicourel was, however, critical towards the probation service and schools that made no attempt to engage with difficult young people therapeutically: "no one is prepared to pay the price of altering their own daily existence as a condition for influencing or altering the juvenile's daily round of activities" (Cicourel 1969, p.223).

More generally, police and probation officers, and judges in the children's court, had to decide whether a young person was in the first stages of a delinquent career, had made a youthful mistake, or was suffering from an illness. These decisions were often made on class and ethnic grounds. For example, a white youth from a middle-class family who was represented by a lawyer had a greater chance of being asked to attend counseling sessions than a black, working class defendant. Cicourel did not demonstrate this statistically, but gave persuasive examples suggesting systematic bias.

There is, therefore, a large body of literature from the 1960s and 1970s that describes the work of criminal justice agencies using ethnographic methods. It is worth re-visiting the labeling tradition as broadly conceived to include both ethnomethodology and symbolic interactionism. I have suggested that it is possible to appreciate the achievements of interactionist studies in describing the work of criminal justice practitioners, without having to accept their relativistic assumptions, or the critical stance adopted towards the police and courts. However, even ethnographic studies that are balanced or have no political motivation, often reveal a different side to institutions, and make one think differently about policy issues.

Two American ethnographies

There have been numerous observational and interview based studies of criminal courts in the USA by researchers influenced by the interpretive tradition.[17] These include two studies about children's courts. The first by Robert Emerson (1969) was conducted in a city "in the northern United States" during the 1960s. The second by Aaron Kupchik (2006) is a mixed methods study, although one with a significant ethnographic component, comparing a children's court and adult court hearing juvenile cases in New York State. They each contain a lot of information on the policy debates around juvenile justice in a particular time and place. They are perhaps most interesting, however, as sociological studies in making visible the institutional practices involved in sentencing young offenders, which it would appear do not vary substantially between Australia and the USA, although there have been significant changes in the last forty years.

Emerson's (1969) *Judging Delinquents* draws on ideas and concepts from both symbolic interactionism and ethnomethodology. It is not always cited in texts on juvenile justice, which is unfortunate since it goes further than many studies in describing the work of professionals, and also addresses underlying issues such as how judicial officers make sense of criminal behavior by juveniles. It was based on spending a year in a children's court. Emerson was partly interested in the relationship between the court and other institutions. He saw it as having to respond to pressures from the police, schools and probation service to take action against difficult young people, in order to maintain the authority of these institutions. It was effectively a dumping ground for "hard-core" cases in detention centers that made it possible for agencies to employ softer methods on "milder and less threatening cases," despite their own conviction that the former have "the same or even greater need for 'help' in these terms" (Emerson 1969, p.80).

The most interesting part of the study is based on summaries of the evidence and arguments presented in hearings. Emerson argues that young people were charged with similar offences, so the main task of the court was to determine the moral character of the defendant:

> Court staff distinguish three general kinds of juvenile moral character. First, a youth may be normal, i.e., basically like most children, acting for basically normal and conventional reasons, despite some delinquent behavior. Second, a youth may be regarded as a hard-core or criminal-like delinquent, maliciously or hostilely motivated, consciously pursuing illegal ends. Third, a youth may be disturbed, driven to acting in senseless and irrational ways by obscure motives or inner compulsions (Emerson 1969, p.91).

Emerson describes sentencing hearings in dramatic terms in which the police and probation officers sought to establish a delinquent moral character through "pitches and denunciations." The judge often had the role of challenging this assessment, and finding some good in the youth, or the circumstances of the offence. In Emerson's view, this reflected the court's "basic resistance to unwarrantable agency attempts to 'dump' undesirable cases on them for incarceration" (Emerson 1969, p.140). A defendant could try to influence the assessment by offering "justifications" and "excuses." However, this was a dangerous course, especially if it involved making a counter-denunciation of the police. The court always supported "licensed denouncers," and challenging the police would almost certainly undermine the youth's moral character.

Even though it gave many second chances, this children's court was presented in rather bleak terms. The only way of reaching young defendants who still respected authority was through a "threatening tone" and "moralistic lecturing" (Emerson 1969, p.173). In the cases of persistent offenders or the mentally disturbed, it was possible to be matter-of-fact and polite. Youths were regularly made to lose face. An example is that one officer "commonly conducted a delinquent to and from the court's detention cell with one arm around his neck and shoulder" (Emerson 1969, p.177). Middle class youth were often sent to the court clinic, rather than the probation service, and received better treatment, provided they were prepared to go along with accepting medical labels. All the agencies had limited resources, so in practice only the most deserving cases could be helped. Whereas labeling theorists at the time, such as Lemert (1970), criticized the court for being too ready to apply stigmatizing labels, Emerson took a different view. He argued that this children's court was reluctant to intervene in minor cases, but at the same time did nothing for the "hard-core" delinquent.

Kupchik's (2006) *Judging Juveniles* demonstrates how intellectual fashions have changed since the 1960s, since it is a mixed methods study. Kupchik described work in a children's court and an adult court that sentenced young people, drawing on interviews with practitioners. However, he also observed a large number of hearings in order to make a quantitative comparison of outcomes, which is seen as more persuasive evidence by policy makers.[18] Like many liberal commentators in the USA, Kupchik is opposed to the policy of transferring young people to adult courts for sentencing. Nevertheless, the book demonstrates that these transfers have not resulted in a more punitive approach desired by proponents. Instead, judges in adult courts "are asked to punish youth in ways that contradict their culturally inscribed understanding of youthfulness" (Kupchik 2006, p.21; see also Kupchik et al 2012). Kupchik argues that it would be preferable to retain the children's court, especially since this often has greater access to treatment programs and specialist professionals than the adult courts. Perhaps, though, the study is most valuable in showing that even hard-bitten judges in adult courts are swayed by the youth of defendants when sentencing.

Ethnography and Discourse Analysis

This study belongs to the interpretive tradition, and seeks to investigate different professional perspectives and make visible institutional practices inside criminal justice. Within this tradition there are many debates, differences of emphasis and preferences for particular methods. There are interpretive traditions that place a greater emphasis in researching language (for example, Ten Have 2007). There are also long-standing and intellectually productive debates between interpretivists and other theoretical traditions. In criminology, many researchers conceptualize crime as arising from social inequality drawing on ideas from Karl Marx and other critical theorists (for example,Taylor et al 1973, Cohen 1988, Anthony and Cunneen 2008). Ethnographers influenced by these theoretical ideas describe criminal justice agencies using similar methods to interpretivists but within an appreciation and analysis of the wider social context, theorized in terms of power relations. The rest of this chapter will discuss the respective merits of ethnography and discourse analysis which are combined in this study, and offer a view on power from within the interpretive tradition. It will also consider the methodological issues that arise in addressing the experiences of young people from an adult perspective.

Ethnography is sometimes criticized by quantitative researchers for being loose, anecdotal and impressionistic (Blumer 1969, p.38). This is to some extent true in that there is no way of checking independently what was observed. A reviewer of a journal submission, based on chapter 5, advised that it was necessary to arrange for multiple observers, and checking procedures, before being able to claim the findings as objective. In the quantitative tradition, there is also greater emphasis on obtaining a representative sample. Even though a lot of data is presented in this book, it is possible that it gives a partial or misleading account of professional work in these Australian children's courts, or even that I have selected data to support a particular observation. These criticisms can be made of any ethnography. However, it should also be apparent that similar problems arise when collecting and interpreting statistical data. This will be demonstrated in chapter 9 in relation to apparent differences between the juvenile detention rates in three Australian states.

One development which makes it easier for qualitative researchers to produce objective findings, or at least hard data that can be discussed and debated, is to obtain tape-recordings of courtroom hearings. This makes it possible to see what actually happens in more detail, particularly when this is combined with ethnographic fieldwork that attempts to address how lawyers or other practitioners understand what is taking place. In the tradition of conversation analysis (Ten Have 2007), a great deal can be learnt simply by repeated listening to an audio-recording, and the close inspection of how people take turns at talk.

There is a large body of research by conversation analysts on legal settings, but very little of this has influenced mainstream criminology. One example is Doug Maynard's (1984) *Inside Plea-Bargaining*. This was based on recording the plea-bargaining negotiations for adult defendants in an American court. Maynard identified a sequence of actions involved in bargaining. This allowed him to make visible what happens during negotiations which was glossed or taken for granted by ethnographic accounts (Maynard 1989). Another example is Martha Komter's (1998) study of how defendants express remorse during criminal proceedings in Holland. She obtained permission to make audio-recordings of 31 sentencing hearings. Defendants are allowed in this country to make a statement after guilt expressing remorse, which can be taken into account in the sentence. Komter analyses in detail what defendants say in these circumstances, and the difficulties they experience in persuading the judge that they really are sorry for their actions and not just seeking a lighter sentence. These studies show that the language used by lawyers and defendants matters in influencing outcomes.

These studies might appear to represent an advance on ethnography. Who would want to write loosely about different professional perspectives, if it is possible to obtain much harder, reliable data? This is, of course, something of an hypothetical question for most researchers outside the USA, or the Netherlands, since it is not normally possible to obtain audio-recordings of legal hearings. However, even if it was possible what are the respective merits of ethnography and discourse analysis as research methods?

A central principle informing conversation analysis is that the researcher should only make findings that can be demonstrated in a transcript. It is illegitimate to import knowledge obtained from interviewing the participants or background knowledge about the setting (Schegloff 1991), or one can use this for strictly limited purposes (Maynard 2003). This allows conversation analysis to present its findings as objective and scientific: it deliberately limits itself to what can be heard on an audio-recording. It also serves to focus analytic attention on the detail of turn-taking, rather than allowing the researcher to become diverted into considering other issues. The ethnographer, by contrast, sets out to address meaning. The assumption is that one can only understand what matters to people in a particular social setting, and perhaps even what they are doing, by spending a long period of time with a particular social group (Moerman 1988). Each method involves committing a lot of time. As an ethnographer in children's courts, you have to spend time observing hearings and meeting practitioners. By contrast, the conversation analyst might work on a small corpus of audio-recordings. The time here, however, is spent in transcribing and repeated examination of the recordings, with the aim of investigating the properties of language in a scientific framework.

There are, therefore, good reasons why the two fields are largely separate. However, there are also researchers who have tried to combine the two methods. My first study about legal practice was based on the assumption that you cannot understand professional work without looking at language, but that you cannot understand the language without knowing something about the local context (Travers 1997a). Or rather that it was only through learning about this local context over time, that made it possible to appreciate and understand work in this setting. The same is true for the sentencing hearings discussed in this book, except that I did not spend as much time with practitioners and so do not understand the practical considerations in the same depth. A lawyer who had appeared before different magistrates on many occasions could immediately assess whether a sentencing decision was normal or unusual, or harsh or lenient, for that court. I was unable to understand hearings in the same way, although this insider perspective was sometimes revealed in conversations that took place between practitioners after hearings. This suggests to me that what can be heard in an audio-recording, even when this is available, only reveals part of what takes place in a legal hearing. The rest has to do with how the participants understand what is happening.

This provides the rationale for conducting ethnographic fieldwork: for visiting courts and interviewing practitioners, as against only working with audio-tapes. However, at the same time, the account of professional work draws considerably on transcripts, both from audio-recordings (kindly supplied by one court for a few hearings), and from contemporaneous notes made during hearings.[19] The audio-recordings have not been transcribed at the same level of detail as required in conversation analysis. Moreover, the transcript data as a whole is presented as a means of illustrating different aspects of professional work, alongside other ethnographic observations, rather than because I have a technical interest in language. This may, however, understate the extent to which my own approach as an ethnographer has been influenced by conversation analysis, since the transcripts are presented as an harder form of data than summaries of cases from fieldnotes (see Atkinson and Drew 1979). Even without aspiring to conduct a technical analysis of language, they make it possible to see, in a straightforward way, how magistrates address or interact with defendants, collaborate with other professionals and explain sentencing decisions.

The Issue of Power

Another criticism of ethnography, or at least the interpretive variety pursued in this study, is that it accepts how the people in any social setting, whether they are judges, lawyers or young offenders, understand their own activities, and is silent on the issue of power. When writing about the criminal justice system during the 1960s, labeling theorists tended to side with subordinate and disadvantaged groups in society, rather than adopting the perspective of the police or other agencies. However, they were themselves criticized by sociologists and criminologists, influenced particularly by Marx, for not having a fully-worked out view of social structure, or political viewpoint (Taylor et al 1973).

During the ascendancy of critical theories during the 1970s and 1980s, it was common to dismiss interpretive approaches such as symbolic interactionism, ethnomethodology and conversation analysis as only addressing the "micro" level of society. This critique was made possible because critical theorists believed that they had a superior understanding of the underlying structure of society to ordinary people, and were optimistic about the prospects for progressive social change. Today, after three decades in which neoliberal governments have been elected in many developed countries, and with no new ideas on the left that can explain or address current economic and social problems, there is far less optimism or certainty.[20] Progressive thinkers still, however, retain a conflict model of society as a struggle for economic resources and prestige between different social groups. In the USA, critical criminologists and law and society scholars portray law as promoting capitalist ideology, although characteristically in these conservative times these ideas are presented as a generalized critique of inequality, rather than advancing a specific political program (for example, Reiman 2006, Ferrell et al 2008, Wacquant 2009).

There are, in fact, many critical ethnographies and discourse analytic studies about criminal justice agencies and institutions, including a growing body of work in recent years by linguistic anthropologists in the USA who are greatly interested in the relationship between language and power.[21] There have also been some ethnographies of children's courts influenced by these ideas. For a hard-hitting Australian study, based on interviewing young people about their experiences in court, but also observing hearings, I would recommend Ian O'Connor and Pamela Sweetapple's (1988) *Children in Justice.* This presented young defendants as frightened victims who did not understand proceedings.[22] Sheila Brown (1991) offered a critical view of magistrates in England. She described the work of agencies producing social inquiry reports, and of magistrates in interpreting these, as reproducing class domination. This study employs similar concepts to those used by other critical researchers in Youth Studies during the 1970s and 80s (Hall and Jefferson 2006).

There are other ways of being critical outside the Marxist tradition. The French sociologist, Jacques Donzelot (1979), examined the origins of social work and criminology as professions in France through conducting historical research, in addition to conducting observational research in a juvenile court. Donzelot was critical towards experts for constructing theories that create youth crime as a social problem:

> At the start, there are always the figures on delinquency, the statistics of offences committed by minors. Experts in criminology study this first layer and detect in the delinquent minor's past, in the organization of families, the signs they have in common, the invariables of their situation, the first symptoms of their bad actions. With the help of these findings, the typical portrait of the future delinquent, the predelinquent, the child in danger of becoming dangerous, can be drawn up. An infrastructure of prevention will then be erected around him, and an educative machinery will be set in motion, a timely action capable of stopping short of a criminal violation. Not only will he be an object of intervention, but by the same token, he will in turn become an object of knowledge. The family climate, the social context that causes a particular child to become a 'risk', will be thoroughly studied (Donzelot 1979, p. 97).

In this version of the critical tradition, the target is not so much economically advantaged groups, but the new professions, including social workers, criminologists and psychoanalysts. These expand through identifying and claiming to help both "children in danger" and "dangerous children" (Donzelot 1979, p.96). There is a class basis to the critique since they are solely concerned with the "less-favored" classes. However, Donzelot seems most concerned about the growth of bureaucratic organizations and expert fields of knowledge that have undermined the family as an institution.

There are some readers of this book who will want this wider political framework, and feel that the description of hearings is limited because it "only" describes the perspective of magistrates and other practitioners. What, however, the critic should be able to see is that the interpretive tradition results in a fuller description of routine work in children's courts than is possible if the focus is on society as a whole. Moreover, there is a difference between imposing your own political views as an analyst on some institution, and examining how people working there understand their own activities (there may, of course, be a variety of perspectives). Critical theorists, such as Pierre Bourdieu (1977) have advocated trying to overcome these differences, and reach some kind of synthesis between interpretivism and critical theory. Interpretivists, such as Blumer (1968) or Garfinkel (1997) have argued that they are quite distinct ways of conducting, and conceptualizing, research, and should be appreciated in their own terms.

Doing Justice to Children

One complaint in the critical literature is that no one listens to young people, or addresses their experience of the criminal justice process in the same way as older ethnographies such as Patrick (1973) and Parker (1974). This is, in fact, not strictly true since several recent studies by criminologists and social workers are based on spending time with young offenders (for example, Yates 2004, Sanders 2005, Barry 2006, Webber 2007). It is also possible to find interviews in evaluations with young people who comment favorably on their experiences in restorative conferences (for example, Crawford and Newburn 2003). When introducing new legislation in Australia, there are even attempts to consult young people by giving talks in schools and reporting the views expressed in guided discussions on public websites.[23]

One criticism that could be made of this literature is that young offenders are usually presented as an homogeneous group with similar experiences and viewpoints. There is also a tendency to produce a version of young people that suits a particular political or professional agenda. The cultural criminologist presents a picture of young people obtaining emotional thrills from committing minor offences, which is theorized as some kind of secret rebellion against the capitalist system (for example, Ferrell et al 2008). Social work studies present them as conscious of the social and economic obstacles that prevent them from achieving their full potential (Barry 2006). In evaluation studies, young people are earnest consumers, happy to rate the experience of attending a restorative conference. For the purposes of consultations, they are responsible citizens who often express the view that offenders should be punished.

Sheila Brown notes that in much of Anglo-American criminology in the post-war period, "the voices of young people themselves were rarely heard, and then only through the more or less elaborate reconstructions of their lives presented by (adult male) academics" (Brown 2005, p.211). Although an accurate observation, it lacks political bite because most researchers, irrespective of their gender and political objectives, are guilty of this reconstruction. Researchers tend to be adults, so inevitably they adopt this perspective towards young people, rather than seeking to describe appreciatively how they understand offending. The complaint in some studies that young people do not understand the nature of the criminal justice system, or accept responsibility for their actions, expresses an adult viewpoint.[24]

Another problem in this literature is that few researchers investigate the experiences of young people outside courtrooms. It is easy to assume from the transcripts in this study that young people are passive victims because they say little or nothing during sentencing hearings. The same impression can easily be conveyed by interviewing young people immediately after hearings (for example, O'Connor and Sweetapple 1988). However, young people also have lengthy meetings with youth workers and lawyers, and interact with family and friends, including other offenders. It is not easy to address this wider set of experiences. They are, surely, important if the aim is to understand this perspective in juvenile justice.

A Kind of Objectivity

There are two main reasons why there have been so few in-depth, ethnographic studies about criminal justice processes in recent years. The first is that criminology has embraced scientism, even to a greater extent than in previous decades, believing that only quantitative research leads to objective knowledge. The second is that qualitative researchers, partly reacting against this, have turned away from doing empirical research and taken up postmodernism or other varieties of critical theory. In each case, proponents have vigorously promoted an intellectual agenda, constructing the other side in negative terms. The evaluators present themselves as offering the only route to useful knowledge, whereas postmodernists often suggest that this conceals a conservative political agenda, or celebrate the fact there is no such thing as truth.

There are, however, plenty of criminologists who have not been caught up in either of these intellectual excesses.[25] Most researchers would agree that there is value in both qualitative and quantitative methods, even if the methodological basis of qualitative research is not well understood in this field. This book is directed towards this middle ground, but without suggesting that quantitative and qualitative research are complementary since they employ different methods and ask distinctive questions. There are a number of traditions that offer systematic and thoughtful ways of researching the meaningful nature of social life that do not lead to subjectivism or relativism, although they have so far made little impact on criminology. One example is grounded theory, which was developed during the 1960s partly as a response to criticisms of qualitative research for being loose and impressionistic (Glaser and Strauss 1967, Strauss and Corbin 1998). Another is conversation analysis which also presents itself as an hard science, through analyzing audio-recordings using a systematic method (Ten Have 2007).

This is not, however, a study that aspires to this level of rigor or scientific purity. Instead, it owes a greater intellectual debt to older traditions of ethnographic research, before the time when these had to justify their scientific credentials; indeed before the time when there were these divisions in social science.[26] In defending interpretive ethnography against evaluators and quantitative criminologists, and also against critical researchers and postmodernists, this study cannot claim to employ especially sophisticated methods. Instead, what appeals to me about the ethnography pursued by labeling theorists during the 1960s, whether this was informed by symbolic interactionism or ethnomethodology, is that it requires little technical knowledge or expertise. There was no difficult method or set of concepts to be learnt, and the best studies were immediately accessible to a general audience. This is also true of the first Chicago School. In fact, the quality and interest of ethnographic and interview research in these earlier periods is arguably superior to most qualitative research published in recent times.

The challenge for the Chicago-style ethnographer lies in

describing what happens in institutional settings or within a social group in a way that respects how the activities there are meaningful for insiders.[27] As symbolic interactionists have argued, this means describing different institutional perspectives and social worlds, even if it is not possible for practical or political reasons to address these in the same degree of depth. For the ethnomethodologist, the challenge is to describe the activities that take place in an institutional setting, in sufficient detail so the reader can understand their practical character. Although it is never possible to be completely objective, careful description of these everyday practices can achieve a kind of objectivity in writing about children's courts.

4.

Professional Work in the Children's Court

What leaves the most lasting impression when you visit a children's court are the young defendants. They can be between 11 and 17 years in age. Some look like street wise, happy teenagers wearing the latest youth fashions. Others are scruffy, shambling and inarticulate. Many have a contrite, respectful manner, but others slouch casually into the court, have a defiant smirk, or keep their hands in their pockets until the magistrate complains. Some attend court with family members, but most have no supporters, and this is sufficiently normal not to attract comment.

This study cannot go very far towards addressing how particular young people understand offending or the criminal justice system.[1] Instead, the focus will be on the work and perspectives of the professionals around them, particularly during children's court hearings. This chapter will start by considering the physical buildings and hearing rooms in which the legal proceedings described in this book take place. The rest of the chapter will consider the work and professional outlook of the occupational groups that work collaboratively in children's courts, drawing upon interviews with practitioners.

Courts and Hearing Rooms

There were significant physical differences between the courts visited during this study, which illustrate the divide between metropolitan and country areas in Australia. The most impressive buildings were the central children's courts in Victoria and New South Wales. The central court in Victoria was built specifically for this purpose in 1999, and divided into two sections that were intended for criminal and child protection cases.[2] In this building, there are pastel shades and good lighting, and numerous art works. At the side of one hearing room, there is an atrium containing native plants. There are also comfortable waiting areas that feel almost like airport lounges. In the central children's court at Parramatta in New South Wales, defendants waiting for their hearings can watch day-time television on a large screen, buy drinks from vending machines, or even bring in take-away food.

Outside the central courts in these states, and in Tasmania, children's courts were convened as special sessions within ordinary magistrates courts. In some metropolitan areas of Victoria, the children's court was accessed through a separate entrance, with the aim of reducing contact between adult and juvenile offenders. In the Magistrates Court in Hobart, there was a separate hearing room and waiting area, but all defendants entered the court through one entrance. These courts in suburban or metropolitan areas were usually in modern buildings. In smaller hearing centers, outside the big cities, there was a mixed picture. One country town visited had a brand new, purpose built magistrates court. Most had rundown buildings, with furnishings and decoration that looked as if they dated from colonial days, although the court had probably last been refurbished in the postwar period. In Armidale, New South Wales, the state government had promised to build a new court, and in the meantime had refurbished part of an historic building.

Whatever the building, the hearing rooms had a similar layout in that the magistrate sat on a raised platform, with a court clerk sitting on a lower platform. In the older courts, these platforms were higher, and there was a greater distance between the magistrate and the defendant. The practitioners faced the magistrates, in some courts around a semi-circular bar table. Defendants not in custody sat besides or behind their lawyers. The case worker normally sat by the prosecutor rather than with the defendant.

In older courts, there was sometimes no separate entrance to the dock, so defendants were brought in through the main entrance. There was also often no screening, so it was possible to reach the magistrate, or at least throw something across the court. During my visits to the court in Hobart, a defendant absconded by leaping over the barrier. The security guard who tried to restrain him suffered a back injury. In the central court in New South Wales, there were new docks partly enclosed by a perspex security screen. A block of wood was lowered as a restraining device once the defendant was sitting facing the magistrate. I was told that this offered some security against the possibility of assaults or escapes, although it would not stop someone who was determined and small.

Magistrates

Magistrates are ultimately responsible for making decisions in children's courts. They are also judicial officers, and it would be possible to apply and discuss the studies conducted over many years by legal philosophers, political scientists and psychologists that seek to understand decision-making.[3] The vast majority are either based on the analysis of legal cases, especially decisions made in appellate courts (Ashworth 2010), or on attitudinal surveys of judges with the aim of predicting or explaining how they interpret legal rules (for example, Hogarth 1971).

This study will adopt a different approach to these literatures for two reasons. Firstly, the scientific approaches, based on quantification and the correlation of outcomes against causal factors, often tell us what we already know, or certainly what an experienced practitioner knows from working in those courts. There are judges or magistrates with different personalities and attitudes, and they sentence differently. Secondly, in measuring personalities or attitudes, or in identifying models of cognitive processing in experimental conditions, these literatures are not usually concerned with how judges experience or understand sentencing as a practical, occupational task (Lynch 1997). Most of this study will be looking at the considerations that arise in sentencing different types of defendants. To start with, it is worth giving some background on how magistrates were trained, and how they approached their work.

Recruitment and training

In Australian states, magistrates are legally qualified, and must have spent a few years in legal practice. In Victoria and New

South Wales, it is possible to become a dedicated children's court magistrate, in which case you can only hear these cases, and must sit in particular courts. However, most magistrates in these states, and all magistrates in Tasmania, sat mainly in the adult courts. In some cases, they were allocated children's courts cases on a roster. I heard some second hand reports about magistrates who felt uncomfortable with this part of the job. This may be because they disapproved of the leniency required by the legislation, but also because magistrates had a different role in hearings, including the obligation to explain the decision to a young person.[4]

What may seem surprising to outsiders is that surprisingly little formal training was required beyond the skills and knowledge acquired in legal practice.[5] The magistrate was left to learn the procedures and develop a particular style or approach to sentencing without needing much contact with colleagues. The following experiences seem common:

> When I was starting out, I just got a feel for it. Mr. X would tell me what I was doing wrong [if I had any queries]. There was no formal sitting in.

> The magistrate is on his own and relies on others to help in making decisions. Practitioners help you in finding the way. A lot of the work involves problem solving.

> I did a two day training conference – but very little was on Youth Justice.

> I have been doing the job for nine months and am still finding my way.

> I did not receive any training as a magistrate. I was just put in the job.

These magistrates report learning how to make decisions and administer procedural rules as much by informal colleagueship, trial and error, and picking up bits and pieces of knowledge, as formal training.

Individual styles

A central aspect of professional work that does not always receive sufficient emphasis is its individual character. Magistrates reported that they developed a personal style in managing hearings:

> I know I have a certain style – I have been told off for bringing in my own experience, but I feel it is important. It takes up time for the court but I am trying to get through to the offender. I try to make eye contact with them – it doesn't always work.

> I engage in therapeutic justice. I talk to the child, so he or see can see it is wrong. Not all magistrates do this.

> I have developed an approach over time. I explain the sentence and talk directly to the defendant and not to counsel. There is an obligation in the Act to explain.

> For their first appearance when they come to court, they have an opportunity to plead or they can ask for an adjournment to find a lawyer. For the second hearing, I always give them a second chance if they have not found a lawyer – these people are not used to finding lawyers.

> My aim is to not to shout at defendants or be long-winded, but to talk to them. I practice therapeutic justice. I say whatever seems necessary to get through.

> I see being a magistrate as a personal thing – it depends on your experience as a person. I have three children and can draw on this experience.

> If I say I will convict if there is another offence, I will unless there is a change of circumstances.

There were also opportunities to develop an individual approach in the sentencing decision. At first glance, there is only a limited range of sentencing options under the youth justice legislation in the three states. Someone appearing for the first time, or who had committed a minor offence, could be sentenced to minor penalties such as being asked to give an undertaking, or enter into a good behaviour bond,[6] or the offence could be dismissed.

Repeat offenders could be sentenced to a supervision order, such as probation or community service. Those who continued to offend or committed serious offences could be sentenced to detention.

There were, however, other options available to magistrates. They could, for example, require attendance at a community conference as part of a probation order, and give suspended sentences. They could also make convictions in addition to a finding of guilt.[7] There was also scope for magistrates to exercise discretion within the statutory limits on the length of orders or conditions, and through combining orders. Rather than being a mechanical process, sentencing allowed magistrates to develop particular styles, and to "craft" sentences.

Defense Lawyers

Before the introduction of the justice model, which took place in most Australian states during the 1990s, there was little emphasis on following legal rules and procedures in children's courts. Young people were usually unrepresented, and could not easily challenge possible abuses or mistakes by social workers or the courts. Today, however, most young defendants are represented in Australia by Legal Aid (Tomsen and Noone 2006), a government-funded agency, or by private firms of solicitors who can claim back the cost from the government.

Lawyers in adult courts have been criticized for going through the motions and not taking a sufficiently aggressive or robust stance towards the prosecution or magistrates (see Blumberg 1969, McConville et al 1994).[8] In the sentencing hearings that take place in children's courts, there is even less sense of an adversarial relationship, although this is partly because these defendants have pleaded guilty, and there is little place for argument either over the facts or law. In most cases, the defendant agrees with the pre-sentence report so there is little scope for the lawyer to add anything.

The impression that defense lawyers are not needed in sentencing hearings, or never challenge prosecutors or the court can be misleading, given that it was only possible to observe a relatively small number of hearings,[9] and a lot of legal work takes place before the hearing. Legal Aid lawyers interviewed supplied a few examples:

Today a youth was charged with aggravated robbery, committing violence in the company of another person. Working as a team we were able to persuade the prosecution to make a single charge of assault. If he had pleaded guilty to aggravated robbery, it would have been quite a stigma to carry. Other charges like assault and stealing are nowhere near as bad. It is important for future appearances. You have to presume they are coming back – they always do.

The majority of cases I deal with are burglary, stealing, setting fire to buildings, motor vehicle stealing, fraud and dishonesty. There is an issue when receiving stolen property that the police need to prove the defendant knew it was stolen at the time. They need to obtain an admission and push very hard to get it. It is the defendant's right to say nothing but they think they are required to talk and they don't understand the caution. If they are told things would be easier [if they pleaded guilty], this would be an inducement, and they don't say this. But it's the impression that is given.

One can see from these examples how legal representation can make a difference. Prosecutors without a legal training can over-charge, and this lawyer did not feel that the defendant could always rely on magistrates to correct this. From a lawyer's perspective, every defendant is vulnerable in a police station, even if the police act with complete propriety, but young people are particularly prone to answering questions when they would benefit from exercising their legal right to remain silent. Lawyers do not, however, usually attend police interviews with juveniles, and they are not always able to attend the first bail hearing (see chapter 8).

Part of the professional task of lawyers working in the children's court is to know the approach adopted by particular magistrates. This does not necessarily affect outcomes for defendants, but it allows them to predict what is likely to happen, and also influences the arguments used in hearings:

There are consistent magistrates and inconsistent magistrates. There are rehabilitative magistrates and others who might send a kid to Ashley[10] on his first offence. We deal with them in adult court as well. Some magistrates, I would make a suggestion to dispose of this matter by XY and Z, but with others I wouldn't dare. Some magistrates I would say [to the defendant] you are at risk of detention and others I would say that other outcomes are most likely.

A juvenile case worker made some similar comments about the need to tailor comments to particular people:

If some magistrate has a hobby horse or pet hate, I will tailor the report to pre-empt [his or her likely feelings about the sentence] and give reasons.

The work of a defense lawyer also involves meeting defendants before hearings. There is an assumption in the literature on criminal justice generally that even adult defendants, who are often ill-educated and from disadvantaged backgrounds, are easily managed by professionals. In the case of young people, it is even easier to assume that they cannot make decisions for themselves, and are told what to do either by their parents or legal advisors. The few lawyer-client interviews observed in this study through a Legal Aid office in Victoria were mainly concerned with minor offences, with strong or incontrovertible prosecution evidence in which the defendant had already made an admission to the police. Even here, however, the lawyer always asked young people how they wished to plead, and explained the Ropes procedure (described in chapter 5). Young people were also interviewed separately from parents, a policy designed to protect the client from any pressure to make admissions, and which recognized that only the young person could give instructions. Lawyers told me that, in most cases, the same considerations applied as when representing an adult client.

In other cases, young people plead not guilty for the same reason as adult defendants: they dispute the prosecution charges against them. Some contested trials will be described in chapter 8, in which the defense challenged identification evidence. In these cases, the defendant had denied committing the offence at the police station, and instructed his lawyer to plead not guilty. Moreover, the apparent passivity of the defendant during hearings may not necessarily result from feeling ill at-ease before the magistrate:

> We've had some training in taking instructions from people with behavioral problems but ultimately if we have queries about their fitness we have the option of seeking advice from forensic mental health. But even without these problems, with a kid who has not been to court before I will explain how I am their voice in court so all they should say is yes when asked their name. Obviously, I don't do this with an old hand.

This short extract from an interview also suggests that lawyers distinguish between the needs of different types of clients. There is a big difference between representing an "old hand" and someone in court for the first time. Someone with behavioral problems requires special treatment, and in this case other professionals are asked to advise.

Prosecutors

The police are represented by in-house prosecutors who are police officers on secondment from other duties. One experienced officer described himself as a "foot-soldier" working in "kiddies' court," which also reflects the fact that young offenders mainly commit minor offences, and are given what the police regard as lenient penalties. Another told me that while police officers believe that children's courts are too lenient, they are not overly concerned about what happens in any particular case. They are too busy with other matters, and assume that young people in their neighborhood will keep offending, and ultimately receive adult penalties.

The central development that has affected police work in dealing with young offenders in Tasmania and New South Wales, although not in Victoria, has been conferencing. The decision made by Youth Officers over whether to send youths to cautions or conferences or whether they should go to court is governed by guidelines issued by the police. The seriousness of the offence, and whether there are prior offences is one consideration, as well as whether the defendant admits guilt. Inevitably,Youth Officers interpret each case differently, using their own professional judgment:

> Q: Do you have to commit multiple offences before going to court?
>
> A: We have guidelines and instructions to see whether offenders meet the criteria. X when he was in the role sent a lot to court, but before him another officer was prepared to give 3-4 formal cautions, and then 3-4 community conferences. I am in the middle and give them one chance on each. However, you can get the file of a young person who doesn't meet the criteria for a conference but then get another file and he does meet the criteria. When it goes to court, the magistrate has the power to convene a community conference. You could get four offenders and the first two go to court, the third gets a formal caution because he meets the criteria, and then the fourth goes to a community conference.

One also gets a sense of the practical difficulties involved in reviewing the cases of offenders who are usually committing multiple offences. According to this interviewee, the practice in this region at one point was to give offenders the opportunity to reform through attending four cautions and four conferences. This suggests that the most consequential debate between advocates of welfare and punishment approaches takes place in the police, and this early stage of the criminal justice process deserves further study.

Juvenile Case Workers

Although magistrates make decisions on what happens to young offenders, they usually follow recommendations made in pre-sentence reports prepared by juvenile case workers. In Tasmania and Victoria, these are known as Youth Justice workers, and in New South Wales Juvenile Justice workers or "JJs." These agencies were established as part of the separation between the criminal and child protective functions of children's courts during the 1990s.

Their mission is to serve the court in administering orders that are concerned under the legislation with balancing the objectives of rehabilitation and punishment.

Working with offenders

Whereas child protection is a professionalized occupation requiring a social work qualification in senior positions, juvenile case workers have a variety of backgrounds. Some started the job with an arts or psychology degree, and some experience of youth work, and subsequently picked up training when they could:

> I have an arts degree, arts and law. There are people here who have social work degrees. X has the equivalent of a social work degree. When I started I got training in the principles of restorative justice, and the training we have on risk assessment takes this into consideration. I have not been on any social work courses. Training just happens where it can. It is important not to equate this with social work – you can fall into the trap of wanting to give welfare benefits to people and because we are following the justice model now we don't give them this.

Another suggested that, although there was a theoretical base, the practical skills could not be taught:

> I've read fairly extensively but primarily I've had a lot of direct experience with young people sitting alongside them trying to understand what's going on. Seeing them in a formal and informal context builds your relationship or capacity to relate.

The formal responsibility of juvenile case workers for young offenders starts with a court order.[11] This usually results from a sentence of probation, but supervision can also be made the condition of a good behaviour bond, or the deferred order which is used in Victoria as a form of diversion (see chapter 5). Whatever the legal basis, the effect is that a young person becomes "known" to the agency. He or she is assigned a case worker with the task of making an assessment and determining the type of supervision and programs required, and the level of resources to address the offending behavior.

One interviewee summarized the procedures involved:

When doing an assessment, I use the risk tool used in our department. Or I use my own grid which is simpler. I then transfer the information onto the risk tool. There is also a case plan – this has the risk factors and the action required. If I am trying to weave an assessment, I will try to show the information I've got on the grid. If the young person has committed an offence, these are the young person's circumstances, there is his or her health and family accommodation. Then there are the areas that require attention. We arrive at a general supervisory framework. Our case plan. This could be complex or simple. There are different levels of intervention. The young person has to understand this and sign the plan.

We work through the plan with the client. It depends on how honest they are – or we try to figure out what's really going on. The kids will tell you anything – it's how you piece it together. If you have a new client from court, you try to engage them. I will try to get them to look at this form. I will say you can see there's a whole lot of things people get in trouble with. I will try to contrast different lifestyles and behaviors and aim to get through. They usually accept there may be whole number of things that can go wrong. It helps them to increase their awareness of the different factors and what they are doing with their life.

The case notes are the record. But this grid is my operating tool. Sometimes, I do not go through everything but just talk. They get sick of going through this stuff. I won't ask if he needs accommodation because he has no accommodation, so this is pointless. I will just focus on the most pressing issues. A lot of the work is waiting for young people to turn up. Often they don't. Gaining trust is important – the ability to do so means that you find out things. All you know is what they tell you. We see most people once a week – just to keep them on our books. The good behaviour bond is the standard order. Even for difficult cases, we only see them once a week. But we respond to events – for example, if they reoffend, become homeless, have family problems or if a family member dies. We can spend time going to Centrelink or the housing office like a social worker. This is the way to build trust, yet it takes time.

Aside from the problem of young people not turning up, there is also the potential for over-dependence:

If it's going OK, we will suspend the youth supervision. But they might commit offences to keep the support. They are getting personal guidance, affirmation and engagement. They think at least if get in trouble I can call them up. Kids don't want to suspend the supervision.

Persuading young people to stop offending can be an uphill task, requiring great patience and effort:

Q: Are young people working with you?

A: Today is not a good day to ask because I've had a bad day with clients. I would say if you've got a long term relation with clients, a large percentage of my clients are working with me and working actively in their case management. I think they mature and a with a bit of maturation in age they feel maybe I can get something out of it.

Programs and resources

The type of programs offered to young people, or recommended in pre-sentence reports, depended both on the assessment of their needs, and what was available. When sentencing, magistrates often included conditions that the young person should attend alcohol and drugs counseling or workshops in anger management. The number and type of programs differed considerably between states, and local teams drew on their experience of what had worked with similar offenders in the past. In Victoria, there were numerous schemes run by community groups and the police, in addition to Youth Justice, that make it possible to pursue different options during supervision orders. These included self-improvement programs based around sporting activities, and opportunities to learn advanced driving skills under supervision by police officers. In this state, there were programs aimed at particular psychological conditions such as Attention Deficit Disorder or learning difficulties, and specialist forensic psychologists who could advise on personality disorders.

Case workers in New South Wales could draw on fewer programs than in Victoria, especially outside Sydney or other large towns. However, resources were directed effectively at groups with high levels of need. To give an example, case workers in Redfern, an inner city area with high levels of deprivation and a large Indigenous population were well-resourced, and could engage in intensive supervision. The Youth Drugs Court in Sydney similarly directed considerable resources at some repeat offenders who would otherwise have been sentenced to detention. In Tasmania, by contrast, there were fewer programs. Some were only available to serious repeat offenders or those refused bail, and who were in the detention centre for long periods. On the other hand, even Tasmania had some programs such as U-Turn for driving offenders that were successful in reducing recidivism.[12]

The pre-sentence report

The work of juvenile case workers was fully integrated into the children's court in the sense that a pre-sentence report was required before making a supervisory order. Reports contained three or four pages of background information on the defendant's offending history, family circumstances, his or her experiences at school and any health problems, and the case plan being pursued.[13] There was also a recommendation on sentence, including conditions for a probation order such as attendance at a workshop on anger management.

Although it was not possible to investigate the matter systematically, interviews both with juvenile case workers and magistrates suggested that magistrates usually followed recommendations, or at least that there were not the tensions reported in some other jurisdictions (for example, Tata et al 2008):

> I sometimes disagree with magistrates, if for example someone gives a conviction. If some magistrate has a hobby horse or pet hate, I will tailor the report to pre-empt and give reasons.

> I don't find there is a big issue. Normally the magistrates follow our recommendations and normally if we ask for specific conditions on the orders they make these as well.

> Miss X [from Youth Justice] is good and knows what we want. Others have just sat there knowing nothing about the defendant.

The first two comments were made by juvenile case workers. The third comment, from a magistrate, may indicate that they have not always been satisfied by the format as opposed to the recommendations made by reports. Magistrates in one hearing center had complained about reports being too long, and containing information used in case management that was not directly relevant to the sentencing decision. It also suggests that they prefer someone who is fully briefed, and able to help if asked to supply additional information. Only one hearing was observed in which the magistrate criticized a case worker, and this was for inexperience (see chapter 9).

This might suggest that sentencing in the children's court is usually quite straightforward in that everyone usually agrees on the basic sentence, leaving it open for variations depending on the approach of particular professionals. This also came across in reports about discussions between case workers, which have a collegial character, rather than involving deep ideological differences:

> There certainly are differences [within our team]. What I might think is appropriate to recommend might be different to what X might think. However, in my team – I can't speak for other teams – I think we are all pretty much heading in a similar direction.

There was scope for disagreement over the recommendation, for example if a case worker recommended probation (which left the options open), whereas the magistrate wanted more intensive supervision and community service.[14] Although a more serious sentence had legal consequences, and might increase the chances of detention if the young person committed further offences, the difference between these options was not necessarily significant in terms of the level of supervision, or the extent to which it had a punitive element. To give an example, case workers had considerable discretion when asking offenders to do community service. In some cases, attendance at a sporting club, or completing an educational course, was seen as appropriate.

Understanding Professional Work

This chapter has sought to provide an overview of different professional perspectives in these children's courts. There is clearly more that could be discovered through spending more time with practitioners. Nevertheless, you can learn a great deal about the practical issues that concern magistrates, defense lawyers, prosecutors and case workers, even from a few interviews. Two general findings, perhaps not in themselves surprising, but not always acknowledged in the policy or jurisprudential literatures are that professionals exercise considerable discretion; and that expertise in this field draws substantially on common-sense in addition to technical knowledge.

Discretion

One feature of professional work that comes across from these interviews is that practitioners differ when making consequential decisions about young people. Police officers adopt different policies on the number of cautions and conferences that young people should attend before sending them to a children's court. There are "hard" and "lenient" magistrates, and their approaches are known to defense and prosecution lawyers. The fact, however, that professionals can differ is not seen as a problem by these organizations, but is accepted and institutionalized as part of a professional culture. The exercise of professional discretion and judgment is built into the juvenile justice system, as in any social institution concerned with making assessments and allocating resources.[15]

In addition, one practitioner acknowledged that the information available is not always clear-cut, and mistakes are made:

> You can make a decision…that turns out to be wrong. You can. OK, we can learn from that. We can say, well what should we be doing next time.

This seems an important point to recognize in professional training. Expertise develops through experience, and learning from other practitioners. However, there are not always clear-cut answers, and professionals often differ amongst themselves.

Technical and common-sense knowledge

What also seems evident is that professional work in the children's court does not, for the most part, involve drawing on a body of technical knowledge or expertise. The importance of technical knowledge should not be discounted: the lay person could not assess legal challenges to evidence during a trial. One should also not discount the fact that some people have a natural ability to relate to young people, whether through their personalities or life experience, and these skills are highly valued on programs. All these professionals deferred to psychologists as having specialist expertise in diagnosing and treating personality problems. Nevertheless, for the most part no special knowledge or skills are required either in working with young offenders, or in deciding an appropriate sentence.[16]

Because the main options are simple, and the principles quite broad, any reader of this study could make sentencing decisions. This means that in later chapters you can form your own assessment of the decisions made by magistrates. Although there is no access to the full submissions made in court, the pre-sentence report or the defendant's prior record, much of the relevant information is available in how cases are summarized. What most people would find difficult is having to make a decision quickly, and then give reasons to the defendant. In many cases, magistrates read the pre-sentence report during the hearing, which also provided an opportunity to make the defendant think about the possible sentence.

Researchers who interview judges often report that it is difficult getting them to explain these skills, or expand on the reasons given in the sentencing remarks (Lynch 1997). Some have claimed that this is because judicial officers are reluctant to reveal the real reasons for their decisions (Tata 2002). Instead, it seems more likely that this problem arises in any attempt to address what ethnomethodologists call tacit knowledge (Garfinkel 1984b). To give another example, when marking, university teachers are asked to assign essays or examination answers to a few grades.[17] In doing so, they weigh up a number of factors, such as content and clarity of expression. The grade and brief comments given to the student explain this reasoning. All this has to be completed quickly: experienced markers have to make this judgment, and formulate comments, nominally in 20 minutes, for each essay. The marker could, if required, expand on the reasons, and perhaps in the case of an appeal might be willing to adjust the grade. However, this does not explain how the original assessment was made.

There are other similarities with marking essays. In the cases I observed, magistrates had no difficulty reaching a decision, even if they sometimes weighed up different options for effect during the sentencing remarks. Nor when interviewed, did they report that sentencing was ever particularly difficult or required agonizing over different options. There were some occasions in which they consulted colleagues on technical issues, or about the suitability of particular programs. However, for the most part they made decisions routinely through hearing the submissions and reading the pre-sentence report.

To put this differently, when making decisions practitioners mostly draw on what everyone knows from their ordinary life experiences about why young people commit offences, and when punishment or help is required. One does not require much technical knowledge to understand the sentencing options available, or the distinction between sending someone home with a warning, asking them to do community service or imposing a custodial sentence. This is why courts are sociologically interesting. They are not simply the preserve of technical experts, but practitioners are in a real sense representing the wider community, through using knowledge and skills that belong to everyone, in deciding questions of right and wrong, and crime and punishment.

5.

Responding to Minor Offences

The central policy development that has transformed children's courts in Australia since the 1990s has been diversion to restorative conferences. In New South Wales, it has been estimated that seventy per cent of young offenders are sent to conferences, and the vast majority do not re-offend (Chan 2005). Nevertheless, even with diversion, magistrates still send away many young people who plead guilty with a reprimand or small fine. They make others subject to an order requiring good behavior for a year but with no other supervision or punishment, or require them to give an undertaking that they will not re-offend. It would, therefore, be a mistake to assume that children's courts only hear cases relating to repeat or serious offenders.

Although the end of this chapter will consider the effectiveness of diversion, the main focus will be on the nature of minor offences. What kind of offences receive penalties at the bottom end of the tariff? Are there any common features? What assumptions and cultural knowledge do magistrates (or anyone else) employ in order to see the offences as only deserving minor penalties? Looking at the content of cases as these are revealed by the facts and arguments presented in court provides an alternative way of understanding what is at issue in juvenile crime to the statistical analysis of risk factors conducted by some criminologists (Livingston et al 2008). It also, however, provides a different view to those critical criminologists who portray youth crime as romantic rebellion or emphasize the enjoyment young people obtain from breaking the law (Katz 1988, Ferrell et al 2008).

The chapter starts with a summary of the different procedures in the three states. Using a concept first employed by David Sudnow (1965) in relation to plea-bargaining, the "situational offence," it will then provide a summary of cases observed in Tasmania that have similar features.[1] The second part looks at the work involved in sentencing three of these young people in more detail, focusing on the reasons given for the decision.[2] The chapter concludes by considering the policy issue of whether more minor offenders should be diverted.

Procedures for Diversion

Although diversion is often presented as an uniform procedure across Australia, in fact there are significant differences between these three states, and it is possible that there are further variations between regions. In addition, even the level of access obtained by this study suggests that practitioners exercise discretion at each stage of the process: there may be lively debates within the police over whether diversion is appropriate for particular offenders.

Tasmania

In Tasmania, conferencing developed as an initiative within the police during the 1990s, mainly through the efforts of one officer, based in a local force, who succeeded over time in raising awareness among senior offices and securing institutional support. The 1997 Youth Justice Act (Tasmania) that refashioned the entire juvenile justice system introduced a two tier system, in which offenders who plead guilty first attend one or more conferences organized by the police, and then one or more conferences arranged through Youth Justice (Prichard 2004). This decision has been criticized by proponents of conferencing who believe that only properly trained facilitators, independent from the police, can achieve positive results. However, this is arguably how conferencing has become institutionalized within the police in this state.

Victoria

In Victoria, there had been a policy decision during the 1990s[3] to restrict conferencing to a diversionary option for defendants who had committed more serious offences, including assault and burglary.[4] For many years, the police responded to minor offending through giving ordinary cautions, probably a number before the local officers lost patience and referred the matter to the children's court.[5] Since 2007, there has been diversion from the children's court to what is known as the Ropes program (Grant 2009). Minor offenders spend a day with police officers in a climbing centre, and receive a group lecture about responsible behavior. Both the police and magistrates have to agree. Offenders appear in the children's court briefly, but if they complete the program, they do not return to court or obtain a criminal record.

New South Wales

In New South Wales, young offenders were diverted to restorative conferences. This was the state in which a local police force in Wagga Wagga, a relatively isolated country area with an high level of Indigenous offending, had first introduced and promoted this method of reducing crime (Daly and Hayes 1997). The Young Offenders Act 1997 (New South Wales), required police officers to consider conferencing as an option before charging. An evaluation funded by the Department of Juvenile Justice found that these had been successful in reducing re-offending, particularly among Indigenous offenders (Chan 2005).

    After publication of this report, it would appear that there was a change of policy, or at least a shift in resources and political support away from conferencing (personal communication). Instead, political efforts have shifted towards establishing a new program of diversion known as Youth Conduct Orders (Attorney General NSW 2008). These were introduced in two pilot schemes while I was observing hearings in New South Wales. The aim was to divert a maximum of ten offenders to a multi-agency team, modeled on Youth Offending Teams in the United Kingdom.[6] The team would devise a rehabilitative program, but also offer support where required, and monitor progress. If successful, the court could dismiss the original charge or give a low penalty such as an undertaking. The diversionary scheme was voluntary in two respects. In the first place, the defendant had to agree. In the second place, the different agencies had to agree to invest resources in this young person through integrated case working.

Common Minor Offences

David Sudnow (1965) when writing about plea-bargaining in an American court made a distinction between legally defined offences and "situational" crimes. The circumstances in which a crime was committed influenced the response of the court, and in particular whether a plea-bargain was permissible. To give an example, an opportunistic burglary was treated differently by the Public Defenders and District Attorneys to one that had been planned and where valuable items were taken. The defendants were each charged with burglary, but only the first case was suitable for the charge being reduced in return for a guilty plea.

The concept of a "situational" offence is even more relevant to sentencing, since magistrates have to take into account the circumstances in which the offence was committed. In the children's court, the circumstances are often related to the age of the offender, or to put this differently the offences are the kind that are committed by young people rather than adults. Magistrates are not required to give detailed reasons in court, and given there might be a number of mitigating factors, it is not usually possible to be certain what most influenced a decision. The next section will discuss some considerations that seem relevant, and illustrate these with short summaries of hearings.

Crimes of violence between juveniles

In a study about homicide trials in the American "Deep South" during the 1940s, the ethnomethodologist Harold Garfinkel (1948) made some interesting observations about the distinction between inter- and intra-racial homicides for legal practitioners. Black on black killings were taken less seriously than those within the white community or where black offenders had killed a white victim. This was evident in the amount of time spent by the court, the attention given by the media, and in the relatively lenient sentences received by black offenders in intra-racial homicides. There are obviously many differences between adult homicide in a racially-segregated society, and juvenile crime. However, it is striking that most offences by young people are committed against other young people. If the same offences were committed by adults against adults, or by children against adults, they would be seen as deserving serious penalties.

In each of the following cases, there are other factors that explain the lenient sentence. In case 5A, for example, it may be that the victim was viewed as partially responsible through having abused the defendant's girl-friend.[7] In case 5B, the magistrate justified his sentence on the grounds that the female defendant had matured and was expecting a baby. In case 5C, there was a medical explanation for threatening someone with an unloaded shotgun. The surrounding circumstances (including the fact that no evidence was supplied about the effect on the victim) may have also helped the defendant. In the first two cases, the defendant had been drinking, and the violence was a spontaneous response to an insult (although interestingly not always associated with a display of masculinity).[8] Nevertheless, the fact that only young people were involved, and the injuries are not usually serious, seems relevant. Nor would one expect intervention by police and the courts to prevent teenagers fighting amongst themselves, as almost a normal part of growing up.

Case 5A

The 17 year old defendant got into an argument with another youth in a park who had insulted his girlfriend. This youth went on ahead and the defendant called him to come back and head-butted him. The victim had blood on his face and his teeth were knocked out. There was no history of violence. The charge of common assault was dismissed and he was fined $100 and required to compensate the complainant if there was dental work.

Case 5B

A 16 year old female defendant was charged with having taken part in a group assault. The complainant was walking with a friend through a shopping mall when six girls started yelling at them, wanting to know what they had been saying about their boyfriends. The defendant had punched the complainant on the head, and initially said in a police interview this was self-defense, although a witness said she had not been provoked. She was now 18 and expecting a baby. She received a reprimand.

Case 5C

The 15 year old defendant had taken a shot-gun from his grandmother's house, and shortened it with tools there, so it fit in his backpack. The gun was unloaded. He had placed this against the face of a 15 year old girl and threatened to shoot her through the head if anything happened to his girl-friend who had been told some youths would get her with a knife earlier that evening. He had forgotten to take medication, and wanted to apologize to the victim. The magistrate referred the matter back to a community conference and imposed an one year probation order.

"Status" offences

A criticism of the American juvenile justice system, prior to the introduction of the justice model in the late-1960s was that young people could be taken into care for long periods, without having committed a criminal offence, simply for being children who had come to the attention of welfare agencies. Today, there are still "status" offences that can only be committed by young people, such as under age drinking. There are also a larger number of offences that, while they can be committed by anyone, are directed against young people. They are designed to protect them, but also have the unintended consequence of bringing young people into contact with the criminal justice system from an early age.

Many of these offences relate to driving. In case 5D, an unlicensed, uninsured driver crashed into a parked car which might not have happened if she had been accompanied by an adult. In case 5E, the defendant committed other offences while driving without a license, including carrying an under-age pillion passenger and speeding. In other cases observed, defendants appeared in court simply for driving without a license, and being uninsured. There were also youths charged with the offence of "hooning" (for example, excessive revving, or doing "wheelies" on a motorbike). These offences can be committed by adults, but are often committed by young people.

Hearings for two other "status" offences were observed: carrying an alcoholic drink in a public place while under age (case 5F), and riding a bicycle without a helmet (case 5G). The second offence can be committed by adults. However, the objective behind the statute is to protect young people from injury. Some interviewees reported that many youths are regularly charged, after disobeying police warnings, and one defendant in Tasmania may even have ended up in Ashley Youth Detention Centre after disobeying 20 times. This is another example of how enforcing the law, and even attempts at "zero-tolerance," are not necessarily effective and can have unintended consequences. All of these offences involve a lack of thought, as well as having caused or risked causing serious harm, and this may explain the lenient sentence. In Case 5E, a case worker felt that the magistrate had given the wrong impression to other young people, by suggesting that someone who had grown up on a farm was likely to be a safe driver, even though he was speeding. However, there was no disagreement about the sentence, or that this was likely to be an "one-off" offence.

Case 5D

A 16 year old girl drove in her mother's car to the local shop without having a licence, and damaged a parked vehicle. Her mother reported this later that day. She received a reprimand. The magistrate told her that an adult could receive a fine of $2,000 and disqualification for two years.

Case 5E

The 16 year old defendant was speeding on an unregistered motor-cycle with a 14 year old pillion passenger, without a rear tail light and driving license. According to his lawyer, he had gone out riding "aimlessly" after having a "heated argument" with his parents, but was driving competently. He had been riding the cycle on their farm for a few years, and supplied a reference from his employers. He was fined $100, and not disqualified from driving so he could obtain his license.

Case 5F

A 16 year old was charged with carrying a can of liquor in a public place. He was not working. He was fined $50 and given 30 days to pay.

Case 5G

A 14 year old defendant was warned by a police officer not to ride a bicycle without a helmet but continued to do so. He was in an hurry to buy an ice cream. He received a reprimand.

Assaulting or disobeying the police

A common offence committed by young people is assaulting the police. This is also true in the case of adults around clubs and pubs, and is associated with heavy drinking. For young people, alcohol is also a factor, but the problems tend to happen on the street or in public places, where they are allowed to congregate. Many minor offences are committed simply when a young person abuses officers while they are arresting someone else, but they often do more than this.[9]

Case 5I gives a taste of how the wording of charges can change through plea-bargaining, although it seems unlikely this affected the sentence. It seems to suggest either that the police made a mistake, or perhaps that the prosecutor could make what might appear to be a major change to the facts, without contacting the arresting officer, to secure a guilty plea. This is also an example of how new offences are considered, so having a prior record will not necessarily mean an increase in penalties. Magistrates discriminate between types of offences so having a prior conviction for burglary will not necessarily affect sentencing for an assault.

Young people also often appear in court charged with assaulting their parents, and on some occasions restraining orders are sought, although at least one magistrate observed believed that these were an inappropriate remedy for a problem that should be addressed by a parent, school or local police officers.[10] It is perhaps not surprising that police officers have greater protection under the law from being abused or disobeyed than parents. As one prosecutor observed, when an officer has lost patience, he or she can charge the youth and pass on the problem to a case worker or the court. This may, however, be unfair to police officers who deal with disobedience and abuse on a daily basis, and need to maintain their authority to manage public places.

Case 5I

The 17 year old defendant abused and lashed out with his fists at police while they were arresting another young person. There was a plea-bargain in court, in which the defendant pleaded guilty in return for the prosecution amending the charge. This had originally stated that he had kicked an officer in the stomach twice. He had been drinking and was charged with disorderly conduct. He had committed several previous offences and had completed periods of community service. The magistrate gave him a fine, and asked him to keep in touch with Youth Justice.

Case 5J

A 16 year old defendant was with a group of youths drinking in a car park. A police officer asked him to leave but he returned within 15 minutes. He had appeared before the court before and had received a caution (the details of the offence were not described). The magistrate imposed a fine of $50, commenting that he had appeared to have learnt nothing from his previous experience.

Opportunistic offences

One distinction between young people and adults is that adults are expected to think about and be responsible for their actions. It is possible to commit an offence recklessly, which means not considering the consequences of an act that a reasonable adult person would expect to cause harm. Young people, on the other hand, often commit offences spontaneously without thinking about the consequences for victims or themselves. This means that the various practitioners concerned with offenders are concerned with education and socialization as much as punishment. They assume that once a defendant has been brought before the court, he or she will not reoffend. They also assume and count on the fact that offenders will acquire a sense of responsibility as they grow up, so there is no need for punishment:

Case 5K

A 16 year old defendant entered a garden and took two garden lights. He had no prior convictions. The magistrate viewed this as an "opportunistic" offence and dismissed the charge. If he returned to court, he would not be treated as leniently.

Case 5L

A 14 year old defendant removed a chocolate bar from a supermarket without paying, and admitted that he had done this 12 times in the last year, and knew that this was wrong. He had one formal caution. The charge was dismissed, and the defendant was told that if he returned to court he would not be treated so lightly.

Case 5M

A 13 year old defendant had found a mobile phone outside his school, and made two phone calls to his parents. He did not take the phone but was charged with stealing the credits. The magistrate gave him a reprimand.

Influence of peers

Another characteristic of young offenders is that they can fall into bad company and are easily led. This was often raised in mitigation by defense lawyers and mentioned by magistrates, and if successful reduced the sentence. There is a big difference, for example, between stealing a motor-vehicle, and being asked to go for a ride in a car that may be stolen. An adult in this situation might be expected to resist peer pressure and also to recognize that the car was stolen. However, a young person often received the benefit of the doubt:

Case 5N

The 14 year old defendant had accompanied her then boyfriend and another youth in a stolen car. After reviewing the facts, the magistrate concluded she knew that it was stolen, but there was a low level of culpability. She had no prior convictions. She was not attending school owing to problems with bullying, but her intention was to return and she ultimately hoped to become a zoologist. She was distressed and crying in court. The magistrate made an order requiring her to commit no offences of dishonesty for the next 12 months.

Youthfulness

There are usually a few mitigating factors that can reduce a sentence, and these include psychological or medical problems. However, it would also appear that youth itself encourages the court to be lenient, and to allow alternative avenues to be pursued without involving the criminal justice system. In the following case, the defendant was doing a martial arts course which his parents believed helped him to control his temper and act more responsibly. The court seemed reluctant to intervene in this family, partly because only minor offences were committed but also because of the defendant's age.

Case 5O

An 11 year old defendant was charged with burglary and trespass. He had "anger issues" and was doing a course in the martial arts which was helping. The magistrate made a order requiring him to conduct no offences for 12 months.

Reasons for the Decision: Some Sentencing Hearings

Social scientists have often been intrigued by hidden factors, whether social, psychological or ideological, that may explain patterns in sentencing (for example, Hogarth 1971). From a different perspective, those seeking to understand the basis of legal decisions are fortunate in that reasons are usually given either in the form of written judgments, or remarks made in court. In the case of young people, magistrates are required to explain their reasoning in more detail. In doing so, they often seek to persuade the young person that an offence has been committed and why it is wrong, for example, to steal from shops. They often explain why an adult would receive a more serious penalty. They also usually review any mitigating or aggravating factors. The summaries presented above can be misleading in that they do not give full details of each case. However, it should also be noted that the purpose of giving reasons in court is to explain the decision to the defendant, and perhaps to guard against the possibility of an appeal. Since magistrates are not required to mention every factor influencing a decision, it is impossible to reconstruct how it was actually made.[11]

This empirical finding might trouble those legal theorists who believe there should be a rational basis to sentencing (for example, Von Hirsch 1993). On the other hand, one can argue that the need to find reasons or "cognitive models" assumes rather too much about how people make decisions, both in courts of law but also more generally. In a critique of the assumption that rational actions are planned, Lucy Suchman (1987) has argued that reasons are always necessarily given after reaching a decision.[12] The cognitive model also assumes that decision-makers carefully weigh up factors, whereas they are often made in an instant. In the children's court, magistrates are presented with a set of facts, and out of these arrive at a sentence through coming to a view about the defendant. What, of course, makes sentencing interesting is that the same facts can be interpreted in different ways.

The ethnomethodologist, Harold Garfinkel (1984a), has argued that what magistrates or ordinary members of society are doing when provided with a set of facts is identifying a particular element in a set of circumstances as standing for an underlying pattern, and then using the pattern to make sense of both this and other elements. Criminal trials involve a clash between parties who seek to identify a different "underlying pattern" behind a set of events, that point to guilt or innocence. The same methods are used whenever a magistrate or, for that matter, a defense lawyer or case worker forms a judgment about a young offender.

When considering decision-making, it is also important to remember that magistrates and other practitioners are not dealing with a set of abstract facts, but an actual flesh and blood defendant whom they can see and interact with in the courtroom. One magistrate noted that, when talking to young people, he looked into their eyes to see if he was "getting through." This could be understood as a factor such as "showing remorse." However, this seems rather to understate the practical and moral problem faced by magistrates (and also other agencies) in responding to actual young offenders.

To illustrate these observations, it is worth looking at three actual sentencing hearings. In each reasons are given, but there are also a number of elements that might also have been important. In the first case, the young person was charged with assault, although this fails to convey the youthful nature of the offence. In the second case, the defendant was charged with speeding while on a motorcycle without having a license. In the third case, the offence committed was riding a bicycle without a helmet.

An assault

Case 5A

U: John Webster [17 year old youth comes into court, accompanied by his mother.][13]

M: [reads papers] Two charges of common assault – head butting someone – and having been admitted to bail, you failed to appear on [ ]. Are you in a position to enter pleas?

D: Yes guilty to both charges please.

M: Yes Mr. Jones.

P: Sir, the victim was walking ahead and they began having a verbal argument [in which the victim insulted his girlfriend]. He said "Shut your mouth before I knock you out." The defendant called the victim to come back and the defendant head butted him. The victim had blood on his face and teeth were knocked out. The defendant said in interview that he would not let this happen to his girlfriend and is sorry for his actions. He has no priors. [0.3] Oh sorry Your Worship [He passes the priors to the court clerk who gives them to the magistrate. He checks them and nods.] There's one here that was dismissed.

M: John, do you agree with the facts?

D: Yes I do.

M: Is there anything you want to say?

D: No.

M: Nothing at all.

D: Only that I've been in trouble for ages now I...[ ]

M: What are you doing with yourself?

M: Working at [ ]. Then I left and [ ].

M: Do you have any income?

D: Just [ ].

M: And what are your outgoings?

D: [ ]

M: Do you see your father?

D: I don't get along with him.

M: Any particular reason you failed to appear in court?

D: I wasn't aware of that date.

M: Well I see looking at the record that you have no convictions for offences involving violence. You were in court for stealing. I gave you community service. You haven't done this.

D: No.

M: Miss M?

YJ: We have tried to contact him.

M: I assume you left a message.

YJ: He has recently moved to a different address [and we are now in contact].

M: OK. Given the lack of a history of violence, I assume it was a breach of character. If you were a violent young man I would have seen you before. Now what you did [ ]. It may well be he did say something to your girlfriend. But he made no attempt to assault her and you reacted to this excessively. You've got to learn to deal with situations like that in a more appropriate way or you'll end up in prison. As you go through life, a lot of people say things you don't like. You'll have to deal with this as part of growing up. I'm going to fine you and not convict you. I'll dismiss that [ ] common assault without a conviction. I fine you in the sum of $100 and make a compensation order in favor of the complainant, damages to be assessed. So if there is dental work, he can claim this from you and you'll get notice. Now the $100, you don't earn much so how long will it take you?

D: One and an half months.

M: So two months would be fine. Very well. So in future just keep your temper under control. You can go.[14]

This case illustrates how magistrates differentiate between types of offending, so the fact there was a prior offence of burglary was not relevant to deciding how the court should respond to this assault. One can see how the surroundings of the court seldom result in defendants opening up or giving lengthy responses when asked to talk about their offending or other circumstances of their lives. Nevertheless, one can see that the information obtained through these questions was relevant to the sentencing decision. The fact that the defendant could afford to pay a fine made it possible to pursue this option as opposed to dismissing the charge. The magistrate also took the trouble to check what period of payment would be realistic. This is an example of how defendants themselves collaborate in the sentencing process.

It also seems clear that the magistrate, like any observer, obtained other information about the defendant from this exchange. This young person had told the police that "he was sorry for his actions" but would not let his girlfriend be treated in this way again. This is probably why the matter was not suitable for a conference: no apology would be made to the victim. There was no indication from his answers or his demeanor that he had learnt his lesson, or would control his temper in the future. On the other hand, the defendant appeared to be contrite, and anxious to help the court with his answers. The fact that he was unrepresented, even though Legal Aid is available, and did not get on with his father, suggests that he might be vulnerable, even without seeing the pre-sentence report. Once you start to fit together the different elements in this way, not keeping appointments to do community service and not answering to bail become signs of someone who is disorganized rather than seeking to evade punishment. The following exchange has a certain poignancy, especially since he was not interrupted but the answer trailed off, which suggests that he did not have the oral skills or confidence to talk about himself in this setting:

M: Is there anything you want to say?

D: No.

M: Nothing at all.

D: Only that I've been in trouble for ages now I...

The magistrate began by asking an open-ended question, giving the defendant the opportunity to apologize for having acted foolishly, and possibly "out of character." The magistrate's next remark, "nothing at all" can be heard as a reprimand, as much as giving him a second chance to say something. A defendant who appreciated the seriousness of the situation, should have something to say in these circumstances. The defendant knew that his answer was not really adequate in explaining his actions ("only that"), and it might even be heard as an attempt to shift the blame onto others, rather than learning from his recent experiences. "I've been in trouble" does not sound like an admission of wrong-doing, but suggests other factors or people have been responsible. He also seems to be claiming leniency on the grounds that he has already been in contact with the criminal justice system for some time, not the kind of response that would satisfy a magistrate. On the other hand, it would also appear from this answer that a vulnerable, and to some extent inarticulate teenager is struggling to understand his past history of offending ("being in trouble") and perhaps also what is involved in becoming an adult. The court has responded leniently because he is a young person rather than an adult: he cannot be expected to answer to bail or attend to do community service. He is committing the kind of non-serious offences that young people commit without thought for the consequences of their actions, and because of this is not treated like an adult.

A road traffic offence

Magistrates have some discretion in how they conduct sentencing hearings. Some magistrates asked questions in an attempt to discover more about the defendant or involve them in the proceedings, but did not say much when sentencing. Others used the hearing to give a short lecture, which it was hoped would "get through" to a young person by explaining why he or she had committed an offence. The following extract from the audio-file of a hearing shows how this was done in the case of a 17 year old who had gone out riding on a motorcycle after having an argument with his parents:

Case 5E

M: [long pause, while looking through papers] Yes. Thank you for that John [0.2 coughs] I am aware of the ability of most kids who grow up on a farm to competently handle machinery.

D: Yes.

M: I have a five year old step grandson who can competently drive a bull-dozer round his parents' farm. That's one thing on a farm. You don't however go on public streets until you have shown that competency to the license authorities. I don't care how competent you are in paddocks. You must have a license before you get on the road.

D: Yes.

M: Now it seems to me that on this night you did everything wrong. You start off with an argument with your parents. There are some times when people cannot see eye to eye. Jumping on a bike to clear your head is not the way to do it. Driving is one of those interesting aspects of our lives that requires total concentration not the time to be driving when you are trying to clear your head from some argument you've had with your parents. By the way as you get older you might start to realize that you shouldn't argue with your parents. They might actually be right. You should listen to them. And then things went from bad to worse, didn't they? First of all, you didn't have a tail light. Then you picked up a pillion passenger. When you get your learner's permit even then you can't carry a pillion passenger. Then you start speeding and heading up the street on a vehicle that's not registered, therefore uninsured. You can thank your lucky stars you have come before me today in my role as magistrate and not come before me in my other role as the coroner here. You are carrying a pillion passenger, are unregistered, uninsured, speeding. Thank goodness there wasn't an accident with someone being potentially killed. You start to see the seriousness of what you've been doing? I bet you didn't give any thought to any of that when you started

D: [nods head]

M: I want people to learn to think first before they act rather than the thinking coming after they've acted. Now I've noted the reference from your employers. That's good. I think the appropriate way to deal with you is to look at these five matters now as one overall incident and I will just give you one penalty. I'm going to give you a financial penalty as a reminder of what will happen if you continue to break the road laws.

D: Yes.

M: I will make it relatively light in the light of your low wage and your youthfulness so on the complaint there will just be a fine of $100. I thought about disqualifying you from driving but I'm not going to. I think it would be better if you got your license somehow and learn to abide by the laws that come with the license. I think this would be a good test in itself.

D: Yes.

M: [addressing his father] Mr. B time to pay $100?

F: Six weeks to pay, sir.

M: I want you to pay it. I don't want your parents to lend it to you. I want it to come out of your income so it hurts.

F: Thank you, sir.

M: Right, he's free to go.

Although it is not explicitly stated by the magistrate, the main reason for the lenient sentence is that, at the time, this youth was not thinking about the possible consequences of his actions, whereas there is evidence in court that he was remorseful and had matured since the incident. The fact that his father was in court and there was a good employer's reference may also have been significant. Viewed in this way, it becomes difficult not to see this as a basically responsible young man who has gone off the rails after leaving school, but has now got back on track through obtaining a job.[15]

Another feature of this hearing that is interesting is that the defendant is not simply a youthful driver, but a youthful driver who has grown up on a farm in a rural area. This provided cultural resources for the defense lawyer to suggest that he was driving competently. The magistrate was not, therefore, simply sentencing a young person for speeding on a motorcycle, but also attempting to combat, but also acknowledge, the assumption that young children growing up in rural areas are competent drivers. This is an example of how where an offence takes place does make a difference for the criminal courts. It may not necessarily change the sentences imposed, since driving offences are, if anything, taken more seriously by magistrates in rural areas where there are large numbers of deaths and injuries each year. However, in this case it shaped or influenced how the sentence was explained to someone who had grown up on a farm.

Driving a bicycle without a helmet

During the fieldwork in Tasmania, there was a television advertisement being screened that sought to raise awareness about the serious head injuries one can receive through riding a bicycle without a protective helmet. Many young people are cautioned by the police for this offence and some end up in the courts. According to one informant, one youth had eventually been sentenced to Ashley Youth Detention centre for repeatedly refusing to wear an helmet. This may be an apocryphal or exaggerated story, but it raises the issue as to how the legal system should respond to persistent violations that do not result in actual harm to other people. It seems worth giving an example of how a magistrate addressed this offence:

Case 5G

M: Why having been spotted by the police, and cautioned, did you ride by without a helmet?

D: I was in a hurry to get an ice cream.

M: Did you think this is a good reason for not wearing a helmet?

D: No.

M: Do you know why you are wearing a helmet?

D: So you don't get hurt.

M: It's there to protect you from a serious head injury or getting killed. [ ] So you want to pay a big fine?

D: Not really.

M: Where was your helmet? Did you have one at the time?

D: No.

M: Have you got one now?

D: Yes.

M: Wear it all the time?

D: No.

M: Were you wearing it when you came here?

D: Yes.

M: This is your first matter. I accept that you're not going to do it again. If you do it again, I will impose a big fine. On this occasion I will give a reprimand and discharge you. You are free to go.

This is another example of youthful behavior in that the magistrate accepted that this 14 year old defendant did not think. The short answers may suggest that he is going along with the court, rather than taking the matter to heart. He also indicates that paying a fine in the future may be an acceptable outcome. It is unclear whether he is wearing a helmet at the moment although the magistrate lets this pass and gives him the opportunity to give a positive answer. From the court's perspective, it made sense to give this defendant the opportunity to learn that riding without an helmet will not be tolerated without imposing a penalty.[16]

Finally, these hearings illustrate that the magistrate was not simply administering legal penalties, but also attempting to educate a young person as someone representing the responsible, adult community. This defendant was asked some questions designed to test that he was a responsible person. He accepted that being in an hurry does not excuse breaking the law: in this case, not wearing an helmet, and disobeying the instructions of a police officer. He also accepted that there were good reasons for wearing an helmet. Older defendants did not receive tutorials on road safety and respecting the law.

The defendant pleading guilty to driving offences was given some advice on listening to one's parents, and not behaving foolishly after an argument. The defendant who had committed an assault was given a lecture about not losing one's temper when hearing something that offends you. Young offenders have probably received similar advice from many sources: their parents, school teachers, police officers and case workers, in addition to the magistrate sitting in court. The routine work of this court seems nicely to illustrate the regular and continuous work of social institutions identified by American structural-functionalists writing during the 1940s and 1950s in maintaining society as an orderly place, based on respect for common values.[17] This is largely successful in that most first-time offenders, or those who have committed less serious offences, never return to court.

Should More Minor Offences Be Diverted?

From these cases, it is apparent that continuing to offend can, in many cases, by itself result in heavier penalties. The young person who shoplifted 12 times would ultimately receive an higher penalty if he continued to shoplift, even if this meant receiving a supervision order as against a good behaviour bond. On the other hand, it is also apparent that the penalties for offences are decided by their seriousness, and not by the previous record of the defendant. It is possible to spend time in a detention center, and still be asked to make an undertaking on a subsequent offence. Indeed, if an offender who had been committing aggravating burglaries or taking cars, next appeared for shoplifting, this was considered an example of successful rehabilitation.

Many young people who appear before magistrates have committed minor offences, and do not come back to court. However, it should be remembered that any young person who comes before the court, even those who are diverted to the Ropes program in Victoria, has probably been warned and cautioned by the police, possibly on a few occasions.[18] One question raised by these hearings is, therefore, whether diversion is working effectively, or could be used for more young people. One might want to argue whether an 11 year old charged with stealing chocolate bars even on 12 separate occasions (case 5L) should appear before the magistrates. Even the more serious of these minor offences are not especially serious. Why should a youth who goes riding on an unlicensed motor cycle appear before the children's court, rather than attending a conference or receiving a warning? To put this differently, magistrates have been given a number of sentencing options that effectively allow them to dismiss cases. With the exception of those sent on the Ropes program, this still results in a finding of guilt, so they have a criminal record. Should, perhaps, even more of these cases be diverted so magistrates can concentrate on more serious, repeat offenders?

There are a number of reasons why offenders who have

committed minor offences are sent to court, as opposed to being given a caution or asked to attend a restorative conference. The first is that these measures have already been tried and failed. Alternatively, it may not always be easy convening a conference, or the offence may appear too serious to be disposed of without going to court. Each of these considerations was probably relevant to case 5C in which a youth threatened someone with a shot gun. The Youth Officer who reviewed the case accepted the argument that it was a serious offence, and that the victim might not want to meet the offender. This case was sent to the court, and the defendant received a sentence of probation. However, the case was sent back to the officer requiring him to arrange a conference, at which the victim was not required to attend. If the arresting officer had taken a different view, this defendant might never have appeared in the children's court.

Another reason why those committing minor offences are not sent to conferences is because they do not admit guilt unequivocally when they are interviewed by the police. Diversion is only available to defendants who plead guilty.[19] There are also defendants who admit guilt, but are not sufficiently remorseful. In all criminal proceedings, it remains possible, after admitting guilt, to find some way of reducing culpability.[20] In children's courts, this seems particularly evident in cases involving violence between young people and also after assaults on the police. In case 5A, for example, the defendant told police that he was sorry, but also that he would not let his girlfriend be spoken to in that way. In many cases, the defendants were not remorseful or apologetic towards the police, which leaves officers with the option of giving a warning or sending the matter to court. After pleading guilty at a later stage, defendants are not usually asked, and do not offer, to apologize to officers.

There are, therefore, good institutional reasons why offenders who have committed minor offences appear in the children's court, instead of being diverted to a formal caution or restorative conference. This suggests that more can probably always be done in keeping young people out of court, assuming that this is seen as a desirable objective. The justification for diversion to conferences is that this saves money, reduces re-offending more effectively than a court hearing and delays the imposition of heavier penalties, particularly detention orders. Exactly, the same argument could be made in relation to diversion to the Ropes program, which is considerably cheaper than conferencing. Proponents in Victoria believe that a brief court appearance has deterrent value above that of a police caution or attending a conference.

One practical suggestion would be to give offenders even more opportunities to demonstrate a remorseful attitude. This might lead to more cases being diverted and heard more quickly than is possible once a case enters the children's court. Another, perhaps more radical suggestion, would to be to set up some procedure in which independent adjudicators could mediate between the police and young offenders, and also engage in educational initiatives. This would allow children's courts to concentrate on middle-range or more serious offences.

6.

Responding to Repeat and Serious Offences

Practitioners working in these Australian children's courts recognized two distinct types of offenders. Most young people who appeared before the court once or twice were never seen again. This may be because the experience of being in court brought home the seriousness of their behavior, or it may be that many young people simply grew out of offending. Then there were a smaller number of offenders who were in regular contact with the courts, and received supervision from juvenile case workers. Some of these received one or more sentences of detention, and in some cases spent a large proportion of their teenage years in a detention centre.[1] They usually committed more serious offences than fighting amongst themselves, shop-stealing or making trouble for the police. These included robbery, burglary, stealing cars and acts of violence.

Through looking at actual cases, one can see that practitioners recognized further differences within these repeat offenders. The next chapter will consider young people who were considered especially "vulnerable" in some way, whether from being in care, having an Indigenous background, belonging to an ethnic group or suffering from a psychological problem such as a learning disability. This chapter will focus on cases in which these factors were not mentioned during the hearing,[2] or if they were mentioned were not viewed as excusing the offence. These defendants were mainly ordinary working class youths, who have attracted attention from criminologists and social control agencies for anti-social behavior for many years.

My warrant as a sociologist for using the term "working class" is partly because some practitioners, matter of factly, characterized the area in which a court was situated as a "working class" district. It also arises from my own observation of hearings. Although it is often hard to identify class distinctions from clothing, or from the way people speak, in an affluent society such as Australia, it is still possible to see or hear these differences. There were some defendants who were smartly dressed. They were accompanied by their parents and had what I recognized as educated, middle-class accents. There were other youths who jauntily displayed their lack of interest in middle class conventions. Some male defendants wore a jacket and tie (with the top button of the shirt unbuttoned) over jeans. One youth was chastised by the magistrate for dressing inappropriately, although the hearing did proceed. He was wearing a t-shirt that presented him as a gift-wrapped parcel, with the slogan, "God's gift to women – from God".

Sentencing decisions lend themselves to different forms of variable analysis, whether these are concerned with identifying the causes of offending, or factors that influence sentencing decisions. They also invite an evaluative response since there were sometimes striking variations in the way different magistrates sentenced what appeared to be similar offences. However, this often means that sentencing researchers do not describe what happens in hearings, the reasons given for the sentence or specific features of particular offences. By contrast, this chapter seeks to describe hearings in more detail, as these were available to me as an observer. This preserves how practitioners understood the seriousness of the offence, which would not be available from the bare details of the charges. The summaries also provide some insight into how offenders understood the hearing. They do not, however, supply a full interactional record of hearings, or the full ethnographic context. In cases where I had an opportunity to interview a case worker about a particular client, or see the pre-sentence report, I had a better understanding of this context, or rather one perspective within it.[3]

The chapter starts by giving a taste of the administrative work involved before sentencing can take place: the young person has to attend a meeting with a case worker so there will be a pre-sentence report. It then provides some examples of decisions that resulted in defendants receiving a probation order, a combination of probation and community service, and a detention order. The hearings also illustrate some of the communicative work involved in seeking to persuade young people to stop offending. The chapter concludes by considering how practitioners responded to repeat offending with what might be called professional realism. They know that legal sanctions often have no effect, but also that most young people grow out of offending.

Although this chapter will not seek to differentiate between the approaches adopted in the three states, one procedural difference should be explained. In Victoria, there was a power in the legislation to defer sentencing a defendant. This made it possible to dismiss offences, or impose a light penalty such as a good behaviour bond, even after a period of supervision by Youth Justice. If more serious offences were committed during the deferral, it was also possible to make a probation order. Deferred sentences were widely used for what were perceived as middle-range offences. This meant that, in Victoria, some young people received the equivalent supervision of a probation order in other states but without being found guilty of a criminal offence.

Obtaining A Pre-Sentence Report

Before a magistrate can impose a more serious penalty than an undertaking or good behaviour bond, the court normally requires a pre-sentence report. The following hearing illustrates how one magistrate in Tasmania explained the importance of this report to a defendant, who in this study will be called David Riley.[4] This transcript breaks up long stretches of talk, which were delivered briskly and without pauses by the defense lawyer and magistrate, for ease of reading. The transcript includes some details of the defendant's dress and body-language, which seems important since some previous studies give the impression that most youths are terrified by, or do not understand, court proceedings. Everyone in the court could see at a glance that this 17 year old youth belonged to a different social world to the magistrate and other practitioners, who were conventionally dressed. He did not appear at all cowed or frightened by court proceedings:[5]

Case 6A

DL: David Riley. It's 30 and 35 on Your Worship's list this morning.

CC: Call David Riley.

U: [outside the court] DAVID RILEY.

[The defendant came into court. He was wearing a red and black Holden tracksuit with trainers, and had a partly shaved head. He stood facing the magistrate with a relaxed posture.]

CC: You are David Riley.

D: Yes.

DL: Thank you Your Worship. I appear on behalf of David.

M: You can sit next to your counsel [The defendant sat to the right of his lawyer.]

DL: [speaking very fast] I am appearing for David today effectively for the duty solicitor. He approached me outside court. He's given me instructions in relation to these charges and he is in a position to enter pleas of guilty to all of them and I note that in relation to index 34 it's a simple charge of stealing, that's a plea of guilty, and in relation to the matter at 35 there are 3 charges of motor-vehicle stealing which are pleas of guilty to all, and attempted motor-vehicle stealing which is also a plea of guilty, and a contravening of the conditions of the notice relating to a curfew condition which is a plea of guilty as well [draws in breath].

Your Worship, my application in relation to this matter is that it adjourn for Facts and Sentence at a later date and in the meantime I will apply for aid on David's behalf at the Legal Aid office and he will be represented appropriately next time.

M: Thank you for that. Have we got a date there Marian?

CC: [mid-May] at 10am.

M: Right the position is this David. These matters will be

adjourned till [mid-May] at 10am. Now your bail will be changed. It will still have the condition that you must live at...in...during the period of the bail and not change it without the approval of the court. But added to that you also have to report to Youth Justice in... and they will give you some details of that in the bail room...Now the questions they put to you will help me understand you as a person. This is all very useful to you because I just see you as another youth at this point in time and I don't know you as a person. Youth Justice get to know you – they bring out the details.

So while they may ask you some very personal questions the position is that you should be very frank with them about what you think, and that sort of thing. And that will all be to your advantage in determining what I should do with these offences at the end of the day. And, of course, the whole process is to benefit you and rehabilitate you in relation to not doing these sort of things or anything else so you can get on with your life.

So it is a very important process from your point of view. And if they ask you to wait around because they haven't got time to see you immediately, make sure you do and be patient, because if we come back and we haven't got the report because of your fault, I will not be very happy about it OK? So if you'd like to go with the officer to the bail room, he'll look after your bail. Then you can be on your way.

D: Thank you [Looked for confirmation that he could leave from his lawyer, then left the court with the security officer.][6]

This transcript demonstrates the organizational and administrative work around sentencing, and the sequence of actions required before this can take place. Although the prosecutor played no part in this hearing (she was sitting immediately to the right of the defendant), the prosecution case had been disclosed to the defendant. This defendant had also seen the duty solicitor, and chose to plead guilty to all charges. It appears that this lawyer had instructed a colleague to indicate this in court. At the next hearing, when the defendant formally pleaded to the charges, the agreed facts would be presented. However, the magistrate could only sentence once a pre-sentence report had been obtained. This meant that Youth Justice had to meet the defendant, prepare a short report about his or her background, and recommend how he or she should be sentenced.

From this short hearing, one can obtain a sense of the values that informed sentencing in this court, which were explicitly communicated to the defendant. While a central objective of youth justice legislation in each state was to punish as well as rehabilitate, this magistrate told the young offender that "of course, the whole process is to benefit you and rehabilitate you in relation to not doing these sort of things or anything else so you can get on with your life". There was some effort to explain the purpose of the Youth Justice interview rather than simply requiring him to attend, which is similar to how young people are disciplined in other social settings.[7]

In this hearing, the moral failing of not attending an interview, and the possible consequences that might flow, seemed rather to overshadow the moral and legal consequences of stealing or motor-vehicle stealing. Before sentencing could take place, the defendant had to be persuaded to attend an interview with Youth Justice, although with an implied threat if he failed to comply ("I won't be very happy"). The magistrate asked rather than ordered the defendant to go with the officer at the end of the hearing ("So if you'd like to go with the officer") and even showed some consideration for taking up this young person's time ("Then you can be on your way"). It seems significant that the defendant thanked him for giving his own time at the end of the hearing. Even though he was being told to comply with a court procedure, the exchange had a polite character, and it was made clear that the procedures were for the defendant's benefit rather than punishment for breaking the law.

Some Probation Orders

Probation is a more serious order than a good behaviour bond. It does not, necessarily, involve more supervision, although it makes it possible for a magistrate to attach an order requiring completion of a program, rather than leaving this to the judgment of the case worker. Nor is it necessarily the case that having a probation order automatically means that the magistrate must consider more serious penalties on the next offence. However, it does make this more likely, if supervision and some degree of support has not resulted in a change of behavior or what case workers describe as cognitive development.

Very few of the relatively small number of hearings observed received a probation order without conditions to attend programs, or without also being required to do community service. Perhaps coincidentally, the two young people sentenced below were from middle class families. In the first case, the offence was relatively minor. A 17 year old youth breached a deferred sentence imposed in Victoria for taking money from another youth. In the second case in New South Wales, a young woman had joined the "wrong crowd" and was causing a disturbance at house parties, committing driving offences and repeatedly disobeying the police. In each case, the circumstances and response were slightly more complex:

"Rolling" at a party

This 16 year old youth (case 6B) was charged with being drunk, while on a three month deferred order imposed after a previous offence, committed when he was 15. In the first offence, he had taken money by going through the pockets of another youth who was sleeping off a bout of drinking at a party. In this case, I was able to attend an interview with his lawyer before the hearing, and read the pre-sentence report. This suggested nothing in his family background, medical history or educational experiences that might explain the offending. Although he was attending drugs and alcohol counseling, and received a positive assessment, at no point in the report was it suggested that he saw moderate drug use as a great problem. Moreover, he did not view "rolling" in order to obtain money to purchase drugs as a serious offence. This had happened to him on a number of occasions, and he had not involved the police. The pre-sentence report also suggested that he was following other people when he committed the first offence, but without giving details. When asked by the Legal Aid lawyer to explain this, he said that this view was mistaken, and that he acted on his own.

His father then joined the interview. He did not believe that his son had stopped drinking, and complained that he was missing school. The lawyer noted that he had not been suspended, and this was not suggested in the pre-sentence report. He went to a good school, but had done badly. His parents had put him on the "Fresh Start" program, a summer camp used in Victoria to encourage re-engagement with school after difficulties. In this camp, he had received a prize for leadership abilities. In the lawyer's view, the fact that he was going to drugs and alcohol counseling once a week was promising: "It doesn't matter if he is still using. It confirms that he's engaging – that's huge".

Even from this short summary, one can see that the young person, case worker, lawyer and parent all viewed this offence, and subsequent progress differently. From the lawyer's perspective, the defendant had already passed a significant threshold in obtaining a criminal record. If he had responded to supervision during the deferral order, the outcome would have been a good behaviour bond. However, his comments to Youth Justice about the original offence, and the new offence, made it more likely that he would be sentenced to a long period of probation. This was an accurate prediction. Moreover, the magistrate expressed doubts about the judgment of the drugs and alcohol counsellor given that there was a glowing report a few days before the most recent offence. He warned him that an adult would normally receive a sentence of imprisonment for robbery, and that he was lucky not to receive a conviction. The sentence was a period of probation for six months, on the condition that he should continue to see the drugs and alcohol counselor weekly.

Joining the "wrong crowd"

There is no criminal offence for mixing with people from a different social background who are regularly in trouble with the police. Nevertheless, when sentencing young people it was often the situation rather than the specific offences that concerned the magistrate. In this case (6C), a 17 year old girl from a good family was sentenced to probation after being in trouble with the police, and committing a number of minor offences over two years, firstly under a deferral order, then a good behaviour bond and most recently a probation order.

According to the case worker, the concern was not the seriousness of the offences, but the fact she was still offending, and continuing to mix with young people who were targeted by police:

> The offences are not particularly serious comparatively. She was on orders for shouting at police at a party and making loud noises and things like that. She was engaged with some pretty heavy neighborhood activities with peers. The magistrate has no idea about this since it is not in the report. If it was his kids, he would be very worried. There was a lot of drinking and drugs and parties and yahooing, and a bit of rebellion, that sort of stuff. What happened [most recently] is she was at a party and got drunk. The police were eventually called. There were complaints about the amount of noise she was making from four blocks away, and she gave the police a hard time. She had also had her license suspended. She was on bail, and then was pulled up and told not to drive. The next day police observed her driving for a second time. They told her to pull over and she sped up. She cut and run. It suggests she's a bit compulsive and will do what she thinks she wants to regardless of the consequences.

The magistrate spent some time deliberating whether or not to give a further probation order, as recommended by the case worker, or to impose a detention order. It was, nevertheless, unsurprising to anyone at the hearing, including the defendant, that he decided to make a further probation order, and did not ask her to undertake community work. The sentencing remarks were also designed for someone who would find detention far more significant in terms of her future life than other defendants:

> It upsets me to see you before the court on all these matters [long pause while reads papers]. If you come back, you're going to jail and your life will be absolutely ruined. You

are now in the children's court. The court is taking more time with you because you're not 18. If you were 18, you would go to jail. You're then dealing with big overweight unattractive women. There's a lot of problems with young girls going into custody, the same as with young boys [long pause]. We all care for you – Mr. H [the case worker], Mr S [the defense lawyer], the prosecutor. At the end of the day what are you going to do? It's about taking responsibility and not seeing people you don't need to be with. You can turn your back on it.

This short extract from an hearing indicates more vividly than statistics the fact that most defendants come from a different world to ordinary, law-abiding middle class citizens. It is also unusual in that there was no suggestion in the report or during the hearing that any social or psychological factor was blamed for the offending behavior. There was a characteristic mix of objectives. Everyone in the court had her welfare at heart ("We all care for you"). However, if she continued to mix with the wrong crowd, she would be sent to prison. For this offender, this was not presented as having any rehabilitative purpose, but as an environment in which young people are physically and sexually abused by older prisoners.

Paying Back Society: Community Service

When faced with repeat offences, the magistrate could continue giving probation orders. However, a common next step was to combine this with an order of community service. These orders were not always punitive in nature, in the sense of involving hard or unpleasant manual work. Nor was there any expectation that community service, like probation, had a deterrent value. However, the thinking behind the order was that the young person was not simply being helped with support by a case worker, but was receiving a light form of punishment or paying something back to society. Opinion, however, differed. Some practitioners believed that any attempt to require a young person to concentrate on some structured activity was both burdensome, and bound to fail. One Legal Aid lawyer described young people as "having the attention span of a gnat." They regularly breached orders, and this resulted in some being sent to detention centers. For other practitioners, community service offered an additional sentencing option that could be used to delay more intensive supervision or detention.

In the following case, a young woman, aged 15 but 14 at the time of the offences, was charged with stealing letters containing checks and then trying to cash the checks at a bank. These extracts from a transcript of the hearing show how the sentencing decision was communicated:

Case 6D

M: Yes, if you could stand up now Jane, thank you. You have got these priors as you've admitted where you were formally cautioned for stealing in December of 2000 [and two dates in 2003], so to some extent you really haven't taken on board what you were cautioned about. And of course that may be the fact that of course you are a young person, and hopefully you are maturing all the time. But it does indicate that at the point when you entered into these matters, you hadn't learnt your lesson. And of course there has to be some deterrence in relation to these matters. Now I understand that in the report you indicated you wanted to do...I'm not sure what it was now. Was it childcare? Yes, childcare.

D: Yep.

M: And it's important of course when you want to have a specific career for you to have an unblemished record if you possibly can or as unblemished record as you can at the time when you go into that particular profession. The reason being of course is that you have to set an example to the children you are looking after etc and of course parents or whoever you will be working for will obviously want to be very sure that you are a proper person to be looking after their children. So you very much need to change your position [ ] I don't know whether I imposed [the curfew] or somebody else imposed it but we don't impose these things for fun. And whilst New Year's Eve and the party period of the year is a great temptation, I don't regard that as a very good reason for you not obeying that order and it shows a lack of responsibility in regard to that matter. Now in respect of that charge which is X of 2005 I am going to impose 21 hrs of community service in respect of that, and hopefully that will enable you when you are doing that to reflect well was it really worth it going out for New Year's Eve? You might think it was but I certainly wouldn't have thought it was.

CC: Is that with or without conviction?

M: That's without conviction. I don't intend to impose convictions on you despite the seriousness of the charge bearing in mind your age and bearing in mind I would like you to develop so you can in fact become a child-carer [ ]. The other charges of course relate to the checks. You were not the instigator in terms of stealing the checks out of the letter box but certainly you must have been aware at 14, I think you're 14 now is that correct, I think you were 13 at the time, but the position is that in an adult this would call for a serious penalty such as a detention order and even in the Youth Division detention orders do occur so one can be placed at Ashley where there are some rather unpleasant children from time to time. And they certainly do not improve necessarily the people who go into incarceration, they do not necessarily come out better persons. That depends on how they react to the discipline and the assistance that is tried that the authorities try to give them. But in this case I certainly am not going to impose a detention order on you at this stage [ ]. And in relation to that offence there will be 119 hours of community orders[8]. Now that's quite a substantial amount of community service but it will give you a chance to understand that society [ ], and I think that you are starting to understand from the discussions you've had with Youth Justice

D: Yes.

M: how this affects people, because not only the larger

community, but if you for example give it to a shopkeeper and they lose the money they are not covered by insurance so they put up their prices and millions are being lost not only from this, well perhaps not so much from this [offence], but from shoplifting. So that is the sum total of the penalty in relation to those offences. And you're to report to Youth Justice by 4.30 on Tuesday and you are to obey the reasonable requirements of Youth Justice in relation to those work matters. And you will understand that this is all part of paying back society for what we do so we all get penalised if we do the wrong thing for what we do. If we go through a red light we get fined for it or whatever. Now having said all that I do not want to see you back here again. I do not believe I will see you back here again. I feel you understand the seriousness of the position. Young ladies are meant to be mature at 14. It takes men another 11 years apparently and some never mature. You have a chance to go ahead without the convictions and all I can say is good luck.

D: Thanks.

This defendant appeared nervous, but did not look remorseful or repentant. In this hearing, there was no reference to the contents of the pre-sentence report, or to the defendant's demeanour.[9] However, the magistrate did comment that she had not developed a sense of responsibility after previous contact with the police:

so to some extent you really haven't taken on board what you were cautioned about. And of course that may be the fact that of course you are a young person, and hopefully you are maturing all the time. But it does indicate that at the point when you entered into these matters, you hadn't learnt your lesson. And of course there has to be some deterrence in relation to these matters.

Although the official purpose of children's courts is to punish and rehabilitate young offenders, these sentencing remarks suggest that there is also a concern with assisting young people to become adults. This happens when they develop a sense of responsibility in relation to their behavior towards other people, such as the victims of their offending or their parents. It also involves developing an understanding or awareness of the consequences to themselves that follow from breaking the law. In this case, the magistrate expressed the hope that appearing in court had helped this defendant to "understand the seriousness of the position", which meant that she could receive a conviction or possibly detention if she committed further offences.

This transcript also illustrates how magistrates explained the reasons for punishment in some detail. In this case, it appears that Youth Justice already had reported some success in explaining why stealing and attempting to cash checks is an offence, and the magistrate also tried to explain why it, and related criminal activities, damage both small businesses and society:

> M: because not only the larger community, but if you for example give it to a shopkeeper and they lose the money they are not covered by insurance so they put up their prices and millions are being lost not only from this, well perhaps not so much from this [offence], but from shoplifting.

This magistrate presented both probation and community service as a punishment that is "all part of paying back society for what we do". The example he used was receiving a fine for going through a red light, perhaps because the potential harm that might be caused is clearer in this case. He stated at a number of points that the offending behavior was serious which explains why he sentenced her to 70 hours, the maximum period of community service for her age. Although this is not explicitly stated, it may be that the seriousness lies in the fact this was a pre-meditated offence involving an attempt to deceive. There is a contradiction between this and the youthful spontaneous offence of breaching a curfew on New Year's Eve: however, disobeying this court order resulted in 21 hours of community service.

Serious Enough For Detention

The heaviest penalty that can be imposed by children's courts is a sentence of detention, or what in New South Wales is called a control order. The powers given to magistrates in the three states differ, but it is possible in New South Wales to be sent to an institution for a period of two or even three years (although with a date for release on parole set by the magistrate as part of the sentence). However, in most cases the periods of detention were for a few months. According to one magistrate, this had a greater deterrent effect than sending someone away for a shorter period, and made it possible to complete rehabilitative programs while in detention. It was not really expected that detention was effective in reducing crime. The threat initially had a deterrent effect, but this wore off once a young person had experience of being in detention. Moreover, it was recognized that young people learnt from mixing with older and more experienced offenders.[10]

Again, the best way to understand the issues, and get a sense of how repeat offenders respond to the juvenile justice system, is through looking at actual cases. The following hearings in Tasmania give an example of two defendants who were sentenced to detention although, in the second case, this was a suspended sentence. In the first case, the offender had committed many offences, including assaults, to support a drugs habit. However, this was not seen as excusing the crime, or identifying the offender as a "vulnerable" person in need of help rather than punishment. In the second case, the magistrate had to address the difficult but common case of a sexual assault committed by a young person.

A case of "crocodile tears"?

Because offenders sentenced to detention had often already spent a few months as remand detainees, an important consideration for magistrates was whether there was any recent evidence that they had come to recognize they had behaved badly, and would change their pattern of behavior. In this case, the defense lawyer suggested that there was a significant chance of rehabilitation since his client had started to participate in programs, but the magistrate took a different view. The main reason was because the case workers supervising the young person in the detention centre believed that he had not shown any sign of remorse:

Case 6E

M: Thanks Mr. Jones. Stand up please Peter. You've pleaded guilty to 33 separate offences. You indicated that you had stopped offending but you continued till [ ] and that last offence was a very serious offence with four assaults, two were very serious. There were eight breaches of bail. Mary Smith [a security guard] thought she was going to be stabbed by you no one deserves that. The offences also show you're not prepared to obey court orders. You consistently breached police bail. You did not follow the directions of Youth Justice. You were just faulting authority and thinking you can get away with it. You punched and set upon Constable A in a most serious way and abused and spat upon Constable B. Your violence is not going to be tolerated and you should just take some time out to think about the effect on other people.

You are 17. For most offences you have not received convictions but there is violence and dishonesty. You received a good behaviour bond but continued to offend. You are not as powerful and clever as you think. This shows to the court you are a weak person. If you can't change your behavior, you will be sentenced to periods of imprisonment for a very long time. I hope it won't happen. It is possible the changes you made in Ashley will continue. I also note that you pleaded guilty. If you had not pleaded guilty, this would have occupied a large number of days for the court.

The only appropriate sentence is a detention order. The sentence is for ten months, with three months suspended backdated to [ ]. I'll talk about when I think you'll get out in a minute. I will also make a probation order and when you get out 49 hours community service orders [long pause while looks through papers].

It seems, Mr. Jones, Peter has two to three weeks left to serve. I take into account you have spent a long time in detention. You now have three months hanging over your head if you commit further offences. The sentence is a global one. Just go with the officer [leaves the dock]. Thank you Mr. Jones. Thank you Miss Green.[11]

The chronology of offending and sentencing was unclear from the sentencing hearing, since the facts had been presented at a previous hearing. The most serious offences were committed on bail in between periods of detention. Nevertheless, from these remarks, it is possible to see that these were serious offences, both in terms of the number of charges, and their nature. It also seems likely that this defendant had already received penalties for minor offences: there were no other options available than detention. Although drug-taking was involved, this 17 year old was presented as a calculating person with a propensity for violence and no respect for authority.

Perhaps because of the report, the magistrate was not optimistic that he would change, and the emphasis in the remarks was on deterrence, rather than rehabilitation. If he committed a further offence, there would be another three month period of detention. What, though, was most striking about the hearing is that the defendant was crying while the magistrate commented on his behavior and imposed this sentence. After the hearing, the case worker described this as "crocodile tears": he had not really changed his attitude towards taking drugs, or showed remorse for his actions either when formally interviewed, or with staff in the detention centre.[12] He was likely to re-offend, even if he was now engaging with rehabilitative programs such as drug and alcohol counseling.

A sexual assault

The cases observed for this study do not include any offences that were so serious that the courts immediately sentenced the offender to detention. The following hearing, however, shows that in the case of a sexual assault magistrates will consider a detention order, or impose a suspended sentence that would result in detention if there was a similar offence. In this case, a young boy was charged with asking a younger girl staying at his house to undress, getting on top of her and "touching her below her pants." He initially denied committing the offence but later admitted he had "taken advantage of her." This was the only hearing observed where the defense view differed from the magistrate, in that the lawyer asked for a conviction not to be imposed:[13]

Case 6F

[The defense lawyer started to make a submission, talking about the family background]

M: I'm a bit troubled by the comment that he presented with little understanding of the seriousness of the offence and minimal victim empathy.

DL:This is to do with his age and an attention deficit disorder and just his lack of experience.

M: Yes. This was a girl of [ ]. He's [ ] and he tried to take her pants off her and has interfered with her. It's a very serious matter.

DL: It is clear that the victim has no manifest impact. Your Worship, the charges themselves are serious but the state has acknowledged the charge of rape is not appropriate in these circumstances, and the fact penetration has not been alleged. In my submission this sets it apart from more serious sexual offences. Your Worship, otherwise the defendant is of good character and you should take that into account. If Your Worship was minded, you have the ability to give a suspended detention order without a conviction so he is not held back in later life. I refer Your Worship to [ ] for the considerations that can be taken into account on the conviction. The youth's age and subsection [ ] the aim to rehabilitate the youth, are significant.

M: Thank you. Yes. Stand up. You are age [ ]. The little girl was age [ ]. You have indicated you knew what you were doing was wrong and it was a bad thing. You told the person who wrote the report that you weren't sure how she felt at the time or now although you think she must feel bad now. You understand that this little girl was a child. She would not have known at all when you asked her to take her pants off and climbed on top of her. Fortunately, you were not able to penetrate her with sexual intercourse or with your fingers. It's unknown as to whether this young girl will be affected. No one can work that out. What you did was terrible, quite frankly, and very much deserving of you going to detention and staying there for a long time [long pause].

This is a serious matter and the law regards it like that. Children like that should not have their childhood affected. You're [ ]. You're having sexual feelings and you took advantage. Taking account of the submission there should be no conviction, there will be a conviction. It is a serious case. You should have thought about her. I make an order that you are sent to six months detention. I will return to that in a minute [short pause]. I further make a probation order under the usual conditions for the next six months. I suspend the detention order on condition you commit no offences containing a sexual element for 12 months. Now you have only just escaped going into detention for six months. This is because of your age and because no penetration occurred. If you commit an offence in the next 12 months, I will send you to detention. Do you understand this?

D: Yes.

M: Do you understand how serious the matter was?

D: Yes.

M: Go to the back of the court please.

This magistrate used stronger, retributivist language while sentencing ("what you did was terrible"), but still applied the rehabilitative principles in the legislation. It seemed to be accepted that, when a young person commits an offence of this kind, there must be a psychological disorder, although this does not necessarily justify a lenient sentence.[14] When interviewed by police and Youth Justice this young person was, apparently, unaware that he had done anything wrong. During the hearing, he was looking at the floor, playing with his cap, as if keeping occupied in the presence of adults discussing something he had done wrong in a language he did not understand.[15]

Professional Realism

The hearings considered in this chapter illustrate how magistrates only had a limited range of options in responding to repeat offenders. Unless the offence was particularly serious, such as a violent assault, they tended to give many chances. The legislation made this possible by allowing them to start with a probation order (itself not involving more consequences than a good behaviour bond), and to then combine this with community service orders, or give convictions. In many hearings observed, the young person was given a second chance: a probation order was continued, with longer periods of community service. Detention was often threatened and, eventually, if there was no change in behavior, was imposed for a short period after which the young person might receive further non-custodial orders and periods of detention.

The statistical evidence collected in New South Wales and Queensland (Chen et al 2005, Weatherburn 2007, Livingston et al 2008) indicates that many young people continued offending after age 18, and some spend time in adult prisons. However, the practitioners interviewed for this study believed that most stopped offending while subject to supervisory orders, and that fewer offences were committed after turning 18. They were unable to explain this other than that the threat of going to an adult prison was effective, and that many young people matured around this age, and no longer got into fights, or committed burglaries or took cars.[16] It seemed to be accepted that, after a period of offending or mixing with the wrong crowd, perhaps because of some personal insecurity, most young people grew up. A magistrate in one country area reported that a father who promised to keep his son on a tight rein had himself committed similar offences in his youth.

None of these young people were described by magistrates or in the pre-sentence report as having had particular social experiences, or suffering from specific social or psychological conditions that might be relevant as a mitigating factor in sentencing. They were not in care, did not have learning disabilities, and had been attending (if not engaging with) school. Nevertheless, practitioners knew very well that most repeat offenders were not simply young people, but usually young people from economically disadvantaged backgrounds. In many courts, a large proportion of repeat offenders come from particular neighborhoods, suggesting a social and environmental basis for offending, and some of the worst offenders belong to well-known problem families.[17] Practitioners know that the rehabilitative programs, or the threat or experience of detention, cannot address these social causes of crime, even though in many cases young people do eventually stop offending or "desist" from crime.

An extract from an interview with a case worker in Tasmania indicates the problems faced by practitioners in trying to reach defendants who have different values both from their youthfulness and their social backgrounds:

Q: You are also dealing with people with different social backgrounds to the norm.

A: Yep. And I think that is something we all struggle with as well and we are all quite lucky to have lived in the way we have. I think we have all been to private schools and we have all had fairly stable sorts of family upbringing. To understand the culture that these other people are living in is a real culture shock and also you sort of, you have to really twist around to work out where they are coming from and you have to imagine yourself in that situation because that's challenging to put yourself in that situation. If you were in a situation where I didn't have any food or any money, what would I do? And it's also very difficult for us to see where the responsibility of our client's parents ends and where their's begins, because a lot of the young people have been so badly damaged by their childhood that you almost think what hope have they got of not stealing things when their parents have taught them to steal. And another thing that really strikes me is that a lot of these people find that, say they've knocked off somebody's car or something like that, and then it's a real shock for them to be told that they are going to detention as a result.

Q: They don't see it as a crime?

A: They don't put their action and the consequence together They have a gap in their understanding of what's going to happen to me if I do this. And it's really hard for me to understand that they weren't thinking at the time of stealing somebody's car that a) it belongs to somebody else and b) they deserve to be in trouble for taking it and c) the trouble that they get in is going to have ramifications for them like going to Ashley or something like that. That is just part of their experience.

In addition, young people did not understand sentencing in the same way as adults:

As long as they don't go to Ashley, some of them just don't care what happens. I think that is why dealing with children is quite difficult because you try to get them to that point where they understand that having a probation order's a pretty bad thing. Some of them will come in and they will say, "Oh do you think I'll get a good behaviour bond?" because they think that's an important outcome from the court because they've heard it on the news or whatever and they've come from a family that doesn't understand the system. And so when they say I've got a good behaviour bond they just think it's a big order and they've got in big trouble and they don't really come from an understanding of what court should be about. A lot of them will talk to their friends about it and their friends will say, "Oh as long as you don't go to Ashley, it's all right." So if you're on a probation order, it's OK and nothing's going to happen to you until you actually get put in Ashley.

This interviewee is not suggesting that only physical confinement has an effect on repeat offenders, because in many cases they continue offending after spending periods of time in the detention centre. There are youths who are scarred by this experience, but others for whom having been in detention increases their status among their peers. There are even young people who see a good behaviour bond as a badge of honor.[18]

Another way of stating that young offenders have a cognitive or psychological deficit is that they do not see their actions as wrong. Practitioners working in the children's court know more than most members of society the frustrations involved in trying to rehabilitate young people who have grown up in disadvantaged circumstances and hold different values to respectable members of society. Although one can view the children's court as successful in that the majority of defendants only appear once or twice, it has less success in rehabilitating or changing persistent repeat offenders.

7.

The Vulnerable Offender

The previous two chapters have described how the courts respond to minor offences, such as assaults on other young people and shoplifting, and more serious offences such as burglaries and motor-vehicle stealing. In these cases, the only mitigating factor mentioned in court was the youthfulness of the defendant, and sometimes the influence of peer pressure or "getting into the wrong crowd." The assumption that young people will commit minor offences, and take a long time learning how to behave in a responsible manner like adults, lies at the heart of the youth justice legislation both in Australia and internationally. It explains the emphasis on rehabilitation rather than punishment, and the fact that only the most serious and persistent offenders received a custodial sentence, often after being given several chances to reform. Assumptions about the limited social knowledge and comprehension skills of young people also influence how the sentence is delivered. Magistrates usually give reasons for the sentence in greater detail than when sentencing adults, and often the sentencing remarks have the character of a short tutorial. The magistrate takes on the role of a parent administering discipline, and trying to teach a young person how to behave responsibly.

This might lead one to assume that those who commit repeat or serious offences are much like young people in general. This, however, is not the case since many come from deprived or difficult backgrounds. As one magistrate noted, matter-of-factly:

Offenders are usually unemployed, and suffer from family breakdown or psychological illness. They have done badly in education and dropped out. Some are ordinary youths you might pass on the street – maybe their offence is an aberration. Others are in contact with the police and courts a great deal. A lot of defendants appear to be normal, but there is something in their background such as a missing family member or abuse. Some crime runs in families. A lot of offenders grow out of it which is why I do not give convictions. But others go on to serious crime sprees – assault with knives and taking cars.

Once one starts to think about the causes of crime systematically, it raises many difficult issues. Does crime have biological or psychological causes, or is it mainly caused by influences in one's social environment? Should crime be seen as a legitimate response to growing up in conditions of poverty and disadvantage, and suggest the need to challenge inequalities in the distribution of income and wealth? Or is it a form of deviant behavior, a product of poor socialization or exposure to anti-social subcultures, that requires treatment like an illness? If crime has social causes, why is only a small proportion of the young people who grow up in difficult conditions affected? Does this mean that wrong-doers should be viewed as morally responsible and asked to make a rational choice between continuing to offend and experiencing punishment? Why is most crime committed by young men? What about those groups, such as Indigenous Australians, who have suffered sustained discrimination and disadvantage for a long period, and are significantly over-represented in the criminal justice system? These and related questions have generated discussion among criminologists and other academic disciplines for two hundred years (see, for example, White and Haines 2008), and as one might expect there are a variety of political viewpoints that have implications for how we respond to youth and adult crime.

The objective of this chapter is not to review this literature or advance a particular political line about how we should respond to youth crime. Instead, it seeks to describe how a variety of mitigating social factors are relevant or visible in the everyday work of children's courts in Australia. The aim is to illustrate the kind of problems that face magistrates and other professionals, or form the taken for granted background to their work. They are often dealing with young people who suffer from difficult social problems, resulting from poverty and disadvantage, that cannot be addressed or ameliorated through the legal process.

The Overlap Between Crime and Protection

Although there are significant differences between how juvenile justice has developed in Britain, the USA and Australia, in broad terms there has been a shift away from a welfare system in which all young people were seen as needing protection, if they met certain social criteria, to the present system in which there is a separation between the protective and criminal work of children's courts. In each Australian state, there is a separate statute empowering the court to intervene in cases where abuse or ill-treatment has come to the attention of social workers, and in some cases remove the child into state care.[1] In many courts, protection hearings take place alongside criminal matters. They are, however, still viewed as distinct areas of court business, even if the same young person could be subject to care and criminal proceedings.

Although some texts give the impression that there is an high degree of overlap between care and criminal hearings (Barry and McNeill 2009), I came across different views among practitioners. Some believed that most young people (one estimate was 60%) have "protective issues." This may mean that they are, or have been, subject to care proceedings, or it may mean that in the view of the interviewee they should be subject to some kind of intervention. Most interviewees suggested that the overlap was more in the region of 30%. Those young people who committed criminal offences, while they might have a variety of problems, mainly came from a relatively stable family environment, and did not require intensive support of the kind provided by social workers. One practitioner in a country area reported that the extent of the overlap varied considerably. In the court I was visiting there was almost no overlap: those committing criminal offences were not normally subject to care proceedings. By contrast in a neighboring court (neighboring in Australian terms means that it was a three hour drive), there was a spate of sexual assaults committed by teenagers who had themselves suffered or witnessed abuse as younger children.

Those working in children's courts recognized that offenders in care presented the most difficult problems, even though the actual offences were often quite trivial. This is because children in care sometimes committed offences because they were unhappy with where they were living, or ran away and got into trouble in the community. As one magistrate put it, this could lead to a "revolving door" through which they spent short periods in hostels for the homeless, in psychiatric hospitals, care homes and police cells. Each institution viewed them as either ineligible for assistance (they were not diagnosed as being properly mentally ill, even after claiming to hear voices or having suicidal thoughts) or as creating too many problems for the care organization. The children's court could be asked to send them to a detention center, partly because of the nature of the offences, but also for their protection in the absence of alternatives. The following hearings illustrate some ways in which this took place.

No suitable place to go

The defendant in this case was a 14 year old girl in Tasmania who had run away from a children's home, and committed some minor offences, after a carer had used force to restrain her (case 7A).[2] She had been offered the chance to live at another institution but had refused after alleging that she had been abused or ill-treated by one of the young residents. In the absence of alternatives, she had been remanded to Ashley Youth Detention Centre. She made it very clear, however, that she did not want to remain there. Before the hearing she was screaming and shouting outside the court, and was restrained with hand-cuffs. However, she calmed down, and these were removed during the hearing.

In this hearing, the Youth Justice worker explained the reasons why no suitable accommodation was available, leaving Ashley as the only alternative at least for the next week. The Legal Aid lawyer argued that this was unacceptable and against her client's instructions. The magistrate carefully reviewed the options, noting that he was also concerned about the defendant's explosive temper. The best he could do was agree to hold an hearing the moment an alternative had been arranged. The defendant left the court quietly, but resisted when the officers replaced the hand-cuffs. She was crying and wailing in a way that communicated both anger and complete despair.

It is worth noting that from a professional viewpoint this was a child protection as much as a criminal case and that, given the available resources, the only safe course was for her to stay in Ashley. Three weeks later Youth Justice did find alternative accommodation with the help of child protection workers. When she appeared by video-link from the detention centre while this was being arranged, she appeared much happier. The nature of the relatively minor criminal offences committed, for which she received a reprimand, was over-shadowed by the welfare considerations of helping someone in difficult social circumstances. However, the only way of initially protecting the defendant was through being remanded in custody.

An assault on a care worker

In New South Wales, the Wood Report (2008) has attempted to address a number of problems in the care and protection system. One change that affected the children's court was that care homes could refuse to accept young offenders who caused trouble, whereas previously they would have been forced under the legislation to take responsibility. Magistrates were, consequently, having to persuade care workers to exercise discretion, and give a difficult young person a further chance, unless it was possible to find an alternative institution, or the offence was sufficiently serious to merit a sentence of detention.

Contrary to what one might expect, care homes in New South Wales are often small hostels , rather than institutions with large numbers of staff. In this hearing, a care worker had been assaulted and had her jaw broken (case 7B). She was not present in court but was represented by a colleague, who was only a few years older than the 17 year old female defendant. There were also two case workers from the Department of Juvenile Justice, who had also been assigned to the defendant since she was under a supervisory order for having committed a similar offence in a different home, although one that had not resulted in injury. In this case, the magistrate suggested that the care home should attempt some form of mediation. The alternative for the young person was going to a detention center for a short period or becoming homeless. Neither of these were seen as desirable outcomes, even though the defendant said that they were preferable to the care home. Ultimately, the professionals knew that the young person would adjust to living in care, and eventually find some place in the community through reconciling with family or receiving support from social services. Detention was not seen as a suitable long term remedy, but nor was it possible to compel a care home to look after a difficult young person.

Social Circumstances

Most of the young offenders I observed were not in care. However, this does not mean that their lives were free of problems. One magistrate told me that, when sentencing young people, he started with the offence, and then looked for any mitigating factors. Common factors included psychological problems, homelessness, family circumstances, financial problems, drug addiction, problems with schooling and influence of peers (often seen as part of a psychological problem rather than simply one aspect of youthfulness). The only factors that seemed to make possible a lower sentence were psychological and medical problems, partly because these usually made it possible to argue there was a low degree of culpability. On the other hand, the whole juvenile justice system seeks to rehabilitate as well as punish, and this is the rationale for allocating young people to case workers. Practitioners working in the courts were well aware that most repeat offenders had some kind of problem that distinguished them from "ordinary" young people. Although they did not see this as excusing criminal behavior, it did influence and inform how they responded to each case.

Family breakdown

Some defendants were accompanied by one or both parents when they attended court, or by a grandparent. In the following case, the magistrate addressed the defendant's mother during a bail hearing:

> M: Mum, all this is in his background. You know him and are sick of him playing up. You need to be absolutely convinced he will do what is required. I intend to impose a curfew and, if the police go round and he is not there, he will be arrested.

M: That won't be a problem.

M: I don't know, if home discipline up till now hasn't been successful. Where is he supposed to live?

DL: [Gave this information].

M: What time do you have dinner?

Mth: 6.30.

M: There should be no problem being home by 6.00. [The defendant looked back skeptically at his mother.] Don't say no. If there is any breach, you will be arrested.

D: Yes Sir.

M: [typing] I'm extending your bail conditions. You should spend every night at [ ]. Do what your mother tells you. There will be a curfew from 6pm to 7am.

D: Yes Your Honor.

M: I'm essentially giving you a chance to learn your lesson. If not, you will go back to detention. Mum, if he starts playing up, remind him that he is going back to jail. That's where I'd send him.

In another hearing, a magistrate encouraged the young offender to be grateful to a parent for attending court:

Let's hope you don't commit further offences. If you do, you will get convicted. You're lucky today because you've got your parents here. You should thank them for standing by you. You've hurt them by this. Make sure you don't hurt them again.

Many defendants observed in hearings were on their own. Although there were sometimes good reasons why a family member could not attend, practitioners seemed to take it for granted that these young people received little supervision or support from their families. In some cases, relationships had broken down, although not to the extent that social services could obtain a protective order. It was common for the defendant to have left home and be living with a relative or family friend rather than his or her immediate parent. Three cases were observed in which mothers sought restraining orders from the court, sometimes to protect themselves against being assaulted by a young person. It was not clear if this resolved this type of problem, or what happened if the order was breached.

Another kind of offender came from families in which parents and siblings had spent time in prison, and were well-known to the courts and police. According to one Youth Justice worker in Tasmania, these young people had a stable home, but poor role models. Growing up in this environment led them to see law-breaking, and even acts of violence, as acceptable or routine. Although it would be difficult gaining access as an outsider to these families, it is intriguing to consider how young people may be taught a different set of values to those promoted by children's courts.

Homelessness and financial problems

Young people appearing before the court had often experienced periods of homelessness, even if there was no protective order. The young person above was not technically homeless, but at one point had "no place to go" when he drove off after an argument with his girlfriend. What initially surprised me, as an observer, was that no one seemed surprised when these or other social problems came up during hearings: they were just part of everyday life for young people from low-income families. In one case, a 14 year old youth had been charged with breaking into someone's house, and stealing a bicycle, with an older co-defendant. When the lawyer asked if the police had found him, it came out that this 17 year old was living in a car. This was both disturbing and intriguing to me as an observer (how is it possible to live in a car for a long period?). But neither the lawyer nor the youth saw this as worthy of comment. Similarly, it was almost expected that young people from working class backgrounds would engage in shop-lifting. Items stolen by younger children were often of low value: a make up kit, chocolate bars or a can of lemonade. Older youths stole more valuable property from stores or through committing burglaries, often to fund a drugs habit.

The lack of means of defendants was revealed when magistrates asked them to indicate their income when considering a fine. In one hearing, a 17 year old on youth allowance was asked to pay $100 over two months as punishment for assaulting another youth over an insult to his girlfriend (case 5A). Magistrates were aware that for defendants from well-off families, paying the same amount was not a test of character since the parents were effectively paying the fine:

Case 5E

M: I'm going to give you a financial penalty as a reminder of what will happen if you continue to break the road laws.

D: Yes.

M: I will make it relatively light in the light of your low wage and your youthfulness so on the complaint there will just be a fine of $100. [ ]

M: [addressing his father] Mr. B time to pay $100?

F: Six weeks to pay, sir.

M: I want you to pay it. I don't want your parents to lend it to you. I want it to come out of your income so it hurts.

In one hearing in Tasmania, a 17 year old defendant objected to the amount of a fine for driving over the limit. She had also committed some burglaries, but the magistrate had postponed the sentencing decision on these charges so he could consult with the case workers. She was trying to save up money so that she could rejoin family in another state:

Case 7C

M: You were stopped on a random breath test not because of the manner of your driving. I take account of your explanation and your personal circumstances generally. In relation to [ ] there will be a conviction, a fine of $200 and disqualification for six months.

D: How am I going to pay $200?

M: I'll come to that in a minute.

[The defense lawyer speaks to the defendant, who looks annoyed.]

DL: She gets [ ] per fortnight in youth allowance. She says she can pay five dollars per week.

M: I know people who can afford to pay a lot more than that.

D: I'm saving to go to [ ].

M: Well, your court fine is more important than that. I'm ordering $20 per fortnight.

D: What if I can't afford it?

M: You'll be in trouble if you can't pay it.

This kind of exchange over whether a defendant could afford to pay a fine was unusual. It also shows how there can be more involved to property theft than supplementing a low income. However, many offenders admitted when stopped by store detectives and the police that they had taken items because they had no money.

Problems with schools

National studies indicate that many adult offenders did not complete schooling. This was apparent when listening to children's court hearings. Defendants had often dropped out due to bullying, or were in special schools due to "learning difficulties." In one hearing, the magistrate went through the conditions of a probation order slowly, because he knew that the defendant could not read. In others, magistrates gave advice or encouragement about bullying:

Case 7D

M: And how are you doing at TAFE?

D: I'm doing well. I'm going on to Year 10.

M: I'm pleased to hear that. You've had hard treatment at school with bullying. You should remember that it's not your problem but them. Keep it in mind.

There were also cases where young people had stolen or caused damage to school property or assaulted teachers. In one assault case in Tasmania, the teacher who had a black eye and was wearing a neck collar sat outside the court during the hearing. This may have been a case in which the victim felt that a sentence of community service and probation was too light, and the possibility of a community conference was not discussed. In this state, the closed court room protected the defendant from contact with the victim, at least during the hearing.[3]

Psychological Problems

Many defendants who had committed repeat offences were attending anger management courses while on probation orders or receiving medication for conditions such as Attention Deficit Disorder (ADD). In addition, the court asked for a report from a psychologist, in addition to a pre-sentence report, for any young person who had committed an excessively violent act or behaved oddly in a way that suggested a personality disorder.[4] For some defendants, there was an attempt to find a medical reason to explain troubling behavior that would enable a more lenient sentence. One example is that a female who repeatedly assaulted the police, believing herself to be a vigilante, defending other women, and who showed no remorse, was sent to a psychiatrist. A sexual assault by a young person was also seen as sufficiently disturbing to justify referral. However, it is not clear that the medical or psychological problem resulted in a more lenient sentence, beyond the fact that the magistrate or case workers could require the young person to attend counseling or see psychologists if this was required.

An anger management condition

This 17 year old defendant had experienced medical problems after having suffered head injuries in a car accident, and was receiving counseling for anger management. The facts presented by the prosecutor suggest a level of violence greater than the kind of assaults regularly made on the police, even though other young people used similar language when they were stopped or arrested.

Case 7E

P: Your Worship the following facts relate to matters [ ] Your
    Worship at 3.30pm Miss Green entered premises at…A
    police officer was inside the residence and informed her
    she was not welcome and had to leave…She picked up a
    [ ] and attempted to throw it through the front window.
    The officer dragged her towards the police vehicle, but
    while he was still holding her, she bit him, and this was
    estimated to be of a duration of 40 seconds. When she was
    lying on her back as the attending constable attempted
    to restrain her, she grabbed his pen and stabbed him in
    the left shoulder and the neck. He called for assistance
    and restrained her until other officers arrived and hand-
    cuffed her. She said "I'll f-ing kill you, c-nt. You wait
    till I get out. I'll f-cking find you and f-cking kill you. I
    know you, you f-cking c-nt. I'll kill you like the dog you
    are." The officer had a laceration and there was a deep
    flow of blood. He has had ongoing treatment for this
    and scratches to his forehead, bruises to both arms, and
    he has a soreness to the chest area.

The defense lawyer in a long submission to the court identified
possible mitigating circumstances. Even though she had thrown
the object, the defendant had not broken the window. She had also
been injured by a third party during the incident which contributed
to the explosive reaction. It seems likely that the magistrate was
most influenced by the evidence of medical condition, since she
dismissed the charges subject to an undertaking that the defendant
reported to Youth Justice, attended "educational programs"
and submitted to "medical, psychological help or counseling as
directed".

In this case, the young person had a psychological problem.
Nevertheless, the magistrate still commented on her obligations
and responsibility to other people, and treated her as having the
capacity to understand the consequences of her actions:

M: Would you just like to stand up and I'll say [a few
    words]. I've heard the facts that the prosecution set

out and what your counsel and Miss Thomas [the Youth Justice worker] said. This is a serious offence but I understand it arose from one set of events and I understand that you felt angry and powerless if you like but as a consequence you have ended up in the court. The report is a really positive report and you are now working and that is a big plus and you have a lot to offer. There are a lot of positives there you have to concentrate on and you've got an intention expressed in the report not to attend court again [pause]. Sorry there are other things you have done. You have pleaded guilty at an early stage. I also take into account that you've had the accident. I am going to deal with this matter on the basis that I am not going to record a conviction. I am going to deal with them to be dismissed on your undertaking for a period of 12 months. Do you understand what I'm saying? There will be some benefits to you in having that support. Where does she have to report to? You need to report to the Youth Justice officer who will be assigned to you. You must receive visits from that officer. You must not commit another offence. You mustn't leave the state. You must notify the Youth Justice worker of any change OK and you must obey the reasonable and lawful instructions of the Youth Justice worker and attend educational programs and submit to medical, psychological or counseling as directed so there can be some assistance to you. Did you have any questions? I know I have said a lot all at once.

D: Is all that psychological stuff the ones I am on now?

M: Yes. And any others that might be useful to you.

Although the defendant pleaded guilty to a criminal offence, it seems clear that welfare considerations influenced the outcome. It is also striking how, in this case, the defendant did not receive a lecture on the need to respect the police (common in many assaults) but the court recognized there were special circumstances. One could even argue that the circumstances of the assault (what might be called an "hysterical" or even "frenzied" attack using an improvised weapon) suggested this from the outset without the need for the defense lawyer or pre-sentence report to explain the background. The defendant herself did not seem to view the counseling and medical services as especially useful ("all that psychological stuff"), but the court was simply concerned that, as a vulnerable person, she was receiving whatever help was available.

Adjustment after migration

Another group of young people, who were often referred to psychologists or counselors, were recent migrants. Some had come to Australia as refugees, having suffered or witnessed torture. In many cases, the process of moving, and psychological adjustment to a new country was itself difficult, and was treated by the courts as a mitigating factor. Legal Aid lawyers in Melbourne and Sydney reported that different areas were known for specific problems relating to migration. There was also gang activity, in the sense that young people went around in groups and engaged in confrontations with police.

Following a visit to the central children's court in Parramatta, Sydney, I witnessed a street confrontation between several well-built Samoan youths, and perhaps 15 police officers. Two officers were using pepper sprays to keep the youths at bay, and others were trying to clear the streets of bystanders who appeared to view their work almost as entertainment. A practitioner commented that in this recently arrived migrant group there was no family cohesion or community organization. There were also identity issues that resulted in psychological problems, particularly anger directed at the authorities. The following hearing illustrates the lenient response to a Sudanese defendant by a suburban court in Melbourne:

Case 7F

P: He was in [ ] library and got into an argument with a man. He was extremely aggressive and abusive. He spat at him and kicked him. The defendant said "I'm going to wait for you and break your f-ing legs." The police arrived. The defendant was nervous and could not spell his name. He became agitated and was handcuffed. In the interview room, he was aggressive towards police and used his fists. When searched the police found an health care card with a false name and address. He gave as his reasons "He swore at me." "I don't know about the false names".

DL: The summary is accepted.

M: I find the charges proven.

DL: My client acknowledges what he did on this occasion was wrong and unacceptable. It was angry behavior and he would benefit from anger management. He's now 18 and at the time of the offences he was 17. [ ] I'm asking Your Honour today, bearing in mind his remorse and insight and he's at school and the family difficulties, to deal with this with a good behaviour bond conditional on taking an anger management course. He is too old at 18 for [ ] but they might be prepared to assess him and he could go on a course with the Salvation army.

[They discussed the other charge, and whether a deferral order was appropriate].

M: I'm inclined to deal with this matter in finality today. J would you stand up? Whatever the circumstances, that conduct is unacceptable to decent people. You understand that. You can only make your life miserable by that response. I am dealing with this matter by a good behaviour bond conditional on you attending an anger management course offered by [ ] or [ ]. The matters are dealt with without a conviction being recorded. Once you sign this, you can go.

This is an interesting example of how social problems become re-defined in official records as psychological conditions. In this case, it is possible to hear the sentencing comments as instructing a new immigrant how to behave in Australia when being insulted, although the magistrate left these issues to be addressed on the anger management course. Responding immediately and without thinking happened in many minor offences involving violence. In this case, a vulnerable migrant received a good behaviour bond.

Drug addiction

Drug addiction was not viewed as a mitigating factor, although magistrates knew that this often provided the motivation for theft, and caused or aggravated acts of violence. Some magistrates warned defendants about the link between cannabis and mental illness. There was a national television advertising campaign when I started this project in 2005, although there has been less media coverage subsequently. In the following hearings, magistrates gave health advice to defendants.

> Case 7G
>
> This defendant was wearing beach attire in court: brightly coloured long shorts, a t-shirt and white plimsolls. He had been charged with assaulting his girlfriend.
>
> M: I'm concerned that he's turning 16 and consuming large amounts of alcohol.
>
> DL:He's aware of it. If he does not constrain his drinking now, it will affect his physical development and his mental development.
>
> M: If you could just move to the side. I cannot see you – your lawyer is hiding you. 90% of people in this court are here because of alcohol.
>
> P: He's currently on a good behaviour bond.
>
> M: I would say one for two years with supervision from Juvenile Justice.
>
> DL: Thank you Your Honour.
>
> M: If you put a foot wrong, you'll be looking to be sent to a boy's home. If you are an adult this court regularly sends people to jail [for this offence]. We don't want that to happen. How's it going at home?
>
> F: OK.

M: Watch the alcohol issue. He's too young to be getting into strife with girls. If you are on a bond you can see Mr. Rogers.[5] If they ask you to do an alcohol course, you will do it.

Case 7H

This 17 year old Indigenous youth had been charged with several offences, relating to a fight between two groups of youths. He had also assaulted his mother.

M: This leaves a charge of affray, recklessly causing injury and threats to kill.

P: This took place in the McDonald's car park. The defendant and co-defendant and 20 unidentified youths set upon the victim. The co-defendants used a metal scooter to assault both victims. The victim was hit over the head with a scooter. He had a broken nose, swollen left eyebrow and lacerations to the abdomen. The second victim had a swollen left cheek. Neither sought medical treatment. His reason in the interview: "He was saying stuff to me". The other charges relate to violence at home to his mother. He smashed plates in the kitchen, and threatened his mother with a carving knife. He threw coins, breaking a window. He has no previous matters.

M: It smells of cannabis. Not because I'm smart. But because I've come across this before. I've dealt with most of the people in this punch up. One group is terrorizing the locals. There is a racial element and things have got completely out of hand. It is just part of being part of a group. I locked someone up for 8 months. This is a matter that indicates probation. There must be no consumption of cannabis. Youth Justice will smell it [pause]. I see hundreds of kids a year and, a few years later, some come back with their brains skewed. If you do it again, you'll get locked up. If you smoke cannabis while on this order, your mother or Youth Justice will smell it.

> The worst thing is it rots the stuff inside your head. You
> have no previous history, so there will be no conviction.
> Probation for six months. Don't let your mother down.
> This is the only chance you will get.

These and other hearings present drug-use as a life-style choice rather than resulting from poor social circumstances or family breakdown. There was also usually no acknowledgement in the sentencing remarks that drug addiction might be physically or psychologically difficult to overcome. Nevertheless, any offender with this problem was sent on a drugs and alcohol course, as a condition attached to other orders.

It was, however, recognized that the courts could do more in combating drugs, if given more resources. The NSW government had funded a youth drugs court in some areas of Sydney modeled on diversionary programs in the USA in which judges employ psychologically-based therapeutic techniques with the aim of effecting personal change through the sentencing process (Burns and Peyrot 2003). Those working on this program believed that it was highly effective with repeat offenders who had not responded to probation orders or detention. One practitioner told me that drug-use was in some senses a pretext for directing resources to a small number of offenders with multiple problems. Most offenders had some kind of problem with drugs, although this was not the only or main factor that explained offending.

Indigenous Young Offenders

Australia, like the USA and Canada, but unlike the United Kingdom, is a settler society in which there remain great moral and political challenges in how to address high levels of deprivation and disadvantage among its Indigenous peoples (Clark 1963). While I was conducting research for this study, the Coalition (centre right) government intervened in Indigenous affairs in the Northern Territory with the aim of combating high levels of child abuse (Altman and Hinkson 2007). When the Labour Party won power in 2007, it made an apology for the first time in Australian history on behalf of the settlers for the damage done in pursuing misguided social policies such as taking children from their parents in order to educate them like Europeans.[6] During these discussions, many commentators pointed to the lack of progress in addressing the social and economic problems created by decades of discrimination and neglect. One indicator is the high rate of imprisonment of Indigenous young offenders. In New South Wales, I was told that 50% of those young people in detention centers (a daily average of 400) were Indigenous. Although the detention rates vary between states, this indicates a continuing failure at all levels of government to address the causes of offending, or develop an effective response.[7]

Through conducting an ethnographic study, it is possible to go beyond or beneath the statistics, and the general political debates that take place around these, and see what happens in actual cases. Ethnography also makes it possible to see how a political issue is important within an institution, but without exaggerating its relevance or visibility in all courts and hearings. Because there is only a small Indigenous community in Tasmania, I only saw a few young people who were described by practitioners as having an Aboriginal background. In Victoria, I came across even fewer in the metropolitan courts because this state has established a separate system for sentencing Indigenous defendants (see below). In New South Wales, there were more Indigenous defendants in the metropolitan courts. However, I encountered most when visiting country courts in Victoria and New South Wales. In this book, I will be using the terms "Indigenous" and "Aboriginal" interchangeably. However, each of these terms is mainly used by outsiders, or when presenting a common front to outsiders: insiders in the three states described themselves as Koori, a general term for peoples on the Eastern Seaboard.

The historical and political context

During a visit to Armidale, New South Wales, there was a ceremony when the local Member of Parliament and the Attorney General opened a refurbished courtroom before an audience of invited councillors and government officers. The leader of the council thanked the government for its support for a new court building to be constructed in the next two years, and for increased financial support for a van staffed by volunteers that was intended to assist young Indigenous people on the street, and prevent youth offending.[8] Most of the defendants who appeared before this and neighboring courts were Indigenous, but this was not mentioned during hearings. It was simply a taken for granted, background feature of work in this court.

A practitioner working for the Aboriginal Legal Service in Armidale offered this bleak assessment of the local history of settlement, and how this resulted in high levels of juvenile crime:

> There is underlying unemployment. There is nothing to do except languish around at home – or they take drugs and play cards all day. This happens at Uralla, Moree, Tingha and in parts of Armidale.
>
> This is my personal view. Wherever they were established in New South Wales from the mid-1880s, the Missions did this. You can read about this. New South Wales does not have stable communities as a result of that relocation. There is no ability to reach back and grab hold of the traditional culture or even language. They were put in church settlements and learnt to say our father and do things like Europeans and they lost their traditional culture. This happened till movements in the 1960s where they had the confidence to go searching for this. In some areas, if you wanted to go to the pictures, you had to get the permission of the Mission.
>
> In that time, the only people who got employment had been to the Mission school. There were a few who finished high school and they worked on the railways or in rural occupations. There was no development of intellectuals, professionals or a management group. I have met non-Indigenous ethnic groups who cannot understand this. The Lebanese or Greeks say we got kicked around too. What they had was structure – a professional class, a managerial class. But the Aboriginal elders often got caught up in the church.
>
> The other factor that is overlooked is that there are 10% Koori in the population of say 25,000 people. If you go back over our files, 10% of these people get into trouble. They are the same 10%. Dad never had a job and grandfather never had a job. Or he was in the railways and then they were

closed. Whitlam favored the idea of an universal dole only in the 1970s[9] – previously they got blankets and flour. It was left to charities to help people.

When visiting a country court in Victoria, I received a similar account of the terrible things that had taken place in the past, and which resulted in high levels of offending by Indigenous young people. The magistrate reported that in that area 30,000 of the local Koori people had been massacred during European settlement. The local industries had mostly closed, so most people were on welfare, and this particularly affected the Indigenous population. It was difficult getting through to these young people:

> Kids often have fear or disdain or hatred, and are dissatisfied with life. Some of the time, it is like talking to a rock. There are a lot of kids who are homeless. There are a lot who see being here as having no consequences. They see it as a rite of passage. They don't understand it.

Although the history of settler-Indigenous relations was not mentioned during hearings, it was recognized by these, and other practitioners, as explaining high levels of Indigenous crime. They were also quite open in admitting that neither the court, nor the welfare system, could address the underlying causes. There was no support for the view advanced by some political commentators and academics that racism or discrimination played a significant part in the over-representation of Indigenous youths in detention centers (for example, Cunneen 2001).[10] Nor was there any optimism that following the National Apology it would be possible to improve economic and social conditions for these Australians.

An appeal against sentence

In many respects, Indigenous young offenders suffered from similar problems to other young people from low income families. They often had psychological problems, lived in poor housing or had experienced homelessness, had not completed school, had medical problems, or used drugs. According to my informants, there were different levels of disadvantage. Growing up in families or communities that had been dependent on charity and then state welfare for 20 years explained most of their difficulties as young people, without needing to attribute this to identity problems or language difficulties (see, for example, Eades 2008). When observing hearings in the two country courts, it was noticeable how most youths sentenced to detention, usually for committing many serious offences, were Indigenous. However, there was nothing in the hearings that suggested these were of a different type, or committed for different reasons, to those by other defendants.

There was, however, one case I heard about, without observing the sentencing hearing, that seemed to suggest that particular characteristics of these communities either brought young people into contact with the police, or created special problems for the criminal justice system that might lead to injustice. This was a 15 year old girl who had been found guilty of an offence, while in her absence, by a court in New South Wales, triggering a suspended sentence of nine months in detention (case 7I). Without going into the details of the case, she had left her family after her sister had been abused by a step-father, and after finding it impossible to obtain housing in the local area, went to stay with relatives in another part of the state. This migrant way of life is common among Indigenous youths, who belong to dispersed extended families. In this case, the police could not find her after the court issued a warrant. In these circumstances, the court was entitled under New South Wales law to find her guilty, although she had the right to have the question of guilt reopened, if she could show some grounds for doing so.

Another aspect of this case that seems distinctive is that the charges arose during a neighborhood dispute between two families. This kind of conflict can happen in any community. However, many studies suggest that it is endemic in disorganized communities in which different ethnic groups have been forced to live together. Her contention, successfully advanced in an appeal against sentence, was that the allegation of assault and criminal damage had been fabricated. Even without knowing more details, one can imagine how the police get drawn into these disputes. Young Indigenous people are in a vulnerable position, both in relation to the criminal justice system, and adults in their own communities. This young person was fortunate in that a Legal Aid lawyer was willing to pursue an appeal.

The Koori Court in Victoria

In response to this social problem, the state government in Victoria had funded an initiative known as the Koori Court. This can be understood as part of the same attempt at reconciliation as the National Apology in that it was based on a political agreement with elders from communities in different areas, recognizing the damage done by colonization. The objective was to involve elders alongside the magistrate, lawyers and welfare professionals in the sentencing process, with the aim of making this more meaningful for Indigenous defendants. This had already been introduced across the state for adults. When I was conducting fieldwork, there was one Youth Koori Court but it was hoped that additional funding would allow others to be established in different parts of the state (Borowski 2010).

Hearings took an hour, as against the 15 or 20 minutes in the ordinary children's court. They had a similar format and objectives to restorative conferences used as a form of diversion for all offenders in some states. Members of the community were encouraged to express their feelings of disapproval, and offenders to apologize to victims. The objective was to make young people experience shame, as a cathartic experience, but also show that family members and supporters cared about them. There was also an attempt to recreate a sense that they belonged to the Aboriginal community through displaying its flag and traditional artwork, even if the actual community no longer existed as a political entity with its own institutions. The magistrate interviewed in a country area believed that young Kooris who had no respect for the police or courts would listen to elders from their own community.

Understanding Vulnerability

Since all young people appearing in children's courts are seen as requiring help and protection, rather than simply deserving punishment, the concept of "vulnerability" has perhaps only limited uses for understanding professional work. Nevertheless, this chapter has demonstrated that practitioners do see young offenders in terms of degrees of vulnerability. The risk assessments conducted by case workers, and that are used in allocating resources, recognized that poor family circumstances, homelessness, and having left school due to bullying increased the chances of offending. Another way of putting this is that everyone, including police officers and magistrates, recognized that offending had social causes, principally through poverty and disadvantage, and in the case of Indigenous young people in the history of colonization.

This was simply a taken for granted context to their work, along with the fact that it was not possible to improve these social conditions. Practitioners could, however, also point to examples of how individuals had responded to supervision and programs. The aim of the children's court was to help young people overcome difficult circumstances. The court was also asked to protect the public, and convey public disapproval towards crime. Most magistrates, consequently, felt that it was necessary to sentence repeat and serious offenders to short periods of detention. In some cases, this also provided a means of offering welfare services for example, by providing a stable environment for someone who had previously been homeless.

Although there has been considerable criticism of detention centers, especially in countries where young people have committed suicide after bullying (Goldson 2008), it should be remembered that, for the most vulnerable, being detained may not be the worst outcome. A case worker in a country area explained why some young offenders might prefer this to their home environment:

JJ: I understand the nature of the world for some of these kids. I do not like to see them in detention…For some kids their home environment is horrendous. It's more horrendous than a detention centre and for some kids they're so unstable and unsteady in themselves and their environment is so hard when they bounce against the sharp bits. They get a sense of stability that they can build on or not depending on the individual. How they respond is a big part.

MT: It is hard to understand why someone would want to be in detention.

JJ: You get a bed, you get fed regularly, you get a structured day. You can go to bed without fear of sexual assault. You can actually go to sleep. For kids with drug induced psychosis, their anxiety decreases when they are in custody because they know nothing is going to go wrong. And honestly a lot of young people that I deal with and some I don't deal with because they manage to get through it do not have their own bed, their own room, their own space in the home. They may not even have a drawer in a house that's just theirs. There are young girls that have never had their own room. They've had to live primarily in lounge rooms or, if they're fortunate, share a cousin's room.

Consultancy firms, that have conducted focus groups with young people, often find that they have similar views to adults about the purpose and nature of punishment. They may not, however, represent those from the most vulnerable backgrounds. Some young offenders observed in hearings in New South Wales politely declined the opportunity to leave detention for the Youth Drugs Court. They were reluctant to commit to an intensive program concerned not only with de-toxification but changing their attitudes and life-style. "Vulnerabilty" is one way in which adults, particularly those working in welfare agencies, understand the problem of youth crime. It would be interesting to investigate how young people themselves understand the issue of vulnerability, the social factors that influence or cause offending, and how society should respond to these issues.

8.

Bureaucratic Work or Due Process?

Although this case study has described sentencing hearings in reasonable detail, some readers may feel that something important is missing, and moreover that this is a common mistake made by sociologists when studying legal institutions.[1] Where is the law in all this? One answer might be that there is relatively little discussion of legal cases or statutes in the lower courts. Magistrates referred to the relevant sections in legislation when making orders, but otherwise their sentencing remarks, and how they questioned young offenders or gave informal tutorials are easy to understand without needing a legal background, and do not seem concerned with legal rules or principles.[2]

A common observation made of the lower courts by law and society researchers is that they are bureaucratic organizations concerned with processing cases rather than with rights or justice (Emerson 1991, Blumberg 1969). In relation to children's courts, one could point to the fact that most defendants plead guilty (this also happens in magistrates courts). In these Australian states, there was no funding for legal representation in police stations, other than obtaining telephone advice. You could argue that, although young people have been given rights in the justice model (see chapter 2), their unequal power in relation to adults means that they have to go along with decisions that can be arbitrary or unfair.

There is also a version of this critique that appeals to governments seeking to save money in providing legal services. If magistrates are doing a mainly administrative job, why not allow people without expensive legal qualifications to make decisions about many kinds of minor offences or civil disputes? In the case of children's courts, it was not so long ago when social workers and members of the community made decisions about young people, in a similar way to some tribunals, without needing judicial supervision. Although those arguing for a return to the welfare model do not make their case in these terms, this might also be one means of funding more intensive case work, or supporting initiatives such as restorative justice.

These criticisms or policy proposals depend on seeing the courts as simply bureaucratic organizations. This chapter will, however, seek to show that matters are more complicated. It will start by considering the case, advanced by many sociologists and policy analysts over the years, that judges in the lower courts are effectively bureaucrats, processing cases without needing to consider matters of law. My own argument will be that this politically-motivated viewpoint misrepresents what actually happens in the lower courts. Even though the work is mainly administrative, magistrates also use legal knowledge and skills, and exercise judicial oversight. This is what makes the lower court a legal institution. The rest of the chapter will describe some aspects of this work, including how magistrates manage the daily list and adjudicate in contested hearings. It will conclude by considering policy debates about the extent to which children should have rights, and whether they are sufficiently protected.

Courts As Bureaucratic Organizations

Perhaps the most influential tradition in American law and society research has involved making a contrast between law on the books and law in action (Pound 1931). Researchers during the 1960s were concerned about the bifurcation of the legal system so that the higher courts applied the law to criminal matters or civil disputes with great care and attention to due process, whereas the lower courts and government agencies offered the working class a lower standard of justice, based on arbitrary and unfair decisions.

The critique of law in action

Forceful criticisms of the lower courts have been made by law and society researchers in the USA and Britain. Because these institutions had to process large numbers of defendants, it was inevitable that they received a low level of service. Abraham Blumberg (1969) argued that privately paid lawyers in the USA developed a closer relationship with the court than their clients. The court allowed them to make impassioned speeches about justice in order to persuade defendants to pay their fees, even though everyone knew that most would be convicted. Many studies have documented the arbitrary character of justice in both the lower criminal and the civil courts (for example, Abel 1982). In one study, lawyers along with other agents of an under-resourced welfare state are portrayed as "street level bureaucrats" (Lipsky 1988) who do not have the time to consider cases properly and become hardened to the problems of the poor.

British sociologists of law, influenced by Marxism, went further in portraying the police and courts as representing the interests of economically dominant social groups, and acting with systematic bias and unfairness towards working class defendants. A good example from Britain is Pat Carlen's (1976) *Magistrates' Justice*, an ethnographic account that emphasized the absurdity of crowded, old-fashioned courtrooms in which defendants were not given a fair hearing, partly because they were not legally represented and magistrates always believed the police. Doreen McBarnet's (1981) *Conviction* took this critique further by suggesting that the rights given to defendants, and celebrated by the legal system, concealed the bureaucratic justice taking place in the lower courts. There were "two tiers of justice," and differential treatment was built into the funding and organization of the legal system (see also Bankowski and Mungham 1976).

One empirical study worth mentioning, because it has a different political slant, was conducted by Maureen Mileski (1971). She found that most defendants in the American court she observed were unrepresented, and were processed in groups rather than individuals to save time. Because of this, there was procedural unfairness. However, she was most struck by the fact that cases had to be heard quickly, and that judges did not use moral or evaluative language:

"…the judge typically does not bother to condemn or chastise defendants with his tone or with his words.[3] The fact that the persons processed by the court are official deviants slips beneath the surface of courtroom interaction…There are no formal or informal requirements that the judge be the personal moral spokesman for the state, and he usually is not…The judge's work becomes routinized as do all work roles" (Mileski 1971, p. 530).

In this passage, Mileski seems to express the view that courts, to be effective, must strike fear into those who break the law. Instead, judges for the most part acted "in a routine, bureaucratic, businesslike way toward the defendants, a manner that at least borders on the impersonal" (Mileski 1971, p. 524). She also noted that it was more common for a defendant to be criticized for creating administrative difficulties for the court, than for the substantive offence. Today, critics are more likely to complain that the lower courts have insufficient resources to engage in therapeutic hearings. Mileski, however, makes us realize that it is the processing of large numbers, in a bureaucratic process, that makes any form of meaningful communication difficult, whether this is intended to rehabilitate or punish.

Finding law in children's courts

These criticisms inform many sociological studies about the lower courts. It should though be remembered that the justice model was established from the late 1960s in different countries with the aim of giving young offenders more rights than under the previous system. In Australia, they have a right to legal representation, even though legal aid is not available to most adult defendants. The most important protection is, however, that judicial officers exercise more oversight over sentencing and what happens to young offenders under rehabilitative orders, than under the previous welfare-oriented system. The rest of this chapter will present evidence (more examples of what anyone can see when attending hearings) demonstrating that children's courts are concerned with protecting rights, in addition to processing defendants.

Judicial Work as Quality Control

One way to understand judicial work is as a form of quality control in the administration of justice. This was most evident in hearings where something had gone wrong procedurally, affecting the rights of the defendant, but also in the routine work of getting through the daily list.

Questioning the charges in a guilty plea

A 17 year old defendant in Tasmania had pleaded guilty to charges relating to stealing and motor-vehicle stealing. On his first appearance in court, he had been remanded in custody owing to the seriousness of the charges, and because he had breached bail in the past, and could offer no surety. Subsequently, problems had arisen in Ashley Youth Detention Centre and he was placed on "suicide watch." Youth Justice had been alerted to the problem, and had obtained a psychiatric report which suggested that the defendant was easily led (in fact, he had received help from disability services in the past but this information was not available at the first bail hearing). This hearing took over an hour, considerably longer than most sentencing hearings. The magistrate raised four issues relating to the charges, which resulted in some discussion before she could proceed with the actual sentencing. I will describe two of these:

Possible need for a separate hearing in the Supreme Court

Two charges were listed for hearing, but since then other charges had been brought. One of these was an indictable matter meaning that, since he had committed this offence as an adult, it could not be heard by the children's court. The allegation was that the defendant had, in the company of others, stolen a motor vehicle worth $20,000. The magistrate wanted all the matters heard together, so that everything could be finished that day. After some discussion as to whether this was procedurally possible, the prosecutor amended the charge to $19,999 (below the threshold for becoming an indictable offence). This solved the problem.

> M: So at the moment there's one complaint with other charges listed on the 10th of May. Are you able?

DL:Your Worship, I have taken brief instructions in relation to that other one and it is likely that it will be a plea of guilty. My understanding is that it is currently an indictable matter.

P: I can assist Your Worship. One of the charges on the complaint for 10th May is a special charge of stealing. The allegation is that the defendant in the company of others stole a motor vehicle to the value of 20,000 dollars It is not a case of motor vehicle stealing under the Police Offences Act. It is a case of stealing under the Criminal Code in circumstances where it was not simply used without permission but rather...

M: But this court would have jurisdiction wouldn't it?

P: Uh.

CC: It's an adult complaint.

M: It's an adult complaint?

P: Yes it is.

M: Let's have a look at that then section 9.

P: My er [pause] concern in relation to it was that if the value remained at 20,000 as it is alleged on the complaint it would not be an election for this defendant.

[ ]

M: Oh well that's that then. It can't be dealt with in this court. Not unless there is to be some amendment and there's no suggestion at this stage.

P: Well Your Worship, I really would only need to change the value by one dollar.

[ ]

M: You'd still have that discretion.

P: Yes I've already received, if I can put it that way, in principle approval to change the value. It's a matter of changing it by one dollar to make it 19,999 dollars which is a minor change in the scheme of things I would suggest.

M: Yes.

P: That would enable the defendant to elect to be dealt with in the summary jurisdiction and may enable Your Worship to deal with the matter today with one matter being an adult and the other one being a

M: No difficulty with that?

P: No I have no difficulty at all.

M: Alright. So you want to make an application to amend? Your application is to amend the complaint 6345. We need to list the complaints.

This extract from the hearing shows the court workgroup, at the direction of the magistrate, exploring different ways of solving a procedural problem. The difficulty is that the defendant had been charged with an indictable offence owing to the value of the car stolen. The magistrate initially assumed that the children's court could hear the case. However, the prosecutor and court clerk told her that the offence was committed after the defendant became an adult. The magistrate accepted that, because of this, there was no room for discretion. However, the prosecutor told the court that, if he reduced the value of the car in the charges, the magistrate could use his discretion under the legislation, and ask for the charge to be heard in the children's court.

A dispute over intention

The defendant pleaded guilty to other charges of stealing petrol. However, when the prosecution stated the facts, it became clear that he had only been a passenger in a car during these offences. The magistrate argued in each case that intent was not proved, especially given the psychiatric report suggested that he was easily led and there was "diminished responsibility." The prosecution agreed that it was "a fine line" and stopped some but not all of the charges. The magistrate felt that it was preferable to adjourn the case so that the defense lawyer and prosecutor's office could look at the matter carefully.

P: Yes on 6346 Your Worship. On [ ] of this year, the defendant Black was in the company of Robin Green. While Black was in the passenger seat, he filled petrol on two occasions [without paying]. There was the same modus operandi.

M: Mere presence does not make him a participant so I'm going to need to hear from you in relation to…

P: Well, the prosecution case is based on a discussion that each time the car needed more fuel a discussion was entered into that the car needed more fuel and it would not be paid for…

M: Well, that may or may not be sufficient. Mere presence is not enough. If presence is relied upon there has to be at least an intention to encourage by presence, and encouragement in fact, being involved in a discussion, may be no more than presence and it depends upon the content of that discussion.

P: Well, I make the submission based on the fact that encouragement comes from there being no attempt by any person in the vehicle to make payment for the fuel and no attempt by Black in particular to prevent the act of the stealing of the petrol occurring in a similar…

M: But he is not obliged to prevent people from committing crimes, as a matter of law, is he? It's a question of whether or not he is guilty. And I need to know what the prosecution case is in relation to those pleas. If you are saying, look he did nothing to prevent those crimes occurring that is effectively presence isn't it?

P: Yes I accept that.

M: And the law in relation to presence is that presence can render him guilty if he intended to encourage by his presence and in fact encouraged by his presence. So that becomes critical and I need to know what the prosecution facts are in relation to that.

P: Well, that is precisely on which the prosecution case

is based. His presence. By his presence he encouraged the continued use of the motor vehicle in circumstances where petrol was required for it to continue to run Your Worship.

M: [pause] I'll need to hear from the defence in relation to whether that is admitted in that particular case.

[The defense lawyer reported on her understanding of each incident]

DL: Your Worship, I don't have a great deal of instructions on that in relation to threats. But he felt obliged to stay in the car and keep his mouth shut and continue with the adventure if you may call it. He didn't feel he was able to speak up at any point.

M: He was a reluctant participant. It's a fine line isn't it um

P: Your Worship, if I may respond to that submission. Certainly in relation to count 3 Black was present. But as Your Worship has pointed out it's a very fine line [looks through charges]. There is a joint enterprise for the first two charges, and counts 3,4,5. With a plea of guilty to 1, 6 and 7, I am not going to push to an hearing [on the others]. I will accept Black's plea [on intention]. The reason why I say this is because I have read the psychiatrist's report. I accept that Black's low level of IQ is relevant.

M: Miss Carter are you in a position to provide me with more detail on count 1. Black's state of mind.

DL: Your Worship, my instructions are he said no and Y threatened him.

M: This matter requires some careful attention. But can I draw to you that a special case of stealing needs an intent. So this question cannot be dealt with quickly today. What I'm proposing is that the pleas remain as they are. I'll hear from Miss Carter on Youth Justice matters. I'll adjourn the other matters. Miss Carter this will give you an opportunity to give this matter the careful attention it requires.

This second problem arose because the psychiatrist's report put in doubt whether the defendant had participated in a series of alleged thefts from petrol stations. This hearing also shows a concern with procedural fairness, within the legislation, and that the magistrate was supervising the quality of legal work. This was possible because other cases were not proceeding that morning: everyone had the time to address what may have been seen as a mistake in refusing bail on his first appearance. The defendant waited patiently while these technical discussions took place without being asked to contribute, since no facts were at issue. There was no indication during the hearing that he understood, or needed to understand, what had been decided, other than that he was granted bail, and would continue to see the case worker and psychiatrist.

Getting through the daily list

Although sentencing took place within a legal framework, it did not normally involve technical deliberations about matters of law. It was also striking that most time spent in court on "for mention" days was concerned with adjournments and scheduling cases, as against sentencing. My own estimate would be that about 40% of court time was spent on sentencing, 10% on bail hearings, and the rest on administrative work in preparation for the sentencing decision. This administrative work was mainly concerned with scheduling and adjournments. It included advising defendants at their first and second appearances in court, taking not guilty pleas and arranging a "contest mention" hearing, and directing defendants after guilty pleas to see a case worker in order to prepare a pre-sentence report. The following examples illustrate the routine character of this administrative work:

> This was this 17 year old defendant's first appearance.
>
> D: Can I represent myself? I want to plead not guilty.
>
> M: You should see a lawyer.
>
> D: I was told I could adjourn.
>
> M: Take your hands out of your pockets. The charge is you

stole a camera. Do you plead guilty or not guilty or do you want advice?

D: [slight pause] Advice.

M: OK then we will adjourn till 8th December.

D: Sorry about that.

M: That's OK.

This 16 year old defendant was appearing before the court for the third time.

DL: I appreciate he appeared on a number of occasions. I've been instructed on 3rd November. Obviously, there has been no time to review the complaint or take further instructions. My application is for an adjournment.

M: Well John you appeared before me on 20th October without a lawyer. Why did it take you two weeks?

D: Been busy.

M: Doing what?

D: Working for me Dad and that.

M: I assume you've got a phone?

D: Yeah.

M: You could have rung Legal Aid and spoken to someone. This matter has been hanging around since July. It's not your counsel's fault. It's your fault not her's. I'll adjourn the matter one more time somewhat reluctantly to 8th December for plea. Bail continues till then. If Miss Bell comes back then and says there has been difficulty in getting instructions, I might take a different course. Do you understand?

D: Yes.

M: You can go.

This 14 year old defendant arrived in the court around mid-day, with her mother, W. The magistrate had been reluctant to issue a warrant. The defense lawyer was present.

> M: I adjourned so you could attend for a Youth Justice report. You didn't attend. Why not?
>
> D: I don't know.
>
> M: Well, there's a few avenues open to you. I could put you in Ashley to improve your memory. Would you like that? No. I could put you there so we know where you are and you can get the report there. Where are you living now?
>
> D: [ ]
>
> M: As I don't have the report the condition will be that you reside there. [Looks at the defendant's mother]. She should stay with you until the matter is finalized. Is that OK?
>
> Mth: Yes.
>
> M: Adjourned to 27th October at 9am. You are to attend Children and Family Services on Wednesday 5th October at 1pm. If you don't go there, I'm going to have you arrested and put you in Ashley and you'll stay there.
>
> Mth:That's OK. She wasn't staying with me last time.
>
> M: That's why I'm making sure she stays with you.

In these examples, magistrates can be heard following a set of administrative procedures to establish the conditions for holding a sentencing hearing. Defendants were allowed two appearances before they were required to plead. In most courts, the first adjournment gave them a month to consult a lawyer. They were also allowed a second adjournment for another month, if this did not happen. In many cases, when they pleaded guilty, the court required a pre-sentence report, and so there was a third adjournment. If the young person did not attend the interview, the court could grant a fourth adjournment. The ultimate sanction was treating the lack of cooperation as a breach of bail, and obtaining the report in a detention center. The work involved explaining the rules to each defendant, in a similar way to how administrators talk to the public when delivering services in other bureaucratic organisations.

Is this, though, simply administrative work? Another way of looking at these hearings is that the magistrate is advising defendants of their legal rights. They have a right in the legislation to adjournments. They also have a right to legal representation. In the first hearing, the magistrate advised the defendant to seek advice, and in other cases the magistrate required an adjournment even though the defendant and family in court wanted the matter to be heard without further delay. Similarly, the pre-sentence report was not simply seen as helpful in allowing magistrates to sentence more effectively but was required by the legislation. One cannot, therefore, easily separate administrative and legal work in the lower courts, or see adjournments as of secondary importance to sentencing hearings. Nor were the decisions inconsequential. While imprisoning a defendant to allow welfare agencies to prepare reports was rare, it did happen. In one hearing, observed in a country court in Victoria, an Indigenous defendant with an history of serious offending had missed an appointment to see a psychologist in the children's clinic. The magistrate sent him to a detention centre for a five week period over Christmas in order to obtain the report.

Contested Hearings

The fact that guilty pleas take place within a legal framework does not entirely remove the impression that children's courts are mainly concerned with case processing, rather than questions of justice. This is because we normally associate the exercise of rights within a system based on due process with an adversarial contest between lawyers. In children's courts, certainly in guilty pleas hearings, the practitioners appear to be on the same side, working together with the magistrate and court clerk for the benefit of the defendant. In some hearings observed in one court, a Legal Aid lawyer took her shoes off, and knelt by the prosecutor (who had not been properly prepared by his office) and whispered advice on what to say next into his ear during the hearing. There was no sign here of an adversarial relationship.

More generally, there was little dispute or disagreement about sentencing. Private lawyers, who were being paid, tended to make longer representations than Legal Aid lawyers. However, in the hearings observed, they never asked for a sentence that led to disagreement with the magistrate. In most cases, both the defense lawyer and magistrate accepted the recommendation in the pre-sentence report. It was also striking that the prosecutor said very little aside from summarizing the facts, and had no brief to ask for a particular sentence. This meant that there was little scope for argument or adversarial relations, and there were few examples in the sentencing hearings observed.[4]

This suggests, however, that children's courts were mainly concerned with hearing guilty pleas. In fact, there were also many defendants who pleaded not guilty, and there were also trials and contested bail hearings. Although I spent most time observing guilty pleas, I can provide a more rounded or complete view of these courts through describing some aspects of these adversarial hearings.

Not guilty pleas

There are no statistics on the numbers pleading not guilty in these children's courts. Observation of court hearings, and interviews with practitioners, suggests that many pleaded not guilty, although they often changed their plea. One Legal Aid lawyer noted that some defendants were quite astute and tactical when it came to giving instructions:

> Going from not guilty to guilty with a defendant happens quite a lot because a lot of smarter kids know they can push and push and have had word that the complainant won't turn up.

Others pleaded not guilty because they did not understand criminal procedures:

> Sometimes they feel if you say 'not guilty', the court will say 'Oh off you go' so there is some naivety. Others as a matter of routine push and push till hearing day. Others try it on

with you. Others do it in ignorance. One pleaded not guilty to a robbery on the grounds that the details were wrong – it should not be taking a handbag but trying to get into the handbag, so there is a certain amount of ignorance and misplaced attempts to be cunning, and there is naivety.

According to this lawyer, even in cases where there was DNA evidence, there was some chance of acquittal. If instructed, lawyers should do everything they could to ensure that a client was acquitted. Some magistrates, by contrast, saw changes of plea in a different light, and on occasions admonished lawyers after a hearing where a late guilty plea resulted from a witness attending. One magistrate offered the following analysis:

A lot of defendants plead not guilty and then plead guilty. Most are charged with new matters so the hearing gets postponed. This sends out the wrong message (unless they are in detention). There should be a procedure to review not guilty pleas and stop this. A young kid could have 30 appearances – it would take 18 months to be punished. I would like defense lawyers to have a training day on how they should act if instructed to plead not guilty. The defendants don't know what is good for them and there can be a 9-10 months delay.

The argument here is that, to address offending behavior, it is necessary to intervene quickly. The repeat offender can, however, take advantage of the system and delay a trial for many months. This suggests that defendants are more active and capable than they are often portrayed in the criminological literature. However, this magistrate saw this as another element of their vulnerability: they were unable to know what is in their best interests.

Trials

Although there were relatively few trials, these took up a considerable amount of court time. Three trials were observed in New South Wales during this study, each lasting half a day. Two turned on identification evidence. In the first case, a defendant was alleged to have thrown a pot plant through a window of the house where his ex-girlfriend was staying. The defense case was that she could not have seen him through a gap in the curtains, if she had moved away from the window. In the second case, a youth was charged with having taken part in torching a car. When the police arrived at the scene, someone from the estate who had come to watch, identified him as the person responsible. The defense lawyer argued that the witness could, in fact, have been the culprit, and her client was an innocent by-stander. In each case, the magistrate after summarizing the evidence found for the prosecution.

In a third case, a 14 year old had been charged with shop-lifting DVDs after a security guard searched his haversack.[5] His defense was that he had accompanied two older friends to a mall. They had asked for his haversack, and when he was otherwise occupied, must have placed the stolen items in it. The prosecutor wanted to know why he had given them the haversack. Since it felt heavier, why did he not look inside? In this case, the magistrate decided that the defendant was easily led, and did not realise that he was carrying the items. Because of this, he found him not guilty.

What was surprising about these trials is that, even though the stakes were relatively low in terms of the consequences for the defendants, there was a considerable level of engagement by the advocates. In the third case, this might be explained by the fact the defendant's parents, who were in court, did not want their son to have a criminal record, and had instructed a solicitor.[6] However, even in the first two cases, there was a lengthy examination-in-chief and cross-examination of the prosecution witnesses. On many occasions, both the prosecutor and defense lawyer objected to the way the question was phrased. The magistrate was often called to adjudicate, as illustrated by the following exchange during cross-examination of the main prosecution witness in the first case:

DL: What did you do when the pot plant came through?

W: I started to walk back.

DL: But you said you saw the boys run off.

W: You just asked me. I saw them when the pot plant came through.

DL: How did you see the boys run off if the curtain was across the window?

W: It was open when it was smashed.

DL: I asked you about the curtain when the pot plant came through and you said it was open a fraction.

P: Your Honor, I object. My understanding is that when she was in the process of closing the window she saw them before the pot plant came through not after.

[Magistrate indicated that the defense lawyer could continue.]

DL: I'm saying after the pot plant came through the window, how did you see them if you moved back?

Prosecutors in New South Wales are required to undergo a relatively long period of training, including taking courses in the law of evidence, which may explain why they attempted to win these contests. The advocates for Legal Aid were each junior barristers, who saw these hearings as valuable training for work in the higher courts. They had the character of a no-holds barred, sparring match before a magistrate with considerable experience in adjudicating these disputes. This again makes it difficult to see the lower courts simply in terms of bureaucratic case processing.

Bail applications

Bail is the only aspect of children's courts that has become a political issue in Australia, at least to the extent that there is concern among practitioners and administrators about the growing number of unsentenced defendants in detention centers. In Tasmania, the Commissioner for Children found that 110 young people spent short periods of time in the detention centre during 2005. Although it was not possible to follow up the outcomes of every case, some had received non-custodial sentences after spending a few months in detention while on remand (Fanning 2006).

In Victoria, there had also been an increase in the number of remand detainees, and this was viewed as a problem by the children's court (Grant 2009). In New South Wales, a debate was taking place about how to interpret an amendment to the Bail Act that, on the face of things, prevented fresh applications unless there was a change of circumstances.[7] In one hearing, a magistrate told the court that his own approach would be to treat even a minor change (which could easily be manufactured) as making possible an application. One gets a sense from these exchanges how even judicial officers in the lower courts regularly have to apply new legislation, and there may be different interpretations until an appeal decision.

Bail decisions were difficult to research since most initial hearings took place before Justices of the Peace in a specially convened evening or weekend court at the request of the Youth Officer in the police.[8] In many cases, young people were not represented at these hearings, although legal aid is available, since most lawyers did not work after-hours. One lawyer suggested that representation made a difference:

Q: Do you feel that anything can be done to reduce time on remand?

A: Yes there is. Particularly, when it is the failure of prosecution systems to work that causes an extra delay. I know how many kids are on remand and you always think if there is something you can do. A child might be taken on a Friday and not given bail by Monday or Tuesday. If a lawyer was there it would make a difference. I appeared a few times and know I was able to construct an argument for them. When there is a set of prior matters they can look fairly average but if you can say these charges fit in here and this breach of bail is when the child's carers demanded money and kicked him out, there is less of a case [for refusing bail]. The prosecution can construct a very convincing argument that can be knocked down by a skilled advocate.

While observing sentencing hearings, there was the opportunity to observe several bail applications. Many were opposed by the prosecutor on the grounds that the breach indicated that the defendant might re-offend. In most cases, it appeared that the magistrates used their discretion to keep defendants out of custody. In the following case, a 17 year old defendant had breached bail conditions for a second time, but the magistrate addressed the problem by increasing the amount his mother would have to pay into court as a surety if there was a further breach:

M: Now the question of bail. I made orders that were breached. What is the position with bail now?

P: Your worship I opposed bail on [ ] but the court saw fit to grant bail so I can only ask for the strictest conditions.

M: Sarah Trane [the defendant's mother] come forward. You were a surety. Why did you not make sure he was reporting? Here we have 3 counts of motor vehicle stealing, 9 counts of breaches of bail. I can't bail again. What is to say he's going to abide by them? I thought I made that quite clear to him last time. The only basis I can grant bail is because I can't deal with this till [ ] which is more than 28 days. I will up the ante with the surety to $1000.

DL: Thank you Your Worship. There were a number of personal circumstances. Mr. Trane recognizes this is his last chance. The proof is that he appeared today.

M: I think it's very [inaudible]. Mrs. Trane are you prepared to act as a surety?

Mth: Yes.

M: Make sure he abides by the conditions. Stephen stand up please. I don't take kindly to people who breach bail conditions. I bent over backwards and all you do is kick me in the face. You committed an aggravated burglary. There is an additional condition not to associate with X and you must live with your surety. You must be there between the hours of 8pm and 6am and report to the person on duty at the police station every Monday, Thursday and Friday. You'll report today. The sum of the surety is now $1,000. She might also be looking for $500 from the last lot. It is about time you gave her a break too. I have made a note on the file for 23rd August. Right, you and your mother can get out to the bail room.

This extract illustrates how increasing the surety, and imposing stricter reporting conditions, made it possible for a magistrate to grant bail, even though the defendant had failed to report to a police station. The magistrate initially said that his hands were tied since this was the second breach, but there were special circumstances since he was not available to hear another bail application within the next month. This may also be an example of how informal policies, not set down in the legislation, can be consequential. There were a number of magistrates in this court, each of whom normally sat once a month to sentence, and consider bail applications along with other administrative matters. Bail was normally renewed, or an application allowed once a month. If anyone was on leave, an application could be heard by any magistrate. However, magistrates preferred to make bail decisions on the cases that were initially assigned, rather than treating them as inter-changeable. In this hearing, the magistrate told the court that, if bail was refused, he would not be there to hear the application personally in a month. It appears that this administrative contingency was sufficient, along with "upping the ante" on the conditions, to justify granting bail.

Another application was observed in which a 17 year old defendant had breached a curfew imposed from 6pm until 6am, and was stopped by police while driving an unregistered and uninsured motorbike without an helmet. He had been charged with five counts of stealing and five of burglary, including computer equipment worth thousands of dollars. He had a long offending history, and 22 breaches of bail in the last few years. He did not provide a surety, although on a previous occasion he had entered into a "recognisance" for $1,000, and paid this after breaching bail.

This defendant was described by the case worker as "an extremely intelligent young man" who "could be one of the people who gets paid to come through the doors of the court rather than to come through [from the cells] as a defendant." He had, however, continued offending on many occasions after promising that he wanted to change his life. The defense lawyer argued that, if bail was not granted, he would spend considerably more time in detention than the sentence that could be imposed for the offences. He argued that breaches of bail in the past had resulted from association with particular people, and this no longer applied. He had failed to meet the conditions of what was a stringent curfew for a 17 year old. The magistrate in this case took a tougher view that the conditions he had attached in initially granting bail had been breached:

> M: Thank you David if you can stand up thank you. My recollection is that these were my bail conditions um I think you are acknowledging that. The position is that when I grant bail, I make it perfectly clear to anybody that if they breach my bail they can go to the Supreme Court to get bail but I'm not going to grant it. Otherwise I'd look a pretty silly person if I'm sitting here making orders and telling people these things and you don't abide by them. Now if you're an intelligent person you will have understood that to be the position at the time, and to me intelligence means that you act in a responsible way, not just that you've got a brain that can get round things. So to me you don't deserve bail in all the circumstances. They were stringent conditions. They were intended to be stringent and I am remanding you into custody until we deal with the matters.

These decisions, made by different magistrates in the same court, suggest that the rules set out in the legislation gave them discretion in weighing up all the circumstances in the same way as when sentencing. In this hearing, the prosecution had argued that the past breaches suggested a risk of re-offending, but these were not mentioned by the magistrate, perhaps because they were not legally relevant to a new application. Instead, he focused on the "intelligence" of the defendant, apparent both from the fact he was doing a further education course, but also because of the sophisticated nature of the offences. This defendant was not seen as qualifying for leniency on the grounds of either youthfulness or vulnerabilty. He was treated like an adult who was capable of behaving "in a responsible way," and expected to understand bail conditions, in addition to his rights of appeal.

In these cases, the facts were clear cut, and there was no dispute over the circumstances, or whether the magistrate had interpreted the law correctly. In hearings observed in another state, the prosecution and defense called witnesses in bail applications. A police officer gave his views on the likelihood of re-offending. The defendant's mother was asked about the arrangements at home, and cross-examined by the prosecutor on her ability to enforce a curfew. Defense lawyers could not predict the outcome of many bail applications. They were, however, taking advantage of the rights given to defendants in the legislation to apply for bail, and in Tasmania and Victoria make new applications every month. If bail was refused, they were also entitled to apply to an higher court. The magistrate in this hearing acknowledged that there was a chance of obtaining bail through this route, but he was entitled to refuse bail.

Children's Rights as a Political Agenda

There is a tradition in the critical literature in criminology and law and society studies in portraying the lower courts as mainly bureaucratic organizations in which there is no concern with due process. This chapter has sought to present children's courts in a more positive light. These are courts in which most defendants plead guilty. Nevertheless, it would be a mistake to see this as one step in what some American researchers call the "pipeline from schools to prisons" (Koehler 2009). If there is a pipeline, it takes place as part of a legal process. In fact, under the justice model, there is judicial oversight over decisions that affect children, that did not happen in the earlier welfare-oriented system. There are still, however, many who would like to restore elements of the welfare system, while at the same time doing more to protect the rights of children. Is it possible to reconcile these apparently conflicting objectives?

Proposals and contradictions

In recent years, the only political pressure on governments around the world to improve their response to youth crime has come from the United Nations. After many years of campaigning, child advocates succeeded in securing international agreement to the 1989 Convention on the Rights of the Child. As in other progressive movements, there are different proposals, and some tensions between them. Some campaigners, influenced by the Marxist tradition, believe that only economic and social changes can protect children: giving them more legal protections will not address the underlying causes of offending, and will strengthen the ideological basis of law as promising equal treatment (Zizek 2010). Others argue that the movement should focus on strengthening the legal protections of young people (Freeman and Veerman 1992, Fortin 2003), or believe that the detention of children breaches a fundamental human right (Harris 1982).

There are contradictions within the argument for legal protections. There is a consensus that young people should have greater procedural rights. On the other hand, many also favor a return to the unified children's courts in which social workers exercised more discretion over how difficult young people were treated without judicial oversight (for example, Barry and McNeill 2009, Whyte 2010). Then there are those who argue that children should be treated like adults at an earlier age, for example through obtaining the right to vote at 16. At the same time, they would like to extend the protections given child defendants into early adulthood. The underlying problem with rights campaigns may be that, as adults, we want children to have rights, but do not see them as capable of exercising these or behaving responsibly because they are children. There have, for example, been proposals to give young people a greater say in sentencing their peers, in order to make this more meaningful, but so long as they make decisions under adult supervision (Green and Weber 2008).

Is there adequate protection?

Despite these tensions and contradictions, this emerging reform movement makes one think about whether children's courts in Australia and elsewhere could do better in protecting the rights of young people. Ultimately, as one case worker commented, it was easier to put repeat offenders in detention rather than investing time and resources in community based programs. There was also scope for injustice given that young people have little power in relation to adults:

I understand the nature of the world for some of these kids. I do not like to see them in detention. I do not like to see them get unjustly punished, or punished severely for things that are very circumstantial or inadvertent or not really their fault. I would like to think that justice was always fair. I think it's fairly consistent but there can be problems.

Young people are, in some respects, given greater protection in these states than adult defendants because they are entitled to Legal Aid, irrespective of means or the nature of the case. In other respects, they are treated like second class citizens. In some countries there has been legislation following political pressure by community groups, and evidence supplied by researchers, about abuses of police power when arresting or interrogating adults. The objective has been to force the police to review their own procedures, and to prevent similar abuses. In Australia, young people are not entitled to representation at police stations, although they are allowed free telephone advice. Although no independent research has been conducted, one suspects that many young people make admissions, when they would have relied on their right to silence given legal advice. Within the courts themselves, it is possible that the quality of legal representation is lower in some country areas, or that young people spend time in detention centers through administrative mistakes. In one hearing in New South Wales, a 14 year old Indigenous youth had been in a detention centre for one month, after pleading guilty to stealing a can of lemonade. This was due to an error by a defense lawyer in not making a bail application at a previous hearing, and no one noticing the problem. Appearing by video-link, he seemed quite happy, as did his mother who was in court. Only the practitioners realized that something had gone badly wrong.

One policy recommendation that follows is that there should be external monitoring or inspection of children's courts or detention centers against international benchmarks of good practice (Muncie 2010). Greater accountability does not necessarily improve outcomes, and one could argue that establishing such mechanisms will divert resources away from the institutions that are doing their best to deliver services. Another view is that rights can only be properly exercised within the legal system if there is some degree of independent scrutiny or political pressure from community groups. In these Australian states, the Commissioner for Children already has this role, but there are currently limited powers to investigate possible problems.

9.

Comparing Courts

Previous chapters have described the work of magistrates, and other practitioners concerned with sentencing children, in three Australian states as if the states, courts and individual magistrates were inter-changeable. Despite some differences, there are many similarities between the legislation and the procedures followed in Tasmania, Victoria and New South Wales. If you visited a children's court in each state, you might think that there were no substantial differences in how magistrates conducted hearings, or made sentencing decisions. This initial impression would, however, be misleading. In the first place, although not everyone accepts the statistics, there is some evidence to suggest that magistrates in Victoria sentence considerably fewer young people to detention (Richards and Lyneham 2010). In the second place, there may be significant differences in sentencing practices, and a willingness to grant bail, between metropolitan and country regions. In the third place, if more detailed statistics were collected and made public, as happens in some American states, they would almost certainly show differences between the sentencing practices of magistrates in the same court.

This chapter will be concerned with these differences, drawing on the statistical information where available, but also on what was discovered through observing courts and speaking to practitioners. It will start by considering the evidence for inter-state differences, and particularly the apparent leniency of Victoria. The reason why the word "apparent" is necessary is that, even though there are clear statistical differences, practitioners and policy makers tend to see these as indicating a lower crime rate, rather than that the magistrates sentence young people differently. Through describing some sentencing hearings, I hope to show that children's courts in this state *are* more lenient: a significant finding, especially given the fact that Victoria is the only Australian state that does not divert offenders to restorative conferences.[1]

The chapter will then consider the evidence for differences in sentencing practices between regions, and between magistrates in the same court. There are no statistics available, so I will report how practitioners understood these issues, and how they became visible to me during the fieldwork. The rest of the chapter will consider possible explanations for the differences in detention rates between states, using the concept of court culture employed by some American studies. It will conclude through considering comparison as a political issue: how one might want to change sentencing practices in children's courts; and whether it would be desirable to have greater accountability through monitoring and evaluation.

Differences Between States

There is a large international literature concerned with identifying patterns or regularities in the decisions made by adult criminal courts, and how these have been shaped by different factors, including the social background of judges or the characteristics of defendants (for example, Hogarth 1971, Hood 1992, Engen et al 2002). There is also a smaller literature that compares outcomes in different regions, either between states or at the county level. In one well-known American study, a team of researchers collected comparative data in six courts, and sought to identify the influence of different court cultures defined partly in terms of the political values shared by judges who were elected to office (Eisenstein et al 1988). In a more recent study, Jeffrey Ulmer (1997) identified local policies towards plea-bargaining in four courts that explain different sentencing outcomes, even though national guidelines had attempted to reduce judicial discretion.

None of these studies express matters in the direct language used by some American newspapers that compare courts and even individual judges on their record in sentencing particular offences. They also do not compare statistical outcomes for sentencing juveniles, although there is a recent literature that seeks to determine if offenders transferred to adult courts receive tougher sentences.

In Australia, there are fewer statistics available when researching juvenile crime, and these are not especially reliable, since there are no common protocols for collecting data. There is, however, an annual report compiled by the Australian Institute of Criminology (Richards and Lyneham 2010) based on voluntary reporting by different states. These reports show that detention rates for juvenile offenders have been steadily falling (although the national rate is, apparently, still higher than the rate for many European countries or even America measured by international comparative surveys).[2] There are, however, significant differences between states. In 2008, the rates of sentenced young persons per 100,000 population in detention centers were 50.1 in NSW, 47.6 in Tasmania and 14.3 in Victoria. There are also differences in the over-representation of Indigenous defendants. There was an average rate of 567 in NSW and 166.5 in Victoria.[3] In this section of the chapter, I will only be concerned with the rates for all juveniles. I will argue, firstly, that the bare statistics have limited value in drawing conclusions about differences in sentencing practices, because they could indicate differences in the amount or seriousness of juvenile offending in these states. I will then, however, attempt to show that there is at least a case to answer through describing comparable cases in more detail.

Statistical evidence and its limitations

In criminology, statistics are often used for political purposes. In juvenile justice, there is a continuing debate between the approaches of welfare and justice (Cunneen and White 2007, Muncie 2009). Proponents of welfare measures, who see detention as a last resort, might approve of leniency in Victoria. Some right wing politicians or "shock jocks" believe that a tougher response is needed towards youth crime, even in New South Wales (see, for example, Videnieks 2002). More fundamentally, there is no agreement on whether there are significant differences. Whenever I raised this issue with magistrates in New South Wales, they invariably said that Victoria had less crime. The two states employed a similar approach when sentencing but there were larger numbers of repeat and serious offenders in New South Wales. This could be attributed to the larger distances in New South Wales, urban areas with higher levels of unemployment, and more Indigenous crime.

One way to address this interpretive problem would be to compare how similar juvenile offences are sentenced in different states. This might become possible in the future since New South Wales already has a data base that shows the average sentence received for particular offences, and it is possible that this could be introduced elsewhere. Even here, however, one would have to be careful in drawing conclusions about differences in sentencing practices. These become apparent when one considers a simplified tariff of sentencing options, which is broadly similar in each state:

minor offences	discharge good behaviour bond undertaking
middle-range or repeat offences	probation community service
serious offences	detention

The New South Wales data base assists magistrates by telling them the sentences made for similar offences over a five year period. One might expect that a young person who committed a minor or first time offence would receive a low sentence: for example, a discharge or good behaviour bond. A repeat offender would be receiving middle of tariff penalties, and perhaps would even be sent to detention. There are, however, several difficulties in using the data base as a comparative tool to check whether offenders are receiving similar sentences in different states.

The first problem is that each offender has a different offending history. Someone who has committed a particular offence for the first time might be expected to receive a more lenient outcome. However, even if one controlled for this, it would not be possible to predict outcomes. As will be apparent from cases presented in this study, there is no automatic progression through the tariff. It is, for example, possible to have spent time in a detention centre, but for the next offence to receive a good behaviour bond. One might be able to see the number of young people receiving a good behaviour bond for committing theft in different states, but not know whether they were first time or regular offenders.

Another problem is that offences differ in their seriousness. We have already seen in chapter 5 that those receiving minor sentences often commit "situational" offences. Resisting arrest, or getting into a fight with another youth after an insult, are viewed as less serious than committing a burglary or taking cars. Then there is the problem that, for any offence, there may be mitigating features identified by the pre-sentence report. There is a distinction between a planned and opportunistic burglary, or a burglary in which the defendant was influenced by peer pressure. The case worker may also report that a defendant has matured in outlook, or there has been a change in family circumstances, since committing the original offence. The magistrate may feel that, because of these changed circumstances, there is little risk of re-offending, and that a lenient sentence is appropriate. The statistics in a data base cannot tell the whole story: they conceal the set of factors considered by the magistrate in an interpretive judgement.

Given access to the pre-sentence reports, it might be possible to collect information about these possible variables. Even so, it would be hard to demonstrate differences in sentencing practices between states through comparing defendants with similar profiles. This is because magistrates make a decision by weighing up the different factors, and using their own judgment. One might add that it would be worrying if magistrates could be replaced by a computer program, and that there would be great potential for injustice through requiring them to follow a points system.[4] We expect judicial officers like other professional occupations to make decisions on a case by case basis, using their judgment and discretion rather than following prescriptive rules. Because of this, it is hard to model their work through quantitative analysis. It is also difficult to determine whether a particular court is tougher or more lenient from statistical evidence.

A qualitative solution?

Qualitative research is often viewed as having little probative value by quantitative sociologists and policy researchers. It is seen as helpful in identifying hypotheses that can be tested, but otherwise cannot produce objective or reliable knowledge. There is some truth in this criticism. However, in this case qualitative research can help in demonstrating the validity of statistical differences. This is because through observing hearings one can normally obtain more contextual information to enable comparison than from the bare statistics. It is also possible to see whether this is a normal decision for that court by attending the hearing, and speaking to practitioners.

Unfortunately, although I observed many sentencing hearings, it proved impossible to obtain a large enough sample to compare the sentencing of many offences. To give an example, I observed a Tasmanian hearing in which a 15 year old girl was sentenced to one year of probation and 70 hours of community service for stealing checks from a letter box, and attempting to cash these at banks (case 6D). This offence is relatively serious since it involves some degree of planning (many youthful offences have a spontaneous or opportunistic character). Since I did not observe hearings for a similar offence in the other states, it is difficult to make comparative observations.[5] I do not know whether a 15 year old girl stealing checks, with the same offending history and family circumstances would receive a similar sentence in a different state. However, I did observe young people being sentenced for the offence of arson in Victoria and New South Wales, and for violent offences in Tasmania, Victoria and New South Wales. These hearings demonstrate, in a way that supports the statistics, that there is a more lenient approach in Victoria.

Responses to arson

Arson is a serious offence that can lead to loss of life, and causes property damage, even when committed in a moment of carelessness. I observed a sentencing hearing in New South Wales in which a 15 year old, while under the influence of cannabis, had set fire to a couch in the house where he was staying, as a response to being evicted (case 9A). According to the data base used to assist practitioners in that state, offenders who commit arson receive detention orders. In this case, there were mitigating factors and the defendant was sentenced to probation for 12 months, with directions to receive drugs and alcohol counseling and to undertake 25 hours of community service.

By contrast, in Victoria, I observed a case where a 17 year old caused a quarter of a million dollars worth of damage in a town centre, in the company of other youths (an aggravating factor). He had committed prior offences including burglary, theft and dangerous driving. In mitigation, his lawyer told the court that he had a learning disability and attention deficit disorder. He had broken into a golf club which was less serious than the burglary of a private dwelling (see Sudnow 1965). A police officer gave evidence on his behalf. The officer told the court that he was already participating, while on bail, in a pilot program the police were running to address offending behavior, and he should be allowed to continue rather than receive a custodial sentence. Both argued that, even if he was given a short period of detention before continuing the program, this would bring him into contact with "undesirable" young people. After hearing these arguments, the magistrate said that he was considering a sentence of detention, but would defer this decision for three months to see how the defendant responded to the program.

This appears, on the face of things, as a very lenient decision. It should be noted, however, that even though he was regarded as one of the "softer" magistrates, there was no great surprise or disquiet among practitioners after the hearing. It was a perfectly normal, and unremarkable or unreportable, sentence in this court (Sudnow 1965). Moreover, the sentence was made possible on this occasion because the local police were advocating a community based sentence for a serious offence. Although this is only one hearing, it would be enough to show anyone familiar with sentencing in Tasmania or New South Wales that there is greater leniency in Victoria, even though a different magistrate might have made a detention order.

Sentencing violent offenders

To give a second example, consider the following three sentencing decisions for multiple offences involving violent crime. Although there are significant differences between the offences, they were all serious. In each case, the defendants apparently showed no remorse when interviewed by case workers.

In the Tasmanian hearing discussed in chapter 6 (case 6E), a 17 year old defendant was sentenced to 10 months detention after committing a series of offences, including punching a police officer and threatening a security guard with a knife. The sentencing remarks indicate that someone who continues to commit offences involving violence, and does not respond to probation orders or community service, will be sentenced to detention in this state. It was the "only appropriate sentence."

I observed a similar case in Victoria, in which the defendant had committed a sexual assault, in addition to violent offences. The defense lawyer raised the fact that his mother had recently died as a mitigating factor. In this case, the pre-sentence report recommended probation, and programs to address the offending behavior. The magistrate followed this recommendation:

Case 9B

M: Michael. Stand up please. You are lucky today. I had to agree with Mr. X that you should be placed on probation. I first thought about the number of offences and was worried by the number and the type of the offences. A number have involved real violence. This is just totally unacceptable on every level. People who get assaulted and robbed live with that for the rest of their lives. The impact on them and their families is often considerable. No one should have to face that. That's up to you. It is your first time before the court so you get a chance today. A youth supervision order which is more serious than probation would be more appropriate and some magistrates would say this. You did not reoffend on your previous deferral and your last offence was in January this year. You were drunk and 15 years old when you committed the offences. I warn you that next time you might not be so lucky. If you were involved in offending and particularly violence, you might find yourself back in custody. Could I ask you to say that you will engage in no form of offending?

D: Yes.

M: And that you are going to comply with the probation order?

D: [nods head]

M: Alright, take a seat [the magistrate types the order into his computer]. Yes, the formal order is probation for 12 months with the condition that you go to a grief counselor. You should pay restitution of 90 dollars and 120 dollars on the robberies and have three months to pay.

There are differences between this and the Tasmanian hearing, including the fact that this was the defendant's first appearance before the children's court. This may, however, be misleading because in Victoria many first offenders, even if they have committed crimes of violence or sexual assaults, can be given sentences that do not result in a finding of guilt. There are two ways in which this can happen. As described in chapter 5, offenders can be sent on the Ropes program which involves spending a day climbing ropes with the police. Alternatively, they can receive a deferred sentence involving supervision by Youth Justice. If they do not re-offend, the charge can be dismissed. Although the details of the case are not available, the sentencing remarks indicate there may be two prior deferrals. This illustrates not simply that magistrates in Victoria are more lenient, but also that the legislation, and informal practices that have arise for diversion, allow them to give second chances.

By contrast, in the following hearing in New South Wales, a tough approach was adopted towards a young offender who had committed his first violent offence:

M: [addressing the defense lawyer] What do you want me to do with it?

DL: Given it's his first offence, I'd ask Your Honor to give a bond. Juvenile Justice supervision would help this young person with alcohol problems.

M: How can we explain to victims of violence that kids get a bond? This took place at 6.30 in the morning as he was going to work. It's outrageous. Why shouldn't he go to jail?

DL: It's his first time in contact with the criminal justice system.

M: So he gets a free punch?

DL: No Your Honor I'd say he would benefit from a section 3 undertaking with anger management as a condition.

M: How can an anger management issue be demonstrated by what happened at 6 in the morning?

DL: I'd say this had to be an extreme reaction. Obviously something was going on.

M: And the attack on the police I find incredible [ ] Have you apologised to the police?

D: No.

M: Why not? Why shouldn't you go to jail?

D: Dunno.

M: You dunno. You think you're a bit of a hero swearing at the police [ ]. Juvenile Justice recommends a bond since this is a first offence. My view is that a violent first offence merits a custodial sentence. As a second option I am prepared to look at probation supervision [The magistrate adjourned the decision.]

Some care is needed in interpreting this hearing, since it may be that the tough language and the threat of detention is a communicative style designed to "reach" young people, rather than indicating that the courts in New South Wales routinely sentence first offenders to detention for assaulting someone in the street. Nevertheless, one can see that the stakes are higher than in Victoria. The magistrate was "prepared to look at probation supervision" but disagreed strongly with the recommendation of a Juvenile Justice worker that he should receive a bond.

These cases suggest, perhaps not conclusively since every case is different,[6] but persuasively, that Victorian magistrates employ a more lenient or tolerant approach in sentencing to magistrates in Tasmania and New South Wales. Even on the basis of considering a few hearings, it seems possible to say that the statistical variation in detention rates is not simply a mirage, caused by differences in the crime rate.

Differences Between Regions

One objection one can make to statistics, purportedly showing some difference between two populations, is that internal variations may be more significant even though these are concealed in the global figures. In the case of juvenile justice in Australia, one difference which may be relevant is where the hearing takes place. There may be significant differences in sentencing practices between regions. I only have anecdotal evidence, admittedly from knowledgeable sources, to support this view. There is also the problem that, even if statistics were available, they cannot demonstrate either toughness or leniency in sentencing. The magistrates in the two country courts visited told me that, in their region, there were particular social problems resulting in high levels of crime. Even if one could demonstrate that a greater proportion of young people were sentenced to detention, this might reflect the nature of offending in that area rather than greater punitiveness. Nevertheless, it seems appropriate to make some preliminary observations about possible differences in sentencing between metropolitan, country and suburban courts, and also the significance of the Indigenous issue in children's courts.

Metropolitan and country courts

When arranging fieldwork visits, it was immediately clear that there was a distinction between metropolitan and country courts, and also in Victoria and New South Wales between central and suburban courts in metropolitan areas. The central courts were distinctive because magistrates only heard children's court matters. By contrast, cases relating to children in the numerous suburban courts were heard in special sessions by general magistrates. They mostly dealt with adult cases, but when dealing with children followed the principles set down in the relevant legislation. In

Tasmania, the metropolitan courts in Hobart and Launceston were similar to suburban courts in the larger states.

No practitioner suggested that the country courts visited during my fieldwork were tougher than metropolitan courts, for example by sentencing a greater proportion of young offenders to detention. Interviewees in New South Wales believed that some country courts were tougher when sentencing. One informant suggested, however, that any unfairness towards defendants resulted from the police asking for unrealistic bail conditions. Magistrates in country areas tended to accept these recommendations. This resulted in more breaches of bail, and consequently a larger proportion of young offenders remanded to detention centers. One might also expect some differences in attitude or motivation between general magistrates and those who had chosen to specialise in children's cases. No one commented on these differences during my visits to courts: nevertheless this seems worthy of further study.

The Indigenous issue

There was a large Indigenous population in the country courts visited in Victoria and New South Wales.[7] Moreover, it was noticeable in hearings that most defendants were from these communities. The remarkable and, by international standards, disturbing extent to which Indigenous young people are over-represented in detention centers across Australia (Richards and Lyneham 2010), has resulted in initiatives such as the Koori Court in Victoria that are intended to reduce recidivism. Despite receiving much attention from criminologists and others, it remains unclear what causes the over-representation. Is it because these young people commit more crime, or are they targeted by police, and treated unfairly by the courts?[8]

The appeal against sentence described in chapter 7 indicates what might be viewed as procedural unfairness, or perhaps that justice is done differently in country areas.[9] Perhaps the magistrate was too ready to make a finding of guilt without giving the defendant an opportunity to contest the case, since this triggered a suspended sentence of detention. It does indicate that courts in a large state with a sizeable Indigenous population, such as New South Wales, have particular problems: because they belong to extended families dispersed across large distances, some defendants cannot easily be located, or brought to court by police.

Differences Within Courts

Statistical evidence only demonstrates patterns within large populations, in this case sentencing across states. However, it was soon apparent from visiting courts that there were significant differences between individual magistrates. In this section, I will consider the evidence from my fieldwork for "hard" and "soft" magistrates. I will also report some findings on different communicative styles.

"Hard" and "soft" magistrates

When describing their work magistrates tended to compare themselves to colleagues who adopted a tough or lenient approach to sentencing. The following comment gives an example:

> One colleague got appealed a lot, once to the Supreme Court for being wrong in law. He was unrepentant and is now the magistrate in a local court where he hands out absurdly lenient penalties.

As in other jurisdictions, this made it possible for advocates to predict some outcomes (see, for example, Mann 1985, Travers 1997a, Scheffer 2010). To give an example, a lawyer observed in Victoria told a client that "we have a nice magistrate today." On another occasion, I was told that it was fortunate that a particular magistrate was on vacation when the defendant breached bail:

> If Mr. X had heard this application, he would have slotted[10] my client. Mrs. Y is a fair magistrate and I was pleased that she granted bail.

In Tasmania, given the small number of offenders, decisions by a single magistrate can influence the overall detention rate in any year. In the larger states, sentencing variation could probably be represented by what statisticians call a bell curve: most magistrates employ a similar approach, although there are also those who are unusually "hard" or "soft" by the standards of that court. The Victorian magistrate in the arson case described earlier in this chapter was described as "a soft magistrate" who normally gave repeat offenders a warning and a second or third chance.

Communicative styles

Another consideration that arises when considering global statistics is whether they tell us everything important about sentencing. It should already be apparent, from the transcripts presented in this book, that there are a wide variety of communicative styles. Some magistrates employed techniques influenced by therapeutic jurisprudence.   In drugs courts in the USA, judges encourage defendants to talk about their lives, and their progress towards goals, with a therapeutic intent (Burns and Peyrot 2003). There was normally no opportunity for a magistrate hearing guilty pleas in a children's court to establish a personal relationship with defendants, mainly because there was only limited time available to hear each case. Even so, it was possible to employ different communicative styles.

In one court, a magistrate greeted each defendant by his or her first name at the start of the hearing. By contrast, a colleague referred to defendants in the third person ("Master X" or "Miss Y") and did not look at the defendant until starting his sentencing remarks. Some magistrates attempted to engage with defendants, and explain the law, through asking questions in the manner of an informal tutorial.   Others only asked questions when they wanted information. Although I was not able to interview every magistrate, one would expect that they could justify these approaches to managing hearings. The magistrate in hearing 9C told me that he was deliberately trying to bring the defendant and his mother to tears by adopting an abrupt manner: "All I'd say is that it is necessary to be hard to them. It is difficult to get through otherwise. They just don't listen." Some magistrates probably believe that courts should be formal and forbidding places. Others believe that justice should be administered informally in a children's court.

It would be interesting to know whether there was a relationship between communicative style and how magistrates made sentencing decisions. My own impression is that whether a magistrate spoke directly to defendants, or only through their lawyers, had no bearing on the sentencing decision. As already reported, one magistrate justified a tough manner as a means of getting through to defendants: as showing that he cared in the manner of a parent. Nor should it be assumed that, from the perspective of young people, therapeutic justice was seen as preferable to someone making a decision without asking a lot of questions. The magistrate in Victoria known for leniency was not simply characterized as "nice" by the Legal Aid lawyer, but as "nice but you will also find him slow." Later that morning, I observed another lawyer telling his client the name of the magistrate. The young person asked, "Is that the slow one?" This nicely illustrates that young people may see courts in a different way to the sociological analyst concerned with justice and fairness.

The Concept of Court Culture

Even though there may be differences in sentencing practices between regions and individual magistrates, it makes sense to focus on what can be shown from the statistics collected at a state level. It is striking that magistrates in Victoria send considerably fewer young people to detention centers. In 2008, the rates of sentenced young persons per 100,000 population in detention centers were 50.1 in New South Wales, 47.6 in Tasmania and 14.3 in Victoria (Richards and Lyneham 2010). The research reported in this chapter, based on examining similar cases, suggests that there is greater leniency in Victoria. How can one explain these differences?

This section will review the approach commonly used in comparative studies conducted in the USA that explain variation in terms of different court cultures. These are conceptualized in terms of differences in legislation, and informal policies resulting from shared values within a court. This concept offers an useful way of thinking about the distinctiveness of Victoria. In this state, the continuous period of Labour government between 1982 and 2010 seems to have been important in fostering or promoting these values, and investing in welfare services. There are a wide variety of rehabilitative programs that give magistrates more sentencing options.

Explaining statistical variation

Although sentencing research is mostly based on finding relationships between quantitative variables, some researchers have employed qualitative methods to explain statistical variation in outcomes. These include David Nelken (2002, 2010) who has written about the cultural and institutional differences between Italy and England, and uses these to explain why apparently few young people in Italy are placed in detention centers. The best known contribution was Eisenstein et al's (1988) well-funded comparative study of several American criminal courts examining the contextual factors that influenced sentencing. These included the nature of the state criminal code, the attitudes of practitioners, the scheduling arrangements between higher and lower courts, the type of plea-bargaining system employed, and the political values dominant within a court community.

A similar mixed methods approach was employed by Jeffrey Ulmer (1997) in studying four courts in Pennsylvania. The objective was to explain "departures" from the Federal sentencing guidelines that have attempted to introduce greater uniformity into sentencing. Ulmer shows that, despite the guidelines, there were considerable differences between courts both in the likelihood of being imprisoned, and also the average length of imprisonment. He explains this through drawing on interviews with practitioners that show, for example, that there is "interdistrict variation in the role of defendant acceptance of responsibility" (Ulmer 1997, p.271). In other words, the guidelines left judges discretion in taking into account mitigating factors, and this resulted in fewer defendants being imprisoned for particular offences in some courts.

The central concept in each of these studies was "court culture." This is usually defined in terms of the informal policies pursued by the court, which are underpinned by values shared by practitioners in a court, or at least influential judges or decision-makers. Eisenstein et al (1988) were also interested in whether the political climate in a county, as measured by voting behavior, might influence courts, but concluded that courts were largely insulated from mainstream politics. There is a certain vagueness in the literature as to how informal policies arise and are maintained. In the case of plea-bargaining, one might imagine that they arise as organizational solutions to high case loads, rather than through a conscious political decision. In the case of sentencing, it is not clear how a "get tough" policy works, and the extent to which the president of a court can influence other judges. Nevertheless, the concept makes it possible to identify legislation, policies and values in Victoria that explain the low juvenile detention rate.[11]

Legislation, informal policies and values

Although there are minor differences, the legislation on youth justice in these Australian states seems broadly similar.[12] The only significant difference appears to be the power used by magistrates in Victoria to defer sentences. This makes it possible to place offenders under what is effectively a supervision order, or on rehabilitative programs, even though they may eventually only receive a good behaviour bond. Magistrates were not, however, required to use this power under the legislation. What seemed striking during my fieldwork observations was that it was regularly used, and not simply for minor offences. It was possible for a young person to commit a few offences while on a deferral order, without acquiring a criminal record. To put this differently, repeat offending in all states led eventually to detention. The deferral order delayed this process in Victoria through showing greater tolerance towards repeat offending.

Another distinctive feature of children's courts in this state were the procedures employed in diversion. In New South Wales and Tasmania, many young people who committed minor or first offences, and pleaded guilty, were sent to conferences. According to their proponents, conferences are often more emotionally demanding on offenders than attending court hearings. The objective is to cause young offenders to feel shame for having committed an offence, before reintegrating them in the community. By contrast in Victoria, first time offenders attended court, but were offered the opportunity of going on what was known as the Ropes program (see chapter 5). This meant that children's court hearings had a lighter, more informal character to those in Tasmania and New South Wales that only heard more serious cases. Young offenders were told that they would be getting "Ropes," and that they would find this an enjoyable experience:

You should enjoy it. I've not done it but lots of magistrates have. Not that that's important.

You've all been assessed for the Ropes program. What you've done is a serious thing. You want to own cars. It is a terrible thing to find your car is smashed in – it was a write-off apparently. You are all apprentices. It seems you acted out of character. You are a bit old for Ropes but you can still enjoy it. It might help you to talk to the police. Maybe you can mature a bit as well. You won't get another opportunity.

Even without observing hearings in every court, it was clear that most magistrates in this court used the power to defer sentencing, and agreed to "Ropes" applications. This indicates that there was a court culture, in the sense of a set of practices that newcomers learnt, which reflects a tolerant or lenient approach to youth offending. These values were taken for granted in the sense that magistrates did not see themselves as doing anything worthy of comment. They were, however, on public display in an exhibition in the foyer of the central children's court. This celebrated the fact that Victoria had achieved the lowest level of juvenile detentions in Australia. The progressive initiatives pursued by the children's court, such as the Koori Court, were supported by Rob Hulls, a progressive Attorney-General who had been a left-wing lawyer. During my fieldwork, he was canvassing the idea of establishing a teen court in which young people were sentenced by peers, under adult supervision, as happens in some American states (Green and Weber 2008).[13]

Programs and resources

One question that cannot easily be answered, but is perhaps crucial for understanding differences between detention rates, is whether there are other factors at work in addition to sentencing practices, or which influence sentencing in unknown ways. One possible factor is the amount of resources available to the agencies that work with young people. This might go some way to explaining the difference between regions. I was told, for example, that there was a ratio of 1:20 between case workers and clients in a rural area of New South Wales, while this was 1:6 in central Sydney. Practitioners in the north of Tasmania complained that they did not have a detoxification program for drug users, even in the detention centre. It is possible that the quality of contact, and type of interventions available, might reduce the recidivism rate in metropolitan areas. This does not, however, explain the lower overall detention rate in Victoria as against New South Wales since most youth crime is committed in metropolitan areas.

Aaron Kupchik (2006), writing about American children's courts, notes that a variety of programs allows judges to try out different options, and so delays sending young offenders to detention. In Victoria, a variety of programs was offered by Youth Justice, the police or voluntary groups. These included the Clean Slate program for drugs and alcohol abuse, and Hand Brake Turn, a program for young people who had committed driving offences. In one hearing, a defendant from a Torres Strait Islander background had been charged with an offence of violence: she had lost her temper and broken the jaw of someone at her school. The magistrate felt that this was too serious for a good behaviour bond, and was considering probation. However, two workers from a charity were attending court, seeking suitable candidates for a new program called One Ocean. This involved attending 12 sessions at weekends to play rugby, with the aim of teaching violent offenders to channel their aggression. A defense lawyer told me later that this was potentially more difficult for the young person than probation, and there was a risk of breaching the order. Nevertheless, this shows how the availability of the order made possible a lower sentence.

Comparison as a Political Issue

One reason why some agencies approached in this study were wary about the comparative side to this project is because it enables one to evaluate how well institutions are performing. In Australia, this is a particularly sensitive issue, since the states are independent: there is no national program of evaluation, for example, about the time taken in listing cases, or the standard of hearing rooms and other facilities, as happened until recently in Britain through Her Majesty's Inspectorate of Courts Administration (HMICA).[14] It should also be remembered that, in most countries, governments remain at arms length from the judicial process, and respect judicial independence. This raises two political questions in relation to children's courts. The first is how different pressure groups want sentencing to change. The second is whether greater accountability through monitoring and evaluation is desirable.

Changing sentencing practices

The sociology of sentencing, at least in recent years, has been concerned with attempts by political parties seeking to obtain votes, and pressure groups representing victims, to influence how judges make decisions (Tata and Hutton 2002). As economic inequality has increased in developed countries, there has also been greater concern about rising levels of crime. In this political climate, judges are often seen as "soft" on criminals. It has been claimed either that they are reluctant to send offenders to prison, or that sentences are misleading since it is possible to obtain parole.

There have been some legislative attempts in Australia, particularly in West Australia and the Northern Territory during the 1990s, to require children's courts to send more young people to detention centers. The objectives behind the 2008 amendment to the 1978 Bail Act in New South Wales seem similar, and have resulted in a significant rise in youth detentions. However, for the most part there has been limited political interference in sentencing, and indeed tacit support for what is effectively a liberal agenda concerned with reducing detentions, and improving welfare services. Within this consensus, the loudest voices at least within policy making circles belong to pressure groups who would like fewer young people detained than happens at present, and a greater emphasis on welfare.

One issue particularly relevant to the liberal or welfare agenda, is whether country courts are offering either a different level of service or making tougher decisions. As we have seen, there is no hard, statistical evidence for either charge. However, I met some practitioners who believed this. It is also easy to see how having fewer welfare programs or resources for case workers can impact on sentencing. In the first place, it can lead to young people going on the run, because there are no accommodation options if they leave home. In the second place, a lack of programs gives magistrates fewer options. In some cases, the detention centre becomes the only means of accessing welfare programs, including education.

Is more accountability desirable?

Those advocating greater tolerance or leniency in sentencing practices do not usually specify how they would achieve change. One possible mechanism would be legislative reform. However, the existing legislation already states that detention should be used as a last resort. Another measure would be to take greater care to recruit magistrates with liberal values. It is easy to see how this might result in a community backlash, especially in country courts. On the other hand, it should be remembered that the gradual reduction of detention rates in many states was made possible partly through new magistrates being appointed after retirements.

A third idea would be that courts need stronger political leadership. This has already happened in Victoria and New South Wales through appointing judges as presidents of the children's courts. The difficulty for the critic is that any president will never tell magistrates how to decide cases. Judicial officers are allowed to exercise considerable discretion when sentencing, even after Legal Aid lawyers complain about arbitrary or unfair decisions.

This leads into a fourth proposal that is sometimes canvassed. This is that the court should become more accountable to the community through greater monitoring and evaluation. Without comparing individual magistrates, the publication of some basic statistics about regions, along with an independent assessment of the resources available to case workers, would make possible political argument and debate. Going down this route politicizes the work of magistrates and may have the unintended consequence of a tougher sentencing policy, given the influence of the law and order lobby.[15] There would, therefore, seem to be no simple solutions to changing sentencing practices.

Even though they belong to court cultures, magistrates normally work alone, without having much contact with colleagues. This happens in country towns, but also in larger courts:

> It's not a hard and fast rule about how you deal with particular defendants. I can't speak for other magistrates. We are independent by definition.

> I don't know if magistrates have different styles. I have no

time to listen to the recordings of hearings.

I wouldn't know anything about different approaches.

These comments also indicate that magistrates take pride in their independence. They may regularly consult with colleagues, attend training meetings and keep up with developments in their field. Like all professionals getting through a large volume of daily case work (Lipsky 1988), they have no time to reflect on what might be happening in different courts, or on how immediate colleagues handle cases.[16] However, they do not see this as a problem: they do not need to consult to make good decisions.

This should not be especially surprising, since many types of professional work involve working alone, and exercising individual judgment. One does not have to go far to find examples: university teachers rarely consult colleagues when designing courses, or marking assessments. There are perhaps even fewer institutional constraints in magistrates courts other than being appealed, although there may be informal, community pressures in some country towns. It is, therefore, possible to exaggerate the strength and cohesiveness of court culture, or the extent to which one can promote change in country courts through educational programs. Nevertheless, it also makes sense to see court communities, if not as especially dynamic or progressive institutions, but as gradually evolving, often in a liberal direction as new magistrates are appointed. The challenge for legislators and court administrators is to promote change while respecting the important principle of judicial independence.

10.

Implications and Recommendations

This book has described the work of practitioners concerned with sentencing young offenders in Tasmania, Victoria and New South Wales, three states on the Eastern Seaboard of Australia. Chapter 4 looked at the professional perspectives of magistrates, defense lawyers, prosecutors and juvenile case workers and how they work collaboratively in sentencing hearings. Other chapters have examined how the courts respond to particular types of defendants. Chapter 5 looked at the response to minor offenders who often receive the penalty of giving an undertaking to stay out of trouble. Chapter 6 looked at how the courts respond to repeat and serious offenders. Some of these are sent to detention centers, but most receive the sentences of probation and in some states community service. Chapter 7 looked at the challenges posed by vulnerable defendants where welfare considerations outweigh the need to punish. Chapter 8 looked at some of the practical issues involved in bail decisions and contested cases. Chapter 9 looked comparatively at sentencing in the three states, and attempted to demonstrate through using qualitative methods that there really is a more lenient approach in Victoria, while leaving open the question as to whether regional differences may be equally important.

The collection, analysis and presentation of data has been influenced by interpretivism, the position in the philosophy of social science that rejects natural science as a model for the social sciences, and instead requires us to address the meaningful character of human group life (Schutz 1962, Weber 1978, Winch 1988). My own work as an interpretive ethnographer has been influenced by the Chicago School tradition of carefully documenting institutional activities and different occupational perspectives drawing on what anyone could report if they spent time observing hearings (Blumer 1969, Bulmer 1984, Fine 1995). I have also drawn on ethnomethodology, a research tradition often associated with interpretivism, even though it rejects the idea that we are constantly engaged in interpretation as misleading (Cicourel 1968, Garfinkel 1997).[1] Ethnomethodologists and conversation analysts have conducted ethnographic and discourse analytic research that makes visible the practical character of work, often neglected in policy and academic literatures. This concluding chapter will discuss some of the theoretical implications of interpretivism for understanding juvenile justice, and conducting comparative research about criminal justice institutions. It will also make some recommendations for this area of criminal justice policy in Australia, and internationally.

Understanding Juvenile Justice

This study can be read as a description of the work of practitioners in children's courts, without the reader needing to know much about theoretical debate in criminology or the social sciences. It shows some of what happens, and depending on your political views, you can use the materials to support an argument about youth justice policy. I will be doing this myself at the end of this chapter. But, if you are a criminologist, or criminology student, you may be looking for more than this. You will know that there are different theoretical traditions in researching crime, such as strain theory, the labeling tradition, Marxism, control theory among others. Undergraduate courses on criminological theory show how each results in a different understanding of criminal behavior and the criminal justice system. What is often given less emphasis is the way each criminological tradition has a different conception of science: of how research data should be collected, and what counts as good knowledge.

From the perspective of criminologists with an interest in developing explanatory theories, whether informed by consensus or conflict assumptions, the description of sentencing in this study may seem seriously deficient. It deliberately stays on the surface of social life, addressing what matters to people in their practical activities, rather than claiming to reveal hidden forces that shape our actions.[2] Unfortunately, because it is both an applied and inter-disciplinary subject, there has perhaps been less recognition of the distinction between different scientific agendas in criminology than has happened in other areas of social science. It is unusual for criminologists to debate or discuss methodological issues, even though much of criminological theory draws heavily on sociological perspectives and methodologies.   The problem does not, however, just lie in criminology. There are also fewer passionate advocates for different methodologies these days across social science. In fact, if like me you like methodological argument, you will find more passion in criminology than many fields of research, especially from advocates for the quantitative tradition (for example, Sherman et al 1999, Wiles 2002).

The problem is that the conversation in recent years has become rather one-sided. For some years, the most influential approach in criminology was the critical tradition which, even when it tries to incorporate its methods and concepts, is fundamentally opposed to interpretivism. Today, the dominant theoretical approaches are, as during the 1950s, mainly derived from Durkheim in viewing crime as deviant behavior (for example, Farrington 2003). It is again assumed that, to make scientific progress, it is necessary to employ quantitative methods and statistical analysis.

Instead of a dialogue or debate between different viewpoints, each sharpening methodological standards in their respective fields, evaluation research and the experiment modeled on natural science seems to have become the dominant approach. There is no doubt that many valuable and methodologically rigorous studies have been conducted in this framework, not least those informed by varieties of strain and control theory in the USA, Britain and Australia (for example, Farrington 2003, France and Hommel 2007; see also Stewart et al 2011). But they do not offer the only way of approaching the study of crime or criminal justice. At any rate, it is worth contrasting the assumptions in these mainstream criminological theories, with the interpretive tradition which informs this study about professional work in children's courts. A sharp distinction can be made since interpretivists have no interest in constructing explanatory theories. They are instead interested in how practitioners such as magistrates or juvenile case workers understand their work, or young offenders understand their own lives.

Although it remains rather a specialist sub-field at the boundaries of anthropology, sociology, criminology and linguistics, this study forms part of the growing broader tradition of law in action research (for example, Maynard 1984, Matoesian 1993, Travers and Manzo 1997, Burns and Peyrot 2003, Conley and O'Barr 2005, Latour 2010, Scheffer 2010 and Dupret 2011). Although there is nothing new about conducting ethnographic or discourse analytic research about legal settings, law in action has developed considerably in recent years both in the number of studies conducted, and in greater contact between those doing this type of work in sociology of law, anthropology, socio-linguistics and criminology. It is also a theoretically diverse field that demonstrates that there are different ways of making sense of talk in legal settings, and that the ideas of different theorists, and the debates between them are relevant to law.[3]

No one committed to interpretivism as a philosophy of social science should have any illusions that publishing studies or arguments will transform the field of criminology. Those doing applied research are expected to produce clear cut findings leading to policy recommendations that improve the efficiency and effectiveness of public services. The problem for the interpretivist is that there are not usually clear cut findings, since any social setting contains different perspectives on what is happening. Instead, interpretive researchers have produced a large body of work demonstrating the value of investigating everyday understandings without irony (Garfinkel 1997). In investigating the criminal justice process, they have taken seriously the principle that research should be inductive or exploratory, as against seeking answers to narrowly framed questions or confirming pre-conceived assumptions.

Some of the best ethnographies by interactionists and ethnomethodologists, and traditions with similar assumptions in anthropology and sociolinguistics, have been absorbed or integrated into mainstream criminology. This is also true, to some extent, of the concepts and analytic tools developed by interpretivists. A good example is "labeling theory," discussed in chapter 3. This was informed both by symbolic interactionism and ethnomethodology during the 1960s, but has since been taken up and assimilated into approaches with quite different core assumptions. These include different varieties of critical theory that celebrate deviant perspectives (for example, Ferrell et al 2008), but also those that wish to reduce deviance through reintegrative shaming (Braithwaite 1989). One could see this as an example of cross-fertilization and theoretical development that enriches criminology, in the same way it has absorbed feminism and other critical intellectual movements. However, what the interpretivist really wants is for the ideas and objectives to be properly understood, and to be taught to students as one approach among many that can advance our understanding of criminal justice.

The objective of these theoretical traditions is not to say that there is anything wrong with having a moral or political view about any aspect of crime, or with using social scientific data to advance these views and connect with different audiences.   They simply seek to demonstrate that it is also possible to investigate the world carefully, and without taking sides. This results in a more detailed, and perhaps more satisfying understanding of the ordinary work of practitioners than is normally available from the mainstream academic and professional literatures. In the case of magistrates, it is possible to go beyond appreciating how lawyers work in a legal framework, to examining how they make decisions using common-sense knowledge and reasoning on a case by case basis.[4] This does not challenge or undermine the insights of jurists who pursue a formal or philosophically-driven interest in sentencing (for example, Ashworth and Von Hirsch 1998). It does, however, reveal the ordinary character of decision making in courts, which as Garfinkel (1984b) has argued relies on common-sense knowledge, in this case about youthfulness, but also numerous mitigating circumstances.

More generally, interpretivism is valuable in challenging the stereotypes that arise, and have some value, when debating political issues, but often prevent us from appreciating what actually happens inside human institutions. Understandably, juvenile justice raises political passions, and there is no agreement among politicians or members of the general public, about the causes of youth offending or how this can be reduced. There are many people who view the idea of punishing children by putting them in detention centers as morally indefensible, including some magistrates and case workers. Critical criminologists have gone further, and argued that the youth justice system is mainly designed to control working class youth (Wacquant 2009). From this perspective, it seems obvious that unemployment and social deprivation causes crime, and that welfare programs at best contain the problem. Another common argument is that criminal justice institutions contribute to systematic discrimination against women and ethnic groups (for example, Carrington and Pereira 2009). In this literature, there is sometimes an idealistic or romantic celebration of youth rebellion, as if this can substitute for the disappearance of an organized working class seeking structural changes in the distribution of income and wealth.

There are also people across society, including victims of crime, who believe that the courts and police are too soft on offenders. From this perspective, which informs the justice model, young people understand the consequences of their actions in the same way as adults, and should receive punishment from the justice system in addition to help from welfare agencies.[5] Criminology as an academic field often remains polarized between these two political positions although there is much common ground since, in practice, welfare and punishment measures are combined, and it is sometimes difficult to distinguish between them (Smith 2005, Muncie 2009).

Inevitably, professionals on each side of these debates see young offenders from an adult perspective. The administrative criminologist sees shoplifting or burglaries as criminal acts, arising from faulty socialization (for example, Farrington 2003), and requiring a response combining welfare and punishment. The critical criminologist (for example, Brown 2009), sees offenders as victims who should be protected from disadvantage and imprisonment by human rights legislation. Some will, no doubt, seek to explain the riots that took place in England during August 2011 as conscious or unconscious "resistance" against the capitalist economic system.[6] Although, this study did not interview young people, it will be apparent from the thoughtful account given by a case worker in chapter 6, that many young people in Australia do not understand offending in these ways. They neither accept that they have done anything wrong (this is why they keep offending), nor do they necessarily see themselves as victims. This interviewee suggested that for some young people going to a detention centre is seen as a "badge of honour".[7]

You could argue that adopting an appreciative stance towards deviance has no value to policy makers, social workers or those with a critical agenda. However, it is surely central to understanding children's courts as institutions. Having started this study with an instrumentalist view of law, I am now much more sympathetic to the views of legal pluralists (for example, Moore 1973), which fit well with the interpretive tradition. From this perspective, it makes more sense to see children's courts as a place where adults and children meet, often without understanding each other, rather than as institutions that transmit adult values through persuasion and the threat of incarceration.

Interpretivism and Comparison

One criticism of the ethnographic tradition is that it cannot lead to generalizable knowledge of the kind required if sociology is to become a proper science (Hughes and Sharrock 2007). Quantitative researchers have produced a cumulative set of findings about the influence of different variables on sentencing. They have also produced general theories about the relationship between law and society based on data collected in different countries. By contrast, the best one can hope for in qualitative research is a series of well-described case studies. These cannot easily be compared either because the local context differs, or because any two researchers investigating the same social setting may produce quite different findings for a variety of reasons.

One approach that has become common in criminal justice research has been to combine the approaches through employing mixed methods. Jeffrey Ulmer (1997), for example, collected statistical data about variations in sentencing, and then used interviews with practitioners to identify institutional processes that resulted in differences in outcomes. One difficulty with this procedure from an interpretive perspective is that it takes a step away from the practical concerns of practitioners and how *they* understand comparison.

Lawyers and magistrates in these Australian states did not have much interest in what was happening outside their own court, and still less in different countries.[8] Although sentencing involves making numerous comparisons between cases, there was no time to do this either systematically or explicitly.

Similarly, although magistrates knew that colleagues had different approaches, they were not concerned over how they compared. They were permitted within a collegial community to adopt an individualized approach, based on their own professional judgment. This does not prove that the generalizable knowledge produced by comparative research has no value, since it is possible that demonstrating the difference between Victoria and other Australian states may influence policy makers elsewhere, given the right political circumstances. It does, however, demonstrate that there are different ways of understanding comparison. There is no reason, from an interpretive perspective, to accept the assumptions, or use the same methods as quantitative researchers, or to accept that policies can easily be transferred between countries.

In some senses, juvenile justice provides few opportunities to explore the value of comparative ethnographic research, since there have only been a few studies, conducted in different decades. Perhaps what is most striking, if you compare the data in this study and also in Kupchik (2006), with older studies by Emerson (1969) but also by O'Connor and Sweetapple (1988), is the change in the way magistrates talk to young people. Some older magistrates told me that when they started the job, it was common for the "old guard" to shout at defendants. In my transcripts, it will be apparent that most magistrates are polite to defendants, to the extent of asking them if they would like to attend appointments with case workers, or agree to a sentence. These ethnographic studies document an important change in the way young people experience juvenile justice, without necessarily suggesting that the system has become less punitive.

Readers outside Australia, and perhaps especially practitioners, will be able to obtain useful insights from comparing the sentences made for particular offences in this case study with practices in their own countries. When presenting a paper to a conference in the USA, it quickly became clear that the way in which each of these Australian states responds to youth crime is considerably more lenient than in that country. There are, of course, all kinds of other differences, such as the fact that Australia has a publicly funded system of case workers, and in most states diverts young people to conferences. Statistical data also makes possible comparisons, but the qualitative case study is usually more effective in making people reflect on their own practices through seeing how different countries respond to youth crime.

There are other ways in which comparison can be interesting. Before moving to Australia, I had conducted a study about the system of immigration appeals tribunals in the United Kingdom (Travers 1999). The political purpose was to look critically at the institutional processes that produced an high refusal rate. This refusal rate was used by politicians to justify an harsh response to refugees. There was also a political debate about detaining a small proportion of asylum-seekers to deter new applicants (although children were not detained, as has happened in Australia for many years). For a two year period, I attended monthly demonstrations outside a detention centre in Oxford.   NGOs representing asylum seekers were concerned about the extraordinary backlog that had developed in processing applications and holding appeals. What seems interesting, by contrast, about the position of children is that no one is demonstrating outside youth detention centers in Australia or internationally. As a lawyer pointed out, this is because young people have far fewer resources or political influence than adults.

Policy Recommendations

A case study, even when conducted without a political intent, can remind us vividly of the injustices that take place in any institutional system, despite the best intentions of those working there or in senior management positions. Although this issue has not been emphasized, it should be apparent that young people are being incarcerated without good cause in these jurisdictions, often through the courts or practitioners having incomplete information (for example, about the mental state of the young person), and insufficient resources to process cases quickly. There is also the highly disturbing reality that some young people are passed between care homes, psychiatric facilities and detention centers, and the streets, in a process described by one magistrate as a "revolving door." This study has also made visible or reminds us about more deep-seated inequalities. Some are specific to Australia and other settler societies with Indigenous populations. Others, such as class divisions, persist in all developed countries, despite their affluence and the size of the welfare system.[9]

This discussion still remains at a general, academic level. What practically can be done to improve the position of young offenders in Australia or internationally? There has certainly been no shortage of media interest or attention to the problem in Australia. During the five years in which I have been researching the work of children's courts, juvenile justice has featured regularly in the news. There is always a steady stream of minor items about youth crime, hardly to the extent of qualifying as a moral panic (Cohen 2002), but suggesting that there is public concern about the issue.[10] The example at the start of this book illustrates how a newspaper in Tasmania picked up a short story about an 18 year old in Sydney committing a small act of vandalism. The paper was not expecting, and did not receive, an outraged reaction from readers because this young woman was sentenced to three months imprisonment. Perhaps, it is a reassuring story for adults, since it shows that young people are brought before the courts for damaging property, even to the extent of drawing a "30cm by 60cm" symbol on the wall of a cafe, and there is due process allowing an appeal that will be decided by legal professionals.

Then there are recurrent stories about the neglect and ill-treatment experienced by vulnerable young people in the juvenile justice system. During 2010 in Tasmania, there was a report of a teenager dying from meningitis in Ashley Youth Detention Centre (Brown 2010). Few details were given, and there was only an internal inquiry. It was reported that the mother of this young offender had told the detention centre about his condition, but there were not sufficient checks to identify that he had a life-threatening illness. In Victoria, detention has also been in the news. An inspection found insanitary conditions and was highly critical towards Youth Justice for having allowed standards of care to deteriorate (Brouwer 2010). In Sydney, there have been concerns about over-crowding, caused partly by a change to the Bail Act, and partly by the management practices of care homes (Clennell 2009). It has been reported that young people sleep in the corridors of detention centers since there are insufficient beds.   Similar reports regularly appear in newspapers across the developed world.

Although in the past there have been quite divergent political and policy views about juvenile justice, at present there is arguably a consensus. Reformers are not campaigning for great ideological changes, such as a return to the welfare model. They accept that any system should try to balance welfare and punishment considerations. Most government departments responsible for the agencies in the juvenile justice system would like fewer detentions of young children and would support any program that "works" in reducing youth crime.

There is, however, still plenty of scope for debate, and a need for empirical research, within this consensus. One issue raised by this book is that diversion, often portrayed as an highly successful policy, may be less effective than one might suppose. This is not an argument for abandoning the policy, but for investing more resources on young people who become persistent offenders. The case study also indicates that, in these Australian states, the quality of programs and the speed of the whole system depends on obtaining sufficient resources. Every country in the developed world is reducing its welfare services as a consequence of the Global Financial Crisis. It is, though, possible to arrive at smart solutions, such as the Ropes program in Victoria, and the way deferred sentences are employed to help young offenders quickly in that state.

More generally, this study indicates that there is still too much emphasis on control and punishment in juvenile justice systems. If you read Emerson (1969), and this study, it will be apparent that little fundamentally has changed despite numerous new initiatives and apparent changes in philosophy over the last forty years. No one could complain today that case workers and the social services are not prepared to exert themselves to help the delinquent, subject to the resources available. However, juvenile justice still acts as a sorting mechanism in which most young people are saved, but the most difficult young people, often from deprived backgrounds, are sent to detention.

One recommendation, that is easy to make as a social scientist, is for more monitoring and evaluation. Here there is a difficult issue of whether the discretion of the judiciary should be constrained, since proponents have usually wanted judges and magistrates to be more punitive (Tata and Hutton 2002). Any serious or sustained attempt to reduce the number of unsentenced detainees would require regular monitoring and evaluation, if only to maintain pressure on different agencies. On the other hand, if the cause of the problem is under-resourcing, monitoring and evaluation itself is of limited value. Greater managerial control may only create more paperwork and bureaucracy, in organizations that are already stretched, rather than achieving this policy objective.

To some extent the desire for research studies to produce "useful" findings misses the point, in the sense that one cannot know what is possible in any area of policy without understanding the nature of professional work. This study has been influenced by interpretivist sociologists, such as Blumer (1969), who believed that any piece of careful research, that described closely what happened in some area of social life, was potentially valuable in showing the choices available, and the practical issues that arise in pursuing policy objectives. It is possible to approach juvenile justice from different political perspectives, and also to take issue with my selection and interpretation of transcripts, interview material and other ethnographic data. In doing so, however, the reader is already entering into a discussion of professional and political issues, and joining a conversation about what should happen in children's courts.

Appendix 1:

A Youth Justice Statute

The work of the magistrates, and other practitioners, described in this study is informed and constituted by legislation on sentencing young offenders. The main statutes are the Youth Justice Act 1997 (Tasmania), the Children and Young Persons Act 1989 (Victoria) and the Young Offenders Act 1997 (New South Wales). There are many common features to the statutes, which can be explained by their emergence during a period of legislative reform in the 1990s across Australia introducing the justice model (Borowski and O'Connor 1997). The following extracts come from the 1997 Youth Justice Act in Tasmania.

4. Objectives of the Act are –

   (d) to ensure that a youth who has committed an offence is made aware of his or her rights and obligations under the law and of the consequences of contravening the law; and

   (e) to ensure that the youth who has committed an offence is given appropriate treatment, punishment and rehabilitation;

5. General principles of youth justice

   (1) The powers conferred by this Act are to be directed towards the objectives mentioned in section 4 with proper regard to the following principles:

   (a) that the youth is to be dealt with, either formally or

informally, in a way that encourages the youth to accept responsibility for his or her behaviour;

(b) that the youth is not to be treated more severely than an adult would be;

(c) that the community is to be protected from illegal behaviour;

(d) that the victim of the offence is to be given the opportunity to participate in the process of dealing with the youth as allowed by this Act [this refers to the powers to refer youths to a community conference];

(g) detaining a youth in custody should only be used as a last resort and should only be for as short a time as is necessary;

(h) punishment of a youth is to be designed so as to give him or her an opportunity to develop a sense of social responsibility and otherwise to develop in beneficial and socially acceptable ways.

47. Sentences and other orders that may be imposed

(1) If a youth is found guilty of an offence, the Court may do one or more of the following:

(a) dismiss the charge and impose no further sentence;

(b) dismiss the charge and reprimand the youth;

(c) dismiss the charge and require the youth to enter into an undertaking to be of good behaviour;

(d) release the youth and adjourn the proceedings on conditions;

(e) impose a fine;

(f) make a probation order;

(g) order that the youth perform community service;

(h) make a detention order;

(i) in the case of a family violence offence, make a rehabilitation program order.

(4) In determining what orders to make under [subsection 1], the Court must have regard to the circumstances of the case, including –

(a) the nature of the offence; and

(b) the youth's age and any sentences or sanctions previously imposed on the youth by any court or a community conference; and

(c) the impact the sentence will have on the youth's chances of rehabilitation generally or finding or retaining employment.

Appendix 2:

Summary of Data Collected

This study is based on describing how magistrates make decisions when sentencing young people. For this reason, any hearing observed in a children's court would provide good data, and those wanting to know how the cases have been selected, with possible concerns about representativeness or in the belief that more is better, are asking the wrong questions. The first part of this summary gives a rough idea of how many sentencing hearings were observed, and how many interviews were conducted with different professional groups. This has some uses when comparing court ethnographies, although it seems important to appreciate the different methods employed and objectives. Two examples illustrate what is possible, depending on time and resources. Aaron Kupchik (2006) observed 978 hearings in 18 months in a comparative study of how young people were sentenced in children's and adult courts, and conducted 15 interviews with practitioners. Eisenstein et al (1988) was a three year study by a large research team based in different universities. The researchers conducted 300 interviews with practitioners.

The summary also lists the sentencing hearings discussed in each chapter. These were selected because they seemed good examples of different considerations or types of defendants. This list does not include bail applications, trials, deferred orders, or hearings concerned with administrative matters. Those interested in conducting court observations will notice the relatively small number of sentencing hearings observed given the number of days spent visiting courts. In a relatively short period of fieldwork, it is also difficult to observe those hearings of defendants who appear in court infrequently. Very few cases in which young people were sent to detention were observed. Relatively few female defendants were observed. Only one case involved a very young defendant (the sexual assault case described in chapter 6). Most defendants observed received minor sentences, such as a good behaviour bond.

Summary of data collected in the three states

Stage 1, Tasmania: 15 days of fieldwork. 6 days conducted in Hobart, 3 days in Launceston, 3 days in Burnie and 3 days in Devonport. 44 sentencing hearings were observed. 15 interviews were conducted with practitioners, including defense lawyers, prosecutors, juvenile case workers and magistrates.

Stage 2, Victoria: 10 days of fieldwork. 4 days conducted in the Central Children's Court, 4 in metropolitan courts, 2 in a country court. 30 sentencing hearings were observed (half through shadowing Legal Aid). 5 interviews were conducted with practitioners.

Stage 3, New South Wales: 9 days of fieldwork. 3 conducted in the Central Children's Court, 4 in metropolitan courts, 2 in country courts. 20 sentencing hearings were observed. 5 interviews were conducted with practitioners.

Sentencing hearings discussed in this study by chapter

Code	Gender	Age	Type of offence	Sentence
5A	male	17	assault	fine
5B	female	16	assault	reprimand
5C	male	15	threatening behaviour	probation, conference
5D	female	16	driving offence, criminal damage	reprimand

Code	Gender	Age	Type of offence	Sentence
5E	male	16	driving offence	fine
5F	male	16	carrying can of liquor in public place	fine
5G	male	14	riding bicycle without a helmet	reprimand
5I	male	17	assault	fine
5J	male	16	refusing request of police to leave public place	fine
5K	male	16	theft	reprimand
5L	male	14	theft	reprimand
5M	male	13	theft	reprimand
5N	female	14	riding in stolen car	undertaking
5O	male	11	burglary and trespass	undertaking
6A	male	17	theft, motor vehicle stealing, breach of curfew	(pre-sentence hearing)
6B	male	16	being drunk, breach of deferred order after theft	probation
6C	female	17	being drunk, not obeying police, causing a nuisance	probation
6D	female	14	forging checks, breach of curfew	probation, community service
6E	male	17	burglaries, assaults, breaches of bail	detention, community service, probation

Code	Gender	Age	Type of offence	Sentence
6F	male	disguised	sexual assault	suspended detention, probation
7A	female	14	theft	reprimand
7B	female	17	assault	probation
7C	female	17	driving offence	fine, disqualification
7D	male	16	criminal damage	probation
7E	female	17	assault	undertaking
7F	male	17	assault	good behaviour bond
7G	male	15	assault	good behaviour bond
7H	male	17	assault	probation
7I	female	17	assault, criminal damage	detention
9A	male	15	arson	probation and community service
9B	male	15	assaults	probation

Notes

Chapter 1 - Introduction

1   This report appeared in *The Mercury*, the main daily newspaper for Southern Tasmania on 3rd February 2009, p.4. Although the newspaper gave the 18 year old defendant's actual name since there are no reporting restrictions in an adult court, and the actual name of the magistrate, these have been disguised.

2   By and large, young people accept these boundaries created by adults, which makes the occasional objections newsworthy. In 2009, a 14 year old Dutch girl wanted to sail round the world, but was prevented by a court order (Mail Foreign Service 2009). There were no objections to her competence, just that this was inappropriate behavior for her age.

3   There are few commentators today advocating the abolition of prisons in the same way as Mathiesen (1974), although see Davis (2005).

4   For a discussion of the international statistics on youth detentions, see Muncie and Goldson (2006).

5   Gregsons is a pseudonym.

6   These social processes are difficult to research, and only partly described in the "pathways" literature that seeks to identify causal factors (France and Homel 2002, Farrington 2003). It is intriguing to consider if there really are families, outside television dramas such as The Sopranos, in which the children pursue conventional careers, and may not even know that their parents are engaged in criminal activities.

7   See Pitts (2001).

8   One difference is that immigration appeals were always contested hearings, whereas most defendants coming before magistrates plead guilty. Another is that the result of appeals was communicated through a written determination whereas the magistrate sentences through verbal remarks during hearings.

9   If you look out of the window on a train ride through the suburbs of any large city, you will see tags covering the fences of houses for many kilometres, left by young people marking their territory.

10   This has, in fact, been the conclusion of many sociologists from different theoretical traditions who see crime as arising from deep-rooted social causes. One example is Cohen (1955) who argued that youth offending resulted both from inequality, but also because schools promoted social mobility (see also Merton 1938).

11   For more discussion on this methodological problem, see chapter 3.

12   For the population of the states and territories of Australia, see Australian Bureau of Statistics, September 2011 <www.abs.gov.au/ausstats/abs@.nsf/mf/3101.0>.

13   There was an administative change in 2010 so that a dedicated magistrate now hears children's matters in Hobart (see Sheehan and Borowski 2012).

14   The hearings from Tasmania discussed in this book are not identified by particular courts. It is not, therefore, possible to discover the identities of these single magistrates.

15   For discussion, see Freiberg and Ross (1999), chapter 10.

16   In Victoria, there is legislation that prevents the observer from revealing the identities of defendants in a children's court or the specific court in which the hearing takes place.

17   Spending a week in a country town allows you to meet practitioners, and get a feel for the nature of juvenile offending in that area. During my visit to Armidale, I travelled to an even smaller court in Tenterfield, and observed some juvenile matters.

18   The system of ethics review that governs university based social science research was introduced by the 1992 National Health and Medical Research Council Act. For the current regulations, see the National Statement on Ethical Conduct in Human Research (NHMRC 2007).

19   In requiring parental consent, ethics committees are denying young people the opportunity to express their views freely to a researcher.

20   There are large fields in qualitative research, particularly in North America, which do not need to defend their concerns against critics who see them as marginal or unscientific. Even so, they are islands in a sea of those committed to quantitative methods or structural theorising. American criminology, for example, is largely

quantitative. The methodological argument in this book is intended for those interested in a more intellectually diverse criminology that employs a wider range of methods, and engages with long standing debates in sociology (Banakar and Travers 2005).

21   This is partly because the identities of some courts had to be concealed to satisfy reporting requirements in legislation, but also in order to protect the anonymity of magistrates. All the practitioners and defendants have been given pseudonyms.

Chapter 2 - Welfare versus Punishment: A Continuing Debate

1   The five English speaking countries are England, Scotland, the USA, Canada and Australia. Although not a sovereign state, Scotland is normally recognised as a "country" within the United Kingdom, in the same way as England. Wales and Northern Ireland, which have devolved administrations, will not be considered in this review.

2   The reforms are often described as a move from a "welfare" to a "justice" model, although this rather conceals the extent to which punishment was seen as appropriate or even desirable in the new model (Lemert 1970).

3   Those promoting restorative justice have also argued that it is cost-effective in reducing crime, although it is difficult to demonstrate this conclusively from the available evidence. For a debate between a proponent and critic, see Cunneen and Hoyle (2010).

4   As is common in human rights instruments, the principles in the UN Convention on the Rights of the Child were deliberately left vague, not least on the age of criminal responsibility which varies between, and in the case of federal states, within countries. Many commentators, however, believe that there are clear international guidelines on specific issues. See, for example, Kilkelly (2008) on whether there should be closed or open hearings in Irish children's courts.

5   A full review of juvenile justice in the English speaking world should include Wales, Northern Ireland, Ireland, New Zealand and South Africa. Concerns about growing penalisation have been raised in some of these jurisdictions. See, for example, Kilkelly (2008) and Lynch (2008).

6   For two initial responses by sociologists, see Duarte (2011) and Furedi (2011).

7   These are called youth justice workers in Tasmania and Victoria, and juvenile justice workers or "JJs" in New South Wales.

8   One statistical point of interest about Australia is that the figure for the national detention rate is, apparently, higher than the detention rate in the USA (compare Richards and Lyneham 2010 and Sickmund 2010). Such comparative statistics are, however, of limited value given the different ways in which detentions and age groups are defined.

9   This could be understood as a contribution to the welfare-punishment debate, rather than having moved beyond this framework.

10 This study uses the professional fields of juvenile justice and child protection as a vehicle to explore the value of autopoesis theory, as developed by the German sociologist Niklas Luhmann, for understanding the relationship between law and society.

Chapter 3 - Why Observe Sentencing Hearings?

1   This may be because interviewees idealise or misrepresent their actions. It may also be because they simply cannot remember what is involved, for example, in professional training or work (Becker and Geer 1967).

2   Ethnography has a much weaker institutional base in Australia: a methods book to which I contributed (Walter 2009) aimed at undergraduates included ethnography in a chapter on "other methods".

3   There is also the fate of qualitative research becoming part of the criminological tool box in which no one appreciates the philosophical basis of methods. For an exception, see Jupp (1989).

4   Although I am arguing for the value of traditional qualitative research, there is something refreshing about these approaches provided they are not taken to extremes. Criminology has developed as a policy-oriented science, and at present hardly engages with the imaginative or empathetic abilities of students or practitioners.

5   There are traditions with similar assumptions in anthropology and sociolinguistics, for example, Geertz (1973), Spradley (1979) and Gumperz and Hymes (1972).

6   The following discussion of evaluation research is not intended as a blanket criticism of quantitative methods in social science, positivism as a philosophy of social science, or studies that employ mixed methods. It is, however, critical towards the commonly held view, in applied fields such as criminology, that quantitative methods are automatically more useful and valuable than qualitative research.

7   This showed that conferencing was more effective in preventing violent offences, but not property theft.

8   For all their commitment to scientific method, evaluations of diversion in Australia have never compared the offending careers of those given cautions with those attending conferences. Similarly, it is often said that conferences reduce recidivism rates. But no one acknowledges that conferencing is not used in Victoria, the state with the lowest detention rate. Whatever the merits of conferencing, this evaluative literature is not scientific in the Popperian sense of seeking to test a hypothesis by looking at counter-examples.

9   A good example is Philippe Bourgois' (1996) *In Search of Respect*, an ethnography based on living among drug dealers in Harlem.

10   See, for example, Blumer (1968), Cicourel (1968), Kitsuse and Cicourel (1963).

11   For more details and an assessment of this reforming agenda, see Fine (1995).

12   More recently, John Braithwaite (1989) has combined labeling theory with Durkheimian assumptions about the need for social order to arrive at the opposite recommendation: that young people should be shamed for their actions and reintegrated into the community. Matza (1964), by contrast, argued that we should think carefully before intervention.

13   Both structural functionalists and Marxists advanced this criticism. See Becker (1972), chapter 10.

14   For a review, see Hester and Eglin (1992).

15   For a review of the ethnographies influenced by Robert Park, see Bulmer (1984). Everett Hughes' (1971) essays on work provide inspiration for anyone with an interest in describing everyday occupational activities. As a sociologist, he was particularly sensitive towards differences in perspectives, such as between professionals and their clients.

16   Although I have described ethnomethodology as an interpretive tradition, this is potentially misleading. This is because this theoretical tradition recognises that most people do not constantly interpret or reflect on the world around them. See Sharrock and Anderson (1991).

17   For some examples, see Eisenstein et al (1988) and Heumann (1978).

18   See also Ulmer (1997). This symbolic interactionist study about the

sentencing of adults combines qualitative research on social worlds in several courts, with sophisticated quantitative analysis.

19 In good conditions, it is possible to make detailed, contemporaneous notes of courtroom exchanges (see Gubrium 1989). One methodological problem that arose in this study was that it did not always feel appropriate to take notes. There were occasions when I could only write up a summary after the hearing.

20 Another reason for this loss of confidence and certainty is the impact of postmodernism on critical theory. Although this turned out to be a short-lived intellectual movement, it has become difficult to defend any intellectual position as offering a true or scientific view of the world, or rely on what Lyotard (1984) termed the "grand narratives" of the past. For a critique of postmodernism from a symbolic interactionist perspective, see Prus (1996).

21 See Phillips (1998) and Conley and O'Barr (2005).

22 There have been some important changes since this study. Today, most young offenders in Australia are represented by Legal Aid lawyers. In addition, it would be unusual today (and possibly result in criticism within a bench) for a magistrate to shout at a defendant.

23 For an example of consultation with young people from Tasmania, see Department of Health and Human Services (2010).

24 For a partial exception, see Griffiths and Kandel (2005). These researchers interviewed young offenders about their experiences in Scottish children's hearings. They were surprised to find that many interviewees would prefer to represent themselves in court rather than through adult lawyers.

25 I am grateful to Mike Emmison for suggesting this phrase.

26 See Bulmer (1984) and Abbott (1999) on the first Chicago School.

27 This term acknowledges that this book is written in a different time and place but is influenced by this American tradition of qualitative research.

Chapter 4 - Professional Work in the Children's Court

1 The requirements for written consent forms, and parental approval, make this difficult for all but the most committed researchers who have time to make arrangements through agencies (see Barry 2006).

2 Rising numbers of child protection cases have since made it impossible to maintain this strict division.

3   For reviews, see Tata and Hutton (2002), McKenzie (2005) and Wandall (2008).

4   For discussion of the emotional demands on magistrates, see Roach Anleu and Mack (2005).

5   In New South Wales, children's magistrates had two days of specialist training each year.

6   Australian spelling is used for technical terms such as a "good behaviour bond" or proper names such as "New Labour." American spelling has been used for words that do not have a technical meaning, such as "behavior."

7   The threat of receiving a conviction was often made by magistrates. In most states, receiving a conviction meant that offenders had a criminal record into adult life. This meant that they might have to disclose this to an employer, and might be denied obtaining a passport. In practice, few magistrates gave convictions. They saw them as either punitive, or ineffective since employers did not understand their significance. One defence lawyer told me that none of his clients were likely to travel overseas. Potential employers did not check criminal records since a large proportion of young people they might employ were known to the children's court.

8   For sympathetic views of lawyers, see Travers (1997a) and Emmelman (2003).

9   Observing a relatively small number of hearings leaves open the possibility that one would see examples of adversarial relations or disagreements between practitioners over a longer period of time. Erving Goffman (1989) in advocating ethnography as a research method argues that a year of fieldwork is necessary to see variations of this kind.

10 The youth detention centre in Tasmania.

11 It should be noted that some young offenders, according to most interviewees about one third, were already receiving help and supervision from social workers under child protection orders. However, most do not receive supervision, or other assistance, until they are found guilty.

12 This was established through the efforts of an enthusiastic police officer who, by all accounts, was good at "reaching" young offenders. It was, however, only offered in the south of the island. A case worker told me that young people from the north were reluctant to spend a week away from home. This illustrates the difficulties in providing specialist services across the population, even in a small state.

13 For an interesting study about pre-sentence reports in England during the 1980s, see Brown (1991). This suggests that case workers, and also school teachers in their reports to case workers, used moralistic language when describing the failings of working class youth.

14 One case worker told me that intensive supervision involved meeting more than once a week: most offenders found this difficult, so the orders were often breached.

15 For some well-documented studies, see Strauss et al (1964), Garfinkel (1997) and Cicourel (1968).

16 The relationship between technical and lay knowledge has been a central theme in ethnomethodological studies about lawyers, but also about other areas of technical expertise such as science. Garfinkel's (1984b) paper on jurors suggests that 95% of their work in deciding cases involves using common-sense skills and knowledge (although what they take from the judges' instructions is also important).

17 In my university, these are currently NN (below 50), PP (50-60), CR (60-70), DN (70-80), HD (80+).

Chapter 5 - Responding to Minor Offences

1 Similar cases were observed in Victoria and New South Wales, but these are not considered in this chapter. In order to protect the anonymity of magistrates, the Tasmanian hearings discussed in this chapter, which were observed in four courts, are not identified by the court in which the hearings took place. For a summary of the data collected, see Appendix 2.

2 The aim is not to identify differences between magistrates or other statistical regularities such as variations in how male and female defendants were sentenced.   Nor is it intended to contrast the judgement of magistrates with possible "objective" measures of seriousness. Instead, this chapter seeks to explicate the practical reasoning (Garfinkel 1984b) that these magistrates employed, and anyone else would use, in seeing these as minor offences.

3 This is simply mentioned as an aside in the (1984) Carney Report which established the present juvenile justice system in Victoria. It may be that questions of resources, rather than values, explain these decisions: diversion was seen as expensive, given that youth crime was declining in this state.

4 In the hearings observed, it was employed as a form of diversion, rather than as a final sentence. If the conference went well, the

magistrate could dismiss the charge, or give a light penalty such as a good behaviour bond.

5   This is similar to the response to youth offending in England during the 1980s, which resulted in a considerable reduction of detention rates (Muncie 2009).

6   These included police officers, social workers, educationalists and health experts.

7   As Wolfgang (1958) demonstrated from police files, it is rare to find a charge of assault where the victim is a completely innocent bystander, although this is not a legitimate mitigating factor that judges can discuss when sentencing since it reopens the issue of guilt or innocence.

8   Many criminologists see adult crime as arising from "hegemonic masculinity" (for example, Brown 2005). It would appear from these cases that girls also respond to remarks about their boyfriends.

9   Although no statistical significance should be drawn, I observed a few cases in which a young woman had assaulted the police, saying this was to protect a friend from being attacked. One involved a 16 year old jumping on the back of an officer who was trying to restrain another youth. A rise of violence among young women internationally has been suggested by some criminologists (Carrington and Pereira 2009).

10 The complainant in these cases was often a single-mother or grandmother who hoped that appearing in court would "get through" to the child. The difficulty in imposing a restraining order, is that a breach could lead to imprisonment, without a criminal offence necessarily having been committed.

11 One can imagine the hypothetical situation in which a magistrate was influenced by factors not acknowledged in the sentencing remarks, such as the bad attitude displayed by a defendant in court. Magistrates may also have come across defendants before, or perhaps have become concerned about particular types of offences after publicity in a local area. I observed hearings in which all these factors *were* acknowledged in the remarks.

12 It is also possible for the reasons to be available to an audience (in this case practitioners in a court room) even if they are not explicitly stated: this is how a practitioner can see that a magistrate has made a good decision, or at least one that is understandable in relation to the facts presented in court.

13 All names of defendants and practitioners have been anonymised.

14 The following abbreviations are used throughout this study in transcripts for participants in hearings. M: Magistrate; D: Defendant; CC: Court Clerk; U: Usher; DL: Defence lawyer; P: Prosecutor; S: Security Guard; Mth: Defendant's mother; F: Defendant's father; W: Witness.

15 This is an example of how a magistrate (or anyone observing the hearing, or reading a report) uses the documentary method of interpretation: the particular of speeding is interpreted in the light of an underlying pattern of a responsible young man who has gone astray.

16 It would be interesting to know if the police would have preferred an heavier penalty. It seems likely that directions to wear helmets are disobeyed on a regular basis.

17 See Parsons (1954) and Evan (1962). Structural-functionalism was much criticised and marginalised within sociology and criminology between the 1960s and 1990s. Nevertheless, a great deal of policy-oriented research today is informed by similar assumptions.

18 When interviewing a police officer in Hobart, I was shown the internal forms that are not given either to Youth Justice or the children's court. These indicate how young offenders are known to the police: there are numerous warnings and cautions for minor offences such as shop stealing, causing a disturbance and criminal damage.

19 This is effectively an inducement to plead guilty, even though strictly speaking there is no finding of guilt from attending a conference.

20 For a close analysis of hearings in which defendants were encouraged to express remorse in Dutch criminal trials, see Komter (1998). For an analysis of the methods used by a murder suspect for blaming the victim, see Watson (1983).

Chapter 6 - Responding to Repeat and Serious Offences

1 No statistics are collected in Australia on the length of time spent by individuals in detention centres.

2 It is possible that they were available to the magistrate from the pre-sentence report.

3 Like other ethnographers, I am not claiming to produce complete or "objective" findings in the same way as quantitative forms of analysis based on measuring variables (for example, Hogarth 1971) or the close

analysis of tape-recorded courtroom discourse (for example, Atkinson and Drew 1979). Even so, the examples in this study document the considerations involved in sentencing young offenders that are not always recognised or analytically interesting to other studies.

4   The identities of all defendants and practitioners have been anonymised.

5   In some cases observed, defendants appeared nervous, or started crying and were comforted by either their lawyer or the case worker. However, for the most part defendants seemed relaxed and familiar with court procedures and their surroundings.

6   For details of abbreviations used in transcripts for participants, see note 14, chapter 5.

7   There is less emphasis on explaining the purpose of punishment in adult courts.

8   The magistrate later apologised for making a mistake about the defendant's age (she was 15 and had been 14 when she committed the offence), and also the correct amount of community service for this age group. The maximum was 70 hours.

9   When sentencing the co-defendant, the magistrate noted that she had a "slight smile" on her face, which indicated that she had yet to accept the seriousness of the offences.

10 In Tasmania, there were cases of a spree of offences committed by small groups of youths immediately after their release from Ashley Youth Detention centre, partly because they had nothing to do and no money.

11 Miss Green (a pseudonym) was the juvenile case worker.

12 There are some similarities with Goffman's (1961) account of psychiatric patients who had to demonstrate normality in abnormal circumstances. One difference is that many young people have often not acquired these social skills or feel the need to present false selves.

13 Some details are disguised.

14 By contrast, a personality change resulting from physical injuries was viewed more sympathetically (see chapter 7).

15 Although some critics of children's courts might wish to criticise the formality of the courtroom, it should be remembered that case workers, psychologists and defense lawyers, in addition to his parents, had already discussed the offence with him in ordinary surroundings.

16 This is also the conclusion of academic studies on "desistance" (see France and Homel 2007).

17 For discussion of this phenomenon in Tasmania, see Goodwin (2008). There is the Lombrosian implication in such studies that criminality is inherited. Sociologists such as Becker (1972) might argue that these criminal subcultures have developed through a process of labeling, and that the families are also targeted by the police.

18 This has also happened with Anti-Social Behaviour Orders in the UK (Ashworth 2004).

Chapter 7 - The Vulnerable Offender

1 For a study that describes professional work in care proceedings in Victoria, see Sheehan (2001).

2 There was no suggestion that anyone had behaved unprofessionally. The social services, like the police, are permitted and required to use force within their own professional mandates, in this case to protect a child who was at risk.

3 There was an hint during this hearing of a possibly different version of events in that a family friend had supplied a reference that sided with the pupil.

4 During the study, I had the opportunity to meet the humanistic psychologist who ran the clinic attached to the central children's court in Melbourne. She told me that, even though there was a body of scientific knowledge on personality disorders, what mattered was being able to respond to clients with kindness and compassion.

5 Mr. Rogers is a pseudonym for the juvenile case worker.

6 For the text of this apology, see *The Australian* (2008) <http://www. theaustralian.com.au/in-depth/aboriginal-australia/apology-to-the-stolen-generations/story-e6frgd9f-111115535578>.

7 Australia is regularly criticised by the United Nations for not achieving some degree of integration and economic development of its Indigenous peoples within a political settlement in the same way as the USA or Canada (for example, Metherell 2010). For accounts of these social processes, see Cunneen (2001), Blagg (2008) and Eades (2008).

8 You can obtain a sense at such events of the actual and symbolic importance of upgrading public buildings in a country town.

9   Gough Whitlam was Prime Minister in a progressive Labour government from 1972-5.

10 One interviewee did, however, suggest that "too many young Aboriginals are put in custody for minor offences," such as shop-lifting, in country towns.

Chapter 8 - Bureaucratic Work or Due Process?

1   See Banakar and Travers (2005), chapter 2.

2   From an ethnomethodological perspective, this does not have to be viewed as a problem. The decisions made by a magistrate are visibly legal, in the sense of having state support, simply because this work takes place under the coat of arms of the Australian Commonwealth (see Dupret 2007).

3   Most judicial officers in the lower courts during the late 1960s were male. Today, there are many women doing this work, but perhaps of equal significance is a change in emphasis so magistrates are more concerned with helping defendants, in addition to administering justice. For discussion, see Roach Anleu and Mack (2005).

4   Blumberg (1969) alleged that adversarial relations were a sham put on to assist the defence lawyer obtain a fee from privately paying clients.

5   If this defendant had pleaded guilty, he would have been cautioned, and not received a criminal record. A police officer told me later that the defendant had made an admission when arrested . However, when his parents arrived at the police station with a lawyer, he denied any involvement. In these circumstances, the police were not prepared to drop the case, even though he was only charged with shop-lifting.

6   This illustrates how social class can affect outcomes. See Cicourel (1968) for examples of cases where the police were persuaded by intervention by parents and lawyers.

7   This gives a glimpse of the discussions that take place within a court, and the role of professional leadership. For accounts of responses by judicial officers to new legislation, see Paterson (1983), Travers (1999) and Latour (2010).

8   Justices of the Peace are judicial officers with more limited powers than magistrates.

Chapter 9 - Comparing Courts

1   Diversion is normally attributed with having reduced the detention

rate across Australia in the last 20 years (see Richards and Lyneham 2010).

2   See Muncie (2006).

3   There is only a small Indigenous population in Tasmania, making it difficult to calculate a statistically meaningful rate. It should be noted that New South Wales only had the second highest rate of Indigenous detentions: the rate in Western Australia was almost double at 794 per 100,000 according to these statistics.

4   This is, however, one way in which governments have tried to restrict judicical discretion (Tata and Hutton 2002).

5   Nevertheless, in the hearings observed for middle-range offences, there were differences in how magistrates used the sentencing option of community service.   Young offenders in Tasmania were usually asked to do longer periods of community service than in New South Wales. In Victoria, it was striking that community service was only used when sentencing serious offenders, and even then rarely used.

6   The Sudanese youth in the hearing summarised in chapter 7 (case 7F) received a more lenient sentence for an assault. This may have been provoked by a racist remark.

7   The court in Victoria cannot be identified due to reporting restrictions. The court in New South Wales was in Armidale.

8   For discussion, see Cunneen (2001).

9   I did not observe the hearing which took place the week before my visit, but read the pre-sentence report.

10   This term was used by this Legal Aid lawyer as a light-hearted way of describing imprisonment. It becomes possible because many young offenders understand the juvenile justice system in a similar way: almost like a game.

11   For discussion of the differences between Victoria and New South Wales in sentencing adults, see Freiberg and Ross (1999).

12   See the Youth Justice Act 1997 (Tasmania), the Children and Young Persons Act 1989 (Victoria) and the Young Offenders Act 1997 (New South Wales).

13   On 27 November 2010, the Labour government was defeated in the state election by the Liberal/National Coalition which has tougher policies on law and order. Practitioners told me that, while this would not mean a change in policy towards youth crime, the teen court would probably not be funded.

14 Most of its work was taken over by other agencies in 2009, following the recommendations of the Hampton report (2005) on streamlining inspections.

15 In the USA, many judges are elected which is a more direct form of accountability (Aarons et al 2009).

16 As one might expect, practitioners in children's courts also have little interest in how things are done in other states, or other countries.

Chapter 10 - Implications and Recommendations

1 For discussion of these distinctions within interpretivism, see Travers (2004).

2 See the discussion of power and doing justice to children in chapter 3.

3 Unfortunately, because it is theoretically diverse, and requires understanding a number of disciplines, law in action is difficult to teach. What often happens is that the student is introduced to one tradition (for example, conversation analysis or critical theory), and there is little opportunity to consider debates between researchers with different assumptions and objectives.

4 The transcripts of sentencing remarks demonstrate how each decision responded to a particular set of circumstances, in addition to arising from the approach developed by a particular magistrate. The aim of ethnomethodological research is to address professional work, which is often only understood or described by sociologists in general terms such as "labeling," at this level of detail.

5 The assumption that young people should accept responsibility for their actions, and compensate victims, is also central to restorative conferences.

6 News reports about the English riots suggest that resentment built up in deprived areas about the conduct of the police. Some rioters had never been in trouble before, and came from middle class backgrounds, which might suggest that there is a complex relationship between riots and ordinary youth crime.

7 On one occasion while travelling on a train in Victoria, I happened to overhear a youth reporting at some length by mobile phone to a friend his experiences in a detention centre. He clearly felt no need to conceal this from the other passengers.

8 For discussion, see Travers (2008).

9   One issue that has not been considered explicitly in this study is the differential treatment of female young offenders (Carrington and Pereira 2009). This is because only a few of the defendants observed were women. None of these hearings suggested that young girls received either lenient or punitive treatment, or that they are becoming more violent (cf. Bracchi 2008).

10 See, for example, Wallace and Jacobsen (2012).

References

Aarons, J., Smith, L. and Wagner, L. 2009 *Dispatches from Juvenile Hall: Fixing a Failing System*. Penguin, New York.

Abel, R. (ed.) 1982 *The Politics of Informal Justice*. Academic Press, New York.

Abbot, A. 1999 *Department and Discipline: Chicago Sociology at One Hundred*. University of Chicago, Chicago.

Altman, J. and Hinkson, M. (eds.) 2007 *Coercive Reconciliation: Stabilise, Normalise, Exit Aboriginal Australia*. Arena Publications, Melbourne.

Amnesty International 2005 USA: Supreme Court outlaws execution of child offenders. Amnesty International, London. <http://www.amnesty.org.au/news/comments/276/> Accessed March 2012.

Anthony, T. and Cunneen, C. 2008 *The Critical Criminology Companion*. Federation Press, Sydney.

Ashworth, A. 2004 "Social control and anti-social behaviour: The subversion of human rights." *Law Quarterly Review*. Vol.120, pp.263-80.

Ashworth, A. 2010 *Sentencing and Criminal Justice*. Cambridge University Press, Cambridge.

Ashworth, A. and Redmayne, M. 2006 *The Criminal Process*. 3rd Edition. Cambridge University Press, Cambridge.

Ashworth, A. and von Hirsch, A. (eds.) 1998 *Principled Sentencing*. Hart, Oxford.

Atkinson, J. and Drew, P. 1979 *Order in Court: The Organisation of Verbal Interaction in Court Settings*. Macmillan, London.

Attorney General NSW 2008 "New Youth Conduct Orders to tackle anti-social behaviour." Press release, 14th April.

Australian Government 2008 "Apology to the Stolen Generations." *The Australian*, 12th February. <http://www.theaustralian.com.au/in-depth/aboriginal-australia/apology-to-the-stolen-generations/story-

e6frgd9f-11115535578>. Accessed March 2012.

Australian Institute of Health and Welfare. 2011 *Juvenile Justice in Australia 2008-09*. AIHW, Canberra.

Banakar, R. and Travers, M. (eds.) 2005 *Theory and Method in Socio-Legal Research*. Hart, Oxford.

Bankowski, Z. and Mungham, G. 1976 *Images of Law*. Routledge, London.

Barry, M. 2006 *Youth Offending in Transition*. Routledge, London.

Barry, M. and McNeill, F. (eds.) 2009 *Youth Offending and Youth Justice*. Jessica Kingsley, London.

Bartels, L. and Richards, K. (eds.) 2011 *Qualitative Criminology: Stories from the Field*. The Federation Press, Sydney.

Becker, H. 1961 "Whose side are we on?" *Social Problems*. Vol.14, pp.239-47.

Becker, H. 1972 *Outsiders*. 2nd Edition. Free Press, New York.

Becker, H. and Geer, B. 1967 "Participant observation and interviewing: A comparison." In J.Manis and B.Meltzer (eds.) *Symbolic Interaction: A Reader*. Allyn and Bacon, Boston.

Bernard, T. 2002 *The Cycle of Juvenile Justice*. Oxford University Press, Oxford.

Blagg, H. 2008 *Crime, Aboriginality and the Decolonisation of Justice*. Federation Press, Sydney.

Blumberg, A. 1969 "The practice of law as a confidence game." In V.Aubert (ed.) *The Sociology of Law*. Penguin, Middlesex, pp.321-31.

Blumer, H. 1972 " 'Action' versus 'interaction'." *Society*. Vol.9, pp.50-3.

Blumer, H. 1968 *Symbolic Interactionism: Perspective and Method*. University of California Press, Berkeley.

Borowski, A. 2010 *Evaluation of the Children's Koori Court of Victoria*. Children's Court of Victoria, Melbourne.

Borowski, A. and O'Connor, I. (eds.) 1997 *Juvenile Crime, Justice and Corrections*. Longman, South Melbourne.

Bourdieu, P. 1977 *Outline of a Theory of Practice*. Cambridge University Press, Cambridge.

Bourgois, P. 1996 *In Search of Respect: Selling Crack in El Barrio*. Cambridge University Press, Cambridge.

Brachhi, P. 2008 "The feral sex: the terrifying rise of feral girl gangs." *Mail Online* <http://dailymail.co.uk/news/article-566919/the-feral-sex-the-terrifying-rise-violent-girl-gangs.html>. Accessed March 2012.

Braithwaite, J. 1989 *Crime, Shame and Reintegration*. Cambridge University Press, Cambridge.

Brouwer, G. 2010 *Whistleblowers Protection Act 2001 Investigation into Conditions at the Melbourne Youth Justice Precinct*. Ombudsman, Victoria. <http://www.ombudsman.vic.gov.au/resources/documents/

Investigation_into_conditions_at_the_Melbourne_Youth_Justice_
Precinct_Oct_20101.pdf>. Accessed March 2012.

Brown, D. 2010 "Ashley inmate found dead." *The Mercury*, 25th October
<http://www.themercury.com.au/article/2010/10/25/18481_tasmania-
news.html>. Accessed March 2012.

Brown, S. 1991 *Magistrates at Work*. Open University Press, Milton Keynes.

Brown, S. 2005 *Understanding Youth and Crime: Listening to Youth?* Open
University Press, Milton Keynes.

Bruyn, S. 1986 *The Human Perspective in Sociology: The Methodology of
Participant Observation*. Irvington, New York.

Bulmer, M. 1984 *The Chicago School of Sociology*. University of Chicago
Press, Chicago.

Burns, S. and Peyrot, M. 2003 'Tough love': Nurturing and coercing
responsibility and recovery in California drug courts. *Social Problems*.
Vol.50, No.3, pp.416-38.

Carlen, P. 1976 *Magistrates Justice*. Martin Robertson, Oxford.

Carney, T. 1984 *Child Welfare Practice and Legislation Review*. Government
of Victoria, Melbourne.

Carrington, K. and Pereira, M. 2009 *Offending Youth: Sex, Crime and Justice*.
The Federation Press, Sydney.

Chan, J. (ed.) 2005 *Reshaping Juvenile Justice: The NSW Young Offenders Act
1997*. Sydney Institute of Criminology, Sydney.

Chen, S., Matruglio, T., Weatherburn, D. and Hua, J. 2005 "The transition
from juvenile to adult criminal careers." *Crime and Justice Bulletin*.
NSW Bureau of Crime Statistics and Research, Sydney, No.86.

Cicourel, A. 1968 *The Social Organization of Juvenile Justice*. Wiley, New
York.

Clark, M. 1963 *A Short History of Australia*. Penguin, Melbourne.

Clennell, A. 2009 "Juvenile detention assaults blamed on overcrowding."
The Sydney Morning Herald, 10 April. <http://www.smh.com.au/
national/juvenile-detention-assaults-blamed-on-overcrowding-
20090409-a28a.html>. Accessed March 2012.

Clifford, J. and Marcus, G. 1986 *Writing Culture: The Poetics and Politics of
Ethnography*. University of California Press, Berkeley.

Cohen, A. 1955 *Delinquent Boys: The Culture of the Gang*. Chicago University
Press, Chicago.

Cohen, S. 1988 *Against Criminology*. Transaction, New Jersey.

Cohen, S. 2002 *Folk Devils and Moral Panics*. 3rd Edition. Routledge,
London.

Conley, J. and O'Barr, W. 2005 *Just Words: Law, Language and Power*. 2nd
Edition. University of Chicago Press, Chicago.

Corriera, M. 2006 *Judging Children as Children: A Proposal for a Juvenile
Justice System*. Temple University Press, Philadelphia.

Crawford, A. and Newburn, T. 2003 *Youth Offending and Restorative Justice: Implementing Reform in Youth Justice*. Willan, Collompton.

Cressey, P. 1932 *The Taxi-Dance Hall*. University of Chicago Press, Chicago.

Cunneen, C. 2001 *Conflict, Politics and Crime: Aboriginal Communities and the Police*. Allen and Unwin, Sidney.

Cunneen, C. and Hoyle, C. 2010 *Debating Restorative Justice*. Hart, Oxford.

Cunneen, C. and White, R. 2007 *Juvenile Justice: Youth and Crime in Australia*. 3rd Edition. Oxford University Press, Melbourne.

Daly, K. and Hayes, H. 1997 "Restorative justice and conferencing." In Graycar, A. and Grabosky, P. (eds.) *The Cambridge Handbook of Australian Criminology*. Cambridge University Press, Melbourne, pp.294-311.

Davies, H., Nutley, S. and Smith, P. 2000 *What Works? Evaluating Policy and Practice in Public Services*. The Policy Press, Bristol.

Davis, A. 2005 *Abolition Democracy: Beyond Empire, Prisons and Torture*. Seven Stories Press, New York.

Davis, M. and Bourhill, M. 1997 " 'Crisis': The demonization of children and young people." In P.Scraton (ed.) *'Childhood' in 'Crisis'*. UCL Press, London, pp.28-57.

Deming, W. 1986 *Out of the Crisis*. MIT Press, Cambridge.

Denzin, N. 1992 *Symbolic Interactionism and Cultural Studies*. Blackwell, Cambridge.

Department of Justice 2009 "The evolution of juvenile justice in Canada." Department of Justice, Canada. <http://www.justice.gc.ca/eng/pi/icg-gci/jj2-jm2/index.html>. Accessed March 2012.

Donzelot, J. 1979 *The Politics of Families*. Pantheon, New York.

Drew, J. 2010 *Speech to the Youth Justice Convention*. Youth Justice Board, London.

Duarte, F. 2011 "Interview: Zygmunt Bauman on the UK Riots." *Social Europe Journal*. 15th August 2011. <www.social-europe.eu/2011/08/interview-zygmunt-bauman-on-the-uk-riots/>. Accessed March 2012.

Dupret, B. 2007 "What is Islamic law? A praxeological example and an Egyptian case study." *Theory, Culture and Society*. Vol.24, pp.79-100.

Dupret, B. 2011 *Adjudication in Action:An Ethnomethodology of Law, Morality and Justice*. Ashgate, Aldershot.

Eades, D. 2008 *Courtroom Talk and Neocolonial Control*. Mouton de Gruyter, New York.

Eisenstein, J., Flemming, R. and Nardulli, P. 1988 *The Contours of Justice: Communities and Their Courts*. Little Brown, Boston.

Emerson, R. 1969 *Judging Delinquents: Context and Process in Juvenile Court*. Aldine,Chicago.

Emerson, R. 1991 "Case processing and interorganizational knowledge: Detecting the 'real reasons' for referrals." *Social Problems*. Vol.38, pp.198-212.

Emerson, R. (ed.) 2001 *Contemporary Field Research: Perspectives and Formulations*. Wave Tree Press, Illinois.

Emmelman, B. 2003 *Justice for the Poor: A Study of Criminal Defense Work*. Ashgate, Aldershot.

Engen, R., Steen, S. and Bridges, G. 2002 "Racial Disparities in the Punishment of Youth: A Theoretical and Empirical Assessment of the Literature." *Social Problems*. Vol.49, No.2, pp.194-220.

Evan, W. (ed.) 1962 *Law and Sociology*. The Free Press, New York.

Fanning, D. 2006 *Review of Juvenile Remandees in Tasmania*. Children's Commissioner for Tasmania, Hobart.

Farrington, D. 2003 "Key results from the first 40 years of the Cambridge study in delinquent development." In T.Thornberry and M.Krohn (eds.) *Taking Stock of Delinquency*. Kluwer, New York, pp.137-79.

Ferrell, J., Hayward, K. and Young, J. 2008 *Cultural Criminology: An Invitation*. Sage, London.

Fine, G. (ed.) 1995 *A Second Chicago School? The Development of Postwar Sociology*. University of Chicago Press, Chicago.

Fortin, J. 2003 *Children's Rights and the Developing Law*. Cambridge University Press, Cambridge.

France, A. and Homel, R. 2007 *Pathways and Crime Prevention*. Willan, Devon.

Freeman, M. and Veerman, P. (eds.) 1992 *The Ideologies of Children's Rights*. Martinus Nijhoff. Leiden.

Freiberg, A. and Ross, S. 1999 *Sentencing Reform and Penal Change: The Victorian Experience*. The Federation Press, Sydney.

Furedi, F. 2011 "Why London's burning." *The Australian*. 13th August 2011, p.11.

Garfinkel, H. 1948 "A research note on inter- and intra-racial homicides." *Journal of Social Forces*. Vol.4, pp.369-81.

Garfinkel, H. 1984a "Commonsense knowledge of social structures: The documentary method of interpretation in lay and professional fact-finding." In H. Garfinkel *Studies in Ethnomethodology*. Polity, Cambridge, pp.76-103.

Garfinkel, H. 1984b "Some rules of correct decisions that jurors respect." In H.Garfinkel *Studies in Ethnomethodology*. Polity Press, Cambridge, pp.104-115.

Garfinkel, H. 1997 "Practical Sociological Reasoning: Some Features in the Work of the Los Angeles Suicide Prevention Centre." In M.Travers and J.Manzo (eds.) *Law in Action: Ethnomethodological and Conversation Analytic Approaches to Law*. Ashgate, Aldershot, pp.24-42.

Geertz, C. 1973 "Thick description: Towards an interpretive theory of culture." In C.Geertz (ed.) *The Interpretation of Culture*. Basic Books, New York, pp.3-30.

Glaser, B. and Strauss, A. 1967 *The Discovery of Grounded Theory*. Aldine, Chicago.

Goffman, E. 1961 *Asylums*. Penguin, Harmondsworth.

Goffman, E. 1989 "On fieldwork" (transcribed and edited by L.Lofland). *Journal of Contemporary Ethnography*. Vol.18, No.2, pp.123-32.

Goldson, B. 2008 "Child incarceration: Institutional abuse, the violent state and the politics of impunity." In P.Scraton and J.McCulloch (eds.) *The Violence of Incarceration*. Routledge, London, pp.86-106.

Goodwin, V. 2008 "The concentration of offending and related social problems in Tasmanian families." *Briefing paper No.8*, Tasmania Institute for Law Enforcement Studies (TILES), University of Tasmania.

Grant, P. 2009 "Young people, court and youth detentions." Unpublished paper. Children's Court of Victoria, Melbourne.

Green, E. and Weber, K. 2008 "Teen court jurors' sentencing decisions." *Criminal Justice Review*. Vol.33, No.3, pp.361-378.

Griffiths, A. and Kandel, R. 2005 "Half told truths and partial silence: Managing the truth in Scottish children's hearings." In von Benda-Beckmann, F., von Benda-Beckmann, K. and Griffiths, A. (eds.) 2009 *The Power of Law in a Transnational World: Anthropological Enquiries*, Berghahn, Oxford, pp.277-96.

Gubrium, J. 1989 *Court-Ordered Insanity: Interpretive Practice and Involuntary Commitment*. Transaction, New Brunswick.

Gubrium, J. and Holstein, J. (eds.) 2003 *Postmodern Interviewing*. Sage, London.

Gumperz, J. and Hymes, D. 1972 *Directions in Sociolinguistics: The Ethnography of Communication*. Holt, Rinehold and Winston, New York.

Hall, S. and Jefferson, T. 2006 *Resistance Through Rituals: Youth Subcultures in Postwar Britain*. Taylor and Francis, London.

Hammersley, M. and Atkinson, P. 2007 *Ethnography: Principles in Practice*. 3rd Edition.Routledge, London.

Hampton, P. 2005 *Reducing Administrative Burdens: Effective Inspection and Enforcement*. HM Treasury, London.

Harris, J. 1982 "The political status of children." In M.Graham (ed.) *Contemporary Political Philosophy*. Cambridge University Press, Cambridge, pp.35-58.

Harvey, D. 2007 *Neoliberalism*. Oxford University Press, New York.

Hester, S. and Eglin, P. 1992 *A Sociology of Crime*. Routledge, London.

Heumann, M. 1978 *Plea-Bargaining: The Experiences of Prosecutors, Judges and Defence Attorneys*. University of Chicago Press, Chicago.

Hogarth, J. 1971 *Sentencing as a Human Process*. University of Toronto Press, Toronto.

Hood, R. 1992 *Race and Sentencing*. Clarendon Press, Oxford.

Hughes, E. 1971 *The Sociological Eye*. Aldine, Chicago.

Hughes, J. and Sharrock, W. 2007 *Theory and Methods in Sociology*. Palgrave, London.

Israel, M. 2004 *Ethics and the Governance of Criminological Research*. NSW Bureau of Statistics, Sydney.

Jupp, V. 1989 *Methods of Criminological Research*. Unwin Hyman, London.

Katz, J. 1988 *Seductions of Crime: Moral and Sensual Attractions in Doing Evil*. Basic Books, New York.

Kilkelly, U. 2008 "Youth courts and children's rights: The Irish experience." *Youth Justice*. Vol.8, No.1, pp.39-56.

King, M. and Piper, C. 1995 *How the Law Thinks About Children*. Arena, London.

Kitsuse, J. and Cicourel, A. 1963 "A note on the uses of official statistics." *Social Problems*. Vol.11, No.2, pp.35-9.

Koehler, R. 2009 "The school-to-prison-pipeline." CommonDreams. 10 December. <http://commondreams.org/view/2009/12/10>. Accessed March 2012.

Komter, M. 1998. *Dilemmas in the Courtroom: A Study of Trials of Violent Crime in the Netherlands*. Lawrence Erlbaum, New Jersey.

Kupchik, A. 2006 *Judging Juveniles: Prosecuting Adolescents in Adult and Juvenile Court*. New York University Press, New York.

Kupchik, A., De Angelis, J. and Bracy, N. 2012 "Order in the court: Using ethnomethodology to explore juvenile justice settings." In D.Gadd, S.Karstedt and S.Messner (eds.) *The Sage Handbook of Criminological Research Methods*. Sage, London, pp.324-35.

Latour, B. 2010 *The Making of Law: An Ethnography of the Conseil d'Etat*. Polity Press, Oxford.

Lemert, E. 1970 *Social Action and Legal Change: Revolution within the Juvenile Court*. Aldine, Chicago.

Lipsky, M. 1988 *Street Level Bureaucracy: Dilemmas of the Individual in Public Services*. Russell Sage Foundation, New York.

Livingston, M., Stewart, A., Allard, T. and Ogilvie, J. 2008 "Understanding juvenile offending trajectories." *Australian and New Zealand Journal of Criminology*. Vol.41, No.3, pp.345-63.

Lynch, M. 1997 "Some preliminary notes on judges' work." In M.Travers and J.Manzo (eds.) *Law in Action: Ethnomethodological and Conversation Analytic Approaches to Law*. Ashgate, Aldershot, pp.99-132.

Lynch, N. 2008 "Youth justice in New Zealand: A children's rights perspective." *Youth Justice*. Vol.8, No.3, pp.215-28.

Lyotard, J. 1984 *The Postmodern Condition: A Report on Knowledge*. Manchester University Press, Manchester.

MacKenzie, G. 2005 *How Judges Sentence*. The Federation Press, Sydney.

Mail Foreign Service 2009 "Solo sailing girl, 14, arrives back in the Netherlands…to face a police interrogation." Mail Online, 22nd December <http://www.dailymail.co.uk/news/worldnews/article- 1237439/ missing-14-year-old-Dutch-sailor-Laura-Dekker-Caribbean.html>. Accessed March 2012.

Mann, K. 1985 Defending White Collar Crime: A Portrait of Attorneys at Work. Yale University Press, New Haven.

Martinson, R. 1974 "What works: questions and answers about prison reform." The Public Interest. No.35, pp.22-54.

Mathiesen, T. 1994 The Politics of Abolition. Martin Robertson, London.

Matoesian, G. 1993 Reproducing Rape. Polity, Cambridge.

Matza, D. 1964 Delinquency and Drift. Wiley, New York.

Maynard, D. 1984 Inside Plea Bargaining: The Language of Negotiation. Plenum, New York.

Maynard, D. 1989 "On the ethnography and the analysis of talk in institutional settings." In J.Holstein and G.Miller (eds.) New Perspectives on Social Problems. JAI Press, Greenwich, CT, pp.127-64.

Maynard, D. 2003 Bad News, Good News: Conversational Order in Everyday Talk and Clinical Settings. University of Chicago Press, Chicago.

McBarnet, D. 1981 Conviction: Law, the State and the Construction of Justice. Macmillan, London.

McCall, M. and Becker, H. 1990 "Performance Science." Social Problems. Vol.37, pp.17-32.

McConville, M., Hodgson, J., Bridges, L. and Pavlovic, A. 1994 Standing Accused: The Organisation and Practices of Criminal Defence Lawyers in Britain. Clarendon Press, Oxford.

McKenzie, G. 2005 How Judges Sentence. The Federation Press, Sydney.

McNara, L. 2006 "Welfare in crisis: Key developments in Scottish youth justice." In J.Muncie and B.Goldson (eds.) Comparative Youth Justice: Critical Issues. Sage, London, pp.127-45.

Merton, R. 1938 "Social structure and anomie." American Sociological Review. Vol.3, pp.672-82.

Metherell, M. 2010 "UN slams 'apartheid' at Australian hospitals." The Age. <http://www.theage.com.au/national/UN-slams-apartheid-at-australian-hospitals-20100604-xkqy.html> Accessed March 2012.

Mileski, M. 1971 "Courtroom encounters: An observational study of a lower criminal court." Law and Society Review. Vol.5, pp.473-538.

Ministry of Justice 2010 Breaking the Cycle: Effective Punishment, Rehabilitation and Sentencing of Offenders. Ministry of Justice, London.

Moerman, M. 1988 Talking Culture: Ethnography and Conversation Analysis. University of Pennslyania Press, Philadelphia.

Moore, S. 1973 "Law and social change: The semi-autonomous social field as an appropriate subject of study." *Law and Society Review*. Vol.7, pp.719-46.

Muncie, J. 2006 "Repenalisation and rights: Explorations in comparative youth criminology." *Howard Journal of Criminal Justice*. Vol. 45, No.1, pp.42-70.

Muncie, J. 2009 *Youth and Crime: A Critical Introduction*. 3rd Edition. Sage, London.

Muncie, J. 2010 "The United Nations, children's rights and juvenile justice." In W.Taylor, R.Earle and R.Hester (eds.) *Youth Justice Handbook: Theory, Policy and Practice*. Willan, Cullompton, pp.200-210.

Muncie, J. and Goldson, B. 2006 *Comparative Youth Justice*. Sage, London.

National Health and Medical Research Council 2007 *National Statement on Ethical Conduct on Humans*. NHMRC, Canberra.

Nelken, D. 2002 "Comparing criminal justice." In M.Maguire, R.Morgan and R.Reiner (eds.) *The Oxford Handbook of Criminology*. 3rd Edition. Oxford University Press, Oxford, pp.175-202.

Nelken, D. 2010 *Comparative Criminal Justice: Making Sense of Differences*. Sage, London.

Newburn, T. 2007 *Criminology*. Willan, Cullompton.

O'Connor, I. and Sweetapple, P. (1988) *Children in Justice*. Longman, Melbourne.

Parker, H. 1974 *View from the Boys*. David and Charles, London.

Parsons, T. 1954 "A sociologist looks at the legal profession." In T.Parsons *Essays in Sociological Theory*. The Free Press, New York, pp.370-85.

Paterson, A. 1983 *The Law Lords*. Macmillan, London.

Patrick, J. 1973 *A Glasgow Gang Observed*. Methuen, London.

Pawson, R. and Tilley, N. 1997 *Realistic Evaluation*. Sage, London.

Pearson, G. 1983 *Hooligan: A History of Respectable Fears*. Macmillan, London.

Phillips, S. 1998 *Ideology in the Language of Judges: How Judges Practice Law, Politics and Courtroom Control*. Oxford University Press, Oxford.

Piacentini, L. and Walters, R. 2006 "Politicization of youth crime in Scotland and the rise of the 'Burberry Court' ." *Youth Justice*. Vol.6, No.1, pp.43-59.

Pitts, J. 2001 *The New Politics of Youth Crime: Discipline or Solidarity?* Palgrave, Basingstoke.

Platt, A. 1969 *The Child Savers*. University of Chicago Press, Chicago.

Pollner, M. 1974 "Sociology and common-sense: Models of the labelling process." In R.Turner (ed.) *Ethnomethodology*. Penguin, Harmondsworth, pp.27-40.

Pound, R. 1931 "The call for a realist jurisprudence." *Harvard Law Review*. Vol.44, pp.697-711.

Pratt, J. 1989 "Corporatism: The third model of juvenile justice." *British Journal of Criminology.* Vol.29, No.3, pp.236-54.

Prichard, J. 2004 *Juvenile Conferencing in Tasmania.* Phd thesis, University of Tasmania.

Prus, R. 1996 "Betwixt positivist proclivities and postmodernist propensities." In R.Prus *Symbolic Interaction and Ethnographic Research: Intersubjectivity and the Study of Human Lived Experience.* State University of New York Press, Albany, pp.203-44.

Reiman, J. 2006 *The Rich Get Richer and the Poor Get Prison: Ideology, Class and Criminal Justice.* 8th Edition. Allyn and Bacon, New York.

Richards, K. and Lyneham, M. 2010 *Juveniles in Detention in Australia 1981-2008.* Australian Institute of Criminology, Canberra.

Roach Anleu, S. and Mack, K. 2005 "Magistrates' everyday work and emotional labour." *Journal of Law and Society.* Vol.32, No.4, pp.590-614.

Roberson, C. 2011 *Juvenile Justice: Theory and Practice.* CRC, Boca Raton.

Sanders, B. 2005 *Youth Crime and Youth Culture in the Inner City.* Routledge, London.

Scheffer, T. 2010 *Adversarial Case-Making: An Ethnography of English Crown Court Procedure.* Brill, Leiden.

Schegloff, E. 1991 "Reflections on talk and social structure." In D.Boden and D.Zimmerman (eds.) *Talk and Social Structure: Studies in Ethnomethodology and Conversation Analysis.* Polity Press, Cambridge, pp.44-70.

Schrag, Z. 2010 *Ethical Imperialism: Institutional Review Boards and the Social Sciences, 1965-2009.* John Hopkins University Press, Baltimore.

Schutz, A. 1962 *Collected Papers Vol.I.* Martinus Nijhoff, The Hague.

Seymour, J. 1988 *Dealing with Young Offenders.* Law Book Company, North Ryde.

Sharrock, W. and Anderson, B. 1991 "Epistemology: Professional Scepticism." In G.Button (ed.) *Ethnomethodology and the Human Sciences.* Cambridge University Press, Cambridge, pp.51-76.

Sheehan, R. 2001 *Magistrates' Decision-Making in Child Protection Cases.* Ashgate, Aldershot.

Sheehan, R. and Borowski, A. 2012 *Australia's Children's Courts: Today and Tomorrow.* Springer, Berlin.

Sherman, L., Gottfredson, D., MacKenzie, J., Reuter, P. and Bushway, S. 1999 *Preventing Crime: What Works, What Doesn't, What's Promising: A Report to the United States Congress.* National Institute of Justice. University of Maryland, Maryland.

Sickmund, M. 2010 "Juveniles in Residential Placement 1997-2008." *Office of Juvenile Justice and Delinquency Programs Fact Sheet.* February. <http://www.ncjrs.gov/pdffiles1/ojjdp/229379.pdf>. Accessed March 2012.

Smith, R. 2003 *Youth Justice: Ideas, Policy, Practice*. Willan, Cullompton.

Smith, R. 2005 "Welfare versus Justice – Again!" *Youth Justice*. Vol.5, No.3, pp.3-16.

Solomon, E. and Garside, R. 2008 *Ten Years of Labour's Youth Justice Reforms: An Independent Audit*. Centre for Crime and Justice Studies, London.

Spradley, J. 1979 *The Ethnographic Interview*. Holt, Rinehart and Winston, New York.

Spradley, J. and McCurdy, D. 1972 *The Cultural Experience: Ethnography in Complex Society*. Science Research Associates, Chicago.

Stewart, A., Allard, T. and Dennison, S. (eds.) *Evidence Based Policy and Practice in Youth Justice*. The Federation Press, Annandale, NSW.

Strang, H., Barnes, G., Braithwaite, J. and Sherman, L. 1999 *Experiments in Restorative Policing: A Progressive Report on the Canberra Reintegrative Shaming Experiments (RISE)*. Australian Federal Police and Australian National University, Canberra.

Strauss, A. and Corbin, J. 1998 *Basics of Qualitative Research: Techniques and Procedures for Producing Grounded Theory*. 2nd Edition. Sage, London.

Strauss, A., Schatzman, L., Bucher, R., Ehrlich, D. and Sabshin, M. 1967 *Psychiatric Ideologies and Institutions*. Free Press, New York.

Streek, W. 2011 "The crises of democratic capitalism." *New Left Review*. Vol.71, pp.5-9.

Suchman, L. 1987 *Plans and Situated Actions: The Problem of Human Machine Communication*. Cambridge University Press, Cambridge.

Sudnow, D. 1965 "Normal crimes: Sociological features of the penal code." *Social Problems*. Vol.12, No.4, pp.255-64.

Tata, C. 2002 "Accountability for the sentencing decision process – Towards a New Understanding." In C.Tata and N.Hutton (eds.) *Sentencing and Society: International Perspectives*. Ashgate, Aldershot, pp.399-428.

Tata, C., Burns, N., Halliday, S., Hutton, N. and McNeil, F. 2008 "Assisting and advising the sentencing decision process: The pursuit of 'quality' in pre-sentence reports." *British Journal of Criminology*. Vol.48, pp.835-55.

Tata, C. and Hutton, N. (eds.) 2002 *Sentencing and Society: International Perspectives*. Ashgate, Aldershot.

Taylor, I., Walton, P. and Young, J. 1973 *The New Criminology*. Routledge, London.

Taylor, W., Earle, B. and Hester, R. 2010. *Youth Justice Handbook: Theory, Policy and Practice*. Willan, Cullompton.

Ten Have, P. 2007 *Doing Conversation Analysis: A Practical Guide*. Sage, London.

Tilley, N. 2009 *Crime Prevention*. Willan, Cullompton.

Tomsen, S. and Noone, M. 2006 *Lawyers, Conflict and Professional Change: Australian Lawyers and Legal Aid*. Federation Press, Sydney.

Travers, M. 1997a *The Reality of Law: Work and Talk in a Firm of Criminal Lawyers*. Ashgate, Aldershot.

Travers, M. 1997b "Preaching to the converted? Improving the persuasiveness of criminal justice research." *British Journal of Criminology*. Vol.37, No.3, pp.359-77.

Travers, M. 1999 *The British Immigration Courts: A Study of Law and Politics*. The Policy Press, Bristol.

Travers, M. 2004 "The philosophical assumptions of constructionism." In K.Jacobs, T.Manzi and J.Kemeny (eds.) *Social Constructionism in Housing Studies*. Ashgate, Aldershot, pp.14-31.

Travers, M. 2005 "Evaluation research and criminal justice: Beyond a political critique." *Australian and New Zealand Journal of Criminology*. Vol.38, No. 1, pp.39-58.

Travers, M. 2007 "Sentencing in the children's court: An ethnographic perspective". *Youth Justice*, Vol.7, No.1, pp.21-35.

Travers, M. 2008 "Understanding comparison in criminal justice research: An interpretive approach." *International Criminal Justice Review*. Vol.18, No.4, pp.389-405.

Travers, M. 2010 "Welfare, punishment or something else? Sentencing minor offences committed by young people in Tasmania and Victoria." *Current Issues in Criminal Justice*. Vol.22, No.1, pp.99-116.

Travers, M. and Manzo, J. (eds.) 1997 *Law in Action: Ethnomethodological and Conversation Analytic Approaches to Law*. Ashgate, Aldershot.

Ulmer, J. 1997 *Social Worlds of Sentencing: Court Communities Under Sentencing Guidlines*. State University of New York Press, Albany.

Van den Hoonard, W. 2012 *Seduction of Ethics: Transforming the Social Sciences*. University of Toronto Press, Toronto.

Videnieks, M. 2002 "Courts under pressure to get tough," *The Australian*, 5 September, p.1.

Von Hirsch, A. 1993 *Censure and Sanctions*. Clarendon Press, Oxford.

Wacquant, L. 2009 *Prisoners of Poverty*. University of Minnesota Press, Minneapolis.

Wallace, N. and Jacobsen, G. 2012 "Children reoffending as system goes soft." *Sydney Morning Herald*, 28 April. <http://m.smh.com.au/nsw/children-reoffending-as-system-goes-soft-20120427-1xqb0.html>. Accessed March 2012.

Walter, M. (ed.) 2009 *Social Research Methods*. Oxford University Press, Melbourne.

Wandall, R. 2008 *Decisions to Imprison*. Ashgate, Aldershot.

Ward, T. and Maruna, S. 2007 *Rehabilitation: Beyond the Risk Paradigm.* Routledge, London.

Watson, R. 1983 "The presentation of victim and offender in discourse: The case of police interrogation and interviews." *Victimology.* Vol.3, pp.31-52.

Weatherburn, D. 2007 "Screening juvenile offenders for further assessment and intervention." *Crime and Justice Bulletin.* NSW Bureau of Crime Statistics and Research, Sydney, No. 109.

Weber, M. 1978 "Introduction." In M.Weber *Economy and Society.* University of California Press, Berkeley, California.

Weber, M. 1997 *The Methodology of the Social Sciences.* The Free Press, New York.

Webber, C. 2007 "Background, foreground, foresight: The third dimension of cultural criminology." *Crime, Media, Culture.* Vol.3, No.2, pp.139-57.

White, R. 2008 "Class analysis and the crime problem." In T.Anthony and C.Cunneen (eds.) *The Critical Criminology Companion.* Hawkins Press, Sydney, pp.30-42.

White, R. and Haines, F. 2008 *Crime and Criminology.* 4th Edition. Oxford University Press, Melbourne.

Whyte, B. 2010 "Values in youth justice: Practical approaches to welfare and justice for young people in UK jurisdictions." In W.Taylor, R.Earle and R.Hester (eds.) *Youth Justice Handbook: Theory, Policy and Practice.* Willan, Cullompton, pp.221-30.

Wiles, P. 2002 "Criminology in the 21st Century: Public Good or Private Interest? –The Sir John Barry Memorial Lecture." *Australian and New Zealand Journal of Criminology.* Vol.35, No.2, pp.238-52.

Winch, P. 1988 *The Idea of a Social Science.* Routledge, London.

Wolfgang, M. 1958 *Patterns of Criminal Homicide.* University of Pennsylvania Press, Philadelphia.

Wood, J. 2008 *Report of the Special Commission of Inquiry into Child Protection Services in New South Wales.* NSW Government, Sydney.

Yates, J. 2004 "Criminological ethnography: Risks, dilemmas and their negotiation." In G.Mesko, M.Pagon, B.Dobugusek (eds.) *Policing in Central and Eastern Europe: Dilemmas of Contemporary Criminal Justice.* <http:www.ncjrs.pdffiles1/nij/Mesko/208043.pdf>. Accessed March 2012.

Zizek, S. 2010 "Against human rights." <http://libcom.org/libary/against-human-rights-zizek>. Accessed March 2012.

Index

CPSIA information can be obtained at www.ICGtesting.com
Printed in the USA
LVOW08s1738241013

358455LV00003B/738/P